JERUSALEM'S GATES

... A NARRATIVE & DEVOTIONAL JOURNEY THROUGH THE

GATES OF JERUSALEM

& INTO THE STORY OF GOD

A NARRATIVE & DEVOTIONAL JOURNEY

IN ORDINARY TIME—BOOK 2

By

REV. TERRY MATTSON

INTRODUCTION

"Are we there yet?" What parent has not heard the steady drumbeat of a child's frustration with time. Buckled in and with no place to run or hide, to explore and wander freely about, time is suddenly thrust into a child's awareness. It is an unwelcome guest interrupting the fantasies and play of a child's heart.

Before computers and DVD players the only recourse a child had inside the confines of a station wagon (boy does that date me) was imagination. In the world of the child's mind time was no longer a boring reminder of what wasn't happening. We were too busy exploring, catching the bad guys, being the good ones. Deep within imagination's world the miles of the road sped by.

As the universe around us rushes in her orbits around ever larger bodies, we the children of earth, continue to explore and fight, love and argue, laugh and weep. We do not feel the rush of time as the rays of the sun traverse the galaxy at 180,000 miles per second. We are lost in our world of play and hurt, of hope and disappointment.

Even so, the question emerges, "Are we there, yet?" Almost intuitively, we humans seem to have a need to relate our struggles and triumphs, our losses and gains to time. It's simply another way of asking, "Does it all matter? Are we on a journey to somewhere? Are we there, yet?"

For the ancient's, life in a garden seemed too good to be true. The environment was tranquil and timeless. Maybe that was part of the problem. Adam's children busted out of the garden and into the story of humanity, without the creator. Life was chaotic, filled with confusion. Each of the Creator's children played to a different dream. The children could not agree on the rules of the game. Arguments abounded. In the end the children of the story could not even read together what they were writing with each new day. We had lost the ability to write or speak one language.

Still, it was here, in the back seat of God's chariot that the question finally emerged, "Are we there?"

God's answer, like that of any parent, was "not yet." As the planet whirled through the emptiness that is space, the Creator began to envision for all God's children a gift. It was time creating a story and place. "Once upon a time" was no longer good enough. So, "in the beginning", eternity jumped into space and offered a destination, which the children of Eve and Adam would one-day call, Jerusalem.

Slowly, this city has captured our attention. Its importance is neither strategic, nor economic. Jerusalem is not the largest of cities, nor the focus of culture or music or drama. Yet, it has become the center of all God's action in time and space to draw us back into the only Story that really matters.

I suppose this is the reason why this city of peace has rarely been, peaceful. Like children in a car, for whom time passes slowly, we have felt confined. We tire of our streaming videos and I-phones. Our fights are no longer innocent. We have lost the heart of a child that can turn the simplest object into a whole universe. And so we look out the window facing images passing us in the night, and ask, "Are we there yet?"

The City of God

Jerusalem does not pop up out of nowhere, though it emerges in an unlikely place. Although Jerusalem offers nothing of military import, it remains the most contested real estate on the planet. Jerusalem's importance is religious. Three world religions call this city sacred. All the major questions are asked within its walls, both ancient and modern. Jerusalem's history is interwoven with humankind's search for himself/herself and God's embrace of history.

This devotional guide is written in the firm belief that God is guiding and pulling and pushing and cajoling and calling us into a future of hope. But it is a hope born in time, one moment leading to another. It is a hope that takes us from the garden to this city.

In this devotional you are invited to walk through Jerusalem's gates and back into the story of humankind as it is taken up into the Story of God! Near the Old Gate you will meet Melchizedek and Abram visiting. You will witness David and Solomon as they enter in the East Gate; one dancing and nearly naked, the other solemn and majestic. You will see Pilate make his way through the Horse gate with an entourage of Roman soldiers accompanying from Caesarea Philippi, while Caiaphas watches the spectacle from the north, near the Master Gate. Passing, at first unnoticed, through the Dung gate and making her way up from the city of David is a poor widow, who will catch the attention of Jesus (and His Church) with her two pence. Mary, blessed of all the daughters of Eve, will weep here along the Via Dolorosa, as her son passes under the Lion's Gate on his way to the rock of the Skull. And here you will see Jesus, who together with Barabbas has been caught up into the drama that is Jerusalem. What will surely surprise you is the moment you see yourself walking the streets of this city of men and women becoming the City of God.

The City of Humans

I live in the city (Seattle) and pastored for 18 years a small multi-ethnic, culturally and economically diverse community. I remain on staff today as an associate pastor. Our community is Wesleyan in theological orientation, which simply means that we believe God is actively at work in the whole world, doing something bigger than any of us can imagine.

It will be the intent of this devotional to emphasize the Story God is writing by looking at the place where most of God's Story unfolds, among the people of the Divine's choosing. The Gates of Jerusalem offer a unique picture into the story as it unfolded in Israel and continues to unfold in the Church. Each gate had a specific function and history. Each gate offers a spiritual door through which we can see God writing

The Story in Israel and the Church as we move toward the New Jerusalem of John's Revelation. All of God's children will one day witness the Messiah, the Christ as he steps through the now closed Eastern Gate, the gate called "Beautiful" and into our future. It is a story we must know. It is a story to be lived. It is a story worth telling!

It is my hope that as you study the Holy Scriptures you will see anew the Trinity of God, who from eternity enters time, in order that we might be taken up into eternity and bring eternity here. May God allow you to see anew the church, as she is Christ bride living in the city of humans, but living and longing for the city of God. Each of these cities (human/God) has the same name: Jerusalem.

Rev. Terry Mattson

Now: Pastor Emeritus, West Seattle Church of the Nazarene
wscnpastorterry@reachone.com

12/02/2016

UNDERSTANDING THIS BOOK

If this writing has any value for you it will be in the dialogue between you, the Spirit of God and Christ's Church. This book is designed to lead you into Scripture and the stories of the Church in order that Jesus might find room in your life.

Format

The Faith given is both personal and social, always. Therefore, readings from Scripture and the history of the church reflect the social/personal quest for the holy—love of God; God's Story written into ours.

To that end you are given for each of the next nine weeks a:

- ➤ Psalm per week (to be read each day of the week), and;
- ➤ Commandment of the week (to meditate upon), and;
- ➤ Selected Scripture for each day, and;
- ➤ Reflections and questions on the scriptures, imagined stories and my devotional thoughts.

These stories/writings are drawn from my own imagination and experiences or the Biblical settings or traditions of the Church from which The Story of God emerges.

These writings express my own thoughts or reflections on writings from numerous others.

You are encouraged to create a journal, titled "Jerusalem's Gates" and note in it your own feelings, insights, prayers, confessions, praises and conversations with God which you may wish to keep and review at a later time.

So, let us enter Jerusalem, the city of humans, the city of God.

Quotations from other authors will be in italics.

DEDICATION

This book is dedicated to my friend and parishioner, Nickolaus Hendel. Nickolaus is an older gentleman (and he is that: a gentle man) who lives on our church campus temporarily and has been entrusted with the care and management of our facilities.

Nickolaus has been a part of our community for about six years, first becoming acquainted with us through a shelter that we hosted for a homeless non-profit, Share—Wheel, who coordinates the housing of men and women throughout Seattle/King County in Churches, Synagogues and Mosques and who sleep overnight from 7 p.m. to 7 a.m. each evening. Share—Wheel also provides oversight for two Tent Cities in the area.

Our friend Nickolaus always has a ready smile and open, tender heart; especially for those he perceives being taken advantage of. He used to be restless and would take a month (and once about year and half) break from us choosing instead to explore the cities and wilderness of western Washington and northern California...on the road again.

Peace has increasingly replaced his restless spirit, though not the need for creative adventure as he has ever moved closer to Jesus—whom he loves. Nickolaus has traveled the world and now ministers to it as he daily opens the church and his kitchen to feed, talk with, pray with and lead Bible Studies with other persons who do not have the benefit of rented or owned homes.

It is his love of all things Biblical, especially the Old Testament and of cities that causes me to dedicate this book to one who in spirit and by means of the printed and streamed page explores ever the history of western civilization, especially as made real by Israel's journey through time.

The City Gates

The Gates of Jerusalem

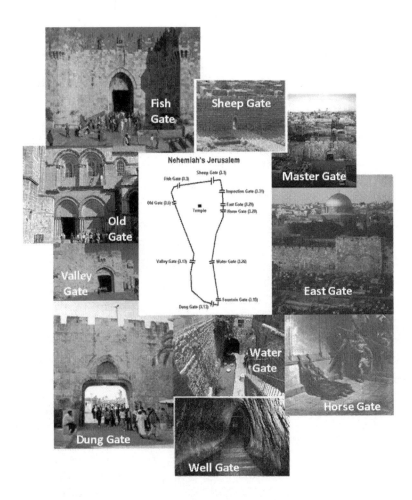

The Old Gate: Some believe the Old Gate belonged to Salem which was first built by King Melchizedek and may represent the oldest of the city gates.

The Sheep Gate: The Sheep Gate is the entrance where the lambs, used for sacrifices in the temple were brought into the city.

The Valley Gate: The Valley Gate overlooked the Hinnom Valley, also referred to as Gehenna... This valley was a place of defilement, idolatry, the sacrificial fires of Molech, and the collection of the city's sewage.

The Well Gate: This gate is near the Pool of Siloam... Water from this pool was brought to the Temple in a golden vessel during the Feast of Tabernacles. It was fed by a conduit which starts at a spring near the Water Gate.

The Water Gate: This gate is located near the only source of fresh water for the whole city of Jerusalem. Since the spring was outside the city wall, a conduit was cut through the 1,780 feet of solid rock and emptied into the Pool of Siloam.

The Fish Gate: At this gate the fish for the local market were brought into the city.

The Dung Gate: The Dung Gate was named because of the piles of rubbish in the Valley of Tophet below it. The garbage was always burned outside the city.

The Horse Gate: The actual Horse Gate was at the end of the bridge which led to the Temple of Zion and allowed the officials and soldiers of the temple access by horse.

The East Gate: This gate, commonly known as the "gate called beautiful," is regarded as the primary gate leading to the Temple.

Decorated with brass and precious metals, it is the largest of the city gates.

The Master Gate: [Inspection Gate] was the gate where persons doing business with the Temple would come. The Temple tax was paid at this gate. It was a meeting place.

Rev. Terry Mattson

CONTENTS

Introduction III

Understanding This Book VII

Dedication IX

The City Gates X

1 WHY JERUSALEM? Pg #14
… The Old Gate

2 THE PERSON Pg #52
... The Sheep Gate

3 TRASH IN THE CITY Pg #92
... The Valley Gate

4 DIGGING DEEP Pg #128
... The Well Gate

5 FRESH WATER Pg #168
... The Water Gate

6 LIFE IN THE CITY Pg #206
... The Fish Gate

7   HEALING   Pg #234
     … The Dung Gate

8   IT'S A WAR!   Pg #272
     ... The Horse Gate

9   HOPE   Pg #302
     ... The Eastern Gate

10   DIVINE APPOINTMENT   Pg #344
     ... The Master Gate

11   CITY OF HUMANS, CITY OF GOD   Pg #386
     ... The New Jerusalem

     Epilogue   Pg #430

     Grateful Acknowledgements   Pg #432

     Other Books by the Author & Their Themes   Pg #436

     About the Author   Pg #439

1 WHY JERUSALEM

... The Old Gate

INVOCATION:

PRAISE BE TO YOU, LORD, CREATOR AND GOD AND FATHER OF OUR LORD JESUS, WHO IS CHRIST. FROM THE HEAVENS YOU HAVE BLESSED US.

IN CHRIST, WE ARE FILLED WITH DELIGHT AS WE MOVE EVER CLOSER TO YOUR VISION BEING FULFILLED IN US, YOUR CHURCH AND IN THE EARTH AND THE HEAVENS. FATHER, YOU HAVE CHOSEN US TO BE HOLY AND BLAMELESS.

IN LOVE YOU HAVE COMMITTED YOURSELF TO MAKE US TRULY YOUR CHILDREN, ALL ACCORDING TO YOUR WILL AND PLEASURE. THANK YOU FOR THE SACRIFICE OF YOUR SON FOR OUR SINS, MADE REAL BY HIS BLOOD POURED OUT. AT JUST THE RIGHT TIME, LORD, JESUS APPEARED AND WITH HIM AND THROUGH HIM AND IN HIM WE ARE ALL SAVED. ALL, LORD, IN THE HEAVENS AND ON EARTH, JUST AS YOU PLANNED SO LONG AGO BEFORE TIME. ALL, LORD, IN CHRIST. AMEN.

ADAPTED FROM EPHESIANS 1: 3-10.

PSALM OF THE WEEK: PSALM 87

COMMANDMENT OF THE WEEK: HEAR, O ISRAEL: THE LORD OUR GOD, THE LORD IS ONE. LOVE THE LORD YOUR GOD WITH ALL YOUR HEART AND WITH ALL YOUR SOUL AND WITH ALL YOUR STRENGTH.

DEUTERONOMY 6: 4,5

DAILY SCRIPTURES:

MONDAY—GENESIS 14:11-24

TUESDAY—GENESIS 22: 1-18

WEDNESDAY—II CHRONICLES 36: 15-23

THURSDAY—DANIEL 6: 1-28

FRIDAY—ISAIAH 40: 1-11

SATURDAY—LUKE 19: 41-48 & 21: 1-6, 20-24

SUNDAY—EPHESIANS 1: 3-18, ROMANS 8: 15-28 REVELATION 5: 1-14 & 21: 9-14

FROM
REVELATIONS 3: 12

AS FOR THOSE WHO EMERGE VICTORIOUS, I WILL MAKE THEM PILLARS IN THE TEMPLE OF MY GOD, AND THEY WILL NEVER LEAVE IT. I WILL WRITE ON THEM THE NAME OF MY GOD AND THE NAME OF THE CITY OF MY GOD, THE NEW JERUSALEM THAT COMES DOWN OUT OF HEAVEN FROM MY GOD. I WILL ALSO WRITE ON THEM MY OWN NEW NAME.

Week-1: MONDAY—GENESIS 14:11-24

STORY 1—A PRE-STORY'S BIRTH

Imaginative Biblical Story

Melchizedek slowly made his way up Mount Moriah, the Mount of the Most-High God. It had been a night with little sleep and he was anxious to see what the new day brought. On this mount he first heard the voice of the Eternal One. Here he learned to wait and listen, trust and weep—to plan and dream.

Looking East and out into the valley toward Jericho, he saw the glistening and golden greeting of the new day's sun as she filtered above the mount that bloomed with the ripening buds of the Olive Tree. 'Oil...' Melchizedek thought to himself. 'The oil of blessing, that together with the wine when it is old, allows for the 'fellowship' of kings, like the one he had enjoyed last evening with Abram. True, Abram was no king. Not just yet, anyway. But Melchizedek knew that in his friend was a man filled with the spirit of the Creator, who like himself, worshiped the One and only, the God of the Heavens.

His mind wandered to the first time he and Abram had met. He had heard the reports of traveling nomads, homeless wanderers, moving through the land. From the kings of the other cities came reports, mostly positive, of a tribal community whose elder walked gently in the land. But this one from Ur of the Chaldeans had grown wealthy and strong. 'It was time', Melchizedek had thought, 'to meet this Abram face to face and see for himself.' With a small entourage the King of Salem, the city of peace, brought offerings of grain, wine and animals and asked for an audience. As they gathered for the days of feasting Melchizedek was both surprised and pleased to hear Abram pray to the God, Most-High with whom he seemed to commune.

But that had been thirty-seven years ago. Last evening Abram had come into his city with a request that horrified him. His friend and the friend of the God Unseen had come to this mountain to sacrifice his one and only son, from Sari's womb. Shocked that Abram would ask such a thing the King had stood in anger and shaking his robe, abruptly departed from his friend's presence. This was the very practice that had first led him to question the gods of the Canaanites and search, on this very mount, his heart, until he met the Creator, God Most-High. True, he had seen in Abram's eyes the sadness and longing that visited other men of good heart and clear mind when looking into the horror of such a sacrifice. "Not on this mount! Not for our God!", Melchizedek had cried as he left Abram alone.

But then, in the middle of the evening the king was suddenly awakened from a frightening dream. In it he had seen two images, both emerging from Mount Moriah and seeming to find birth in Abram's heart. In the first, the King of Salem was standing over a precipice whose skull like shape he had often seen before, just outside the city. He was looking to the east and across the valley towards Jericho, above the mount filled with the oil of the Olive Tree. Descending in the clouds had been a city that shone *with the glory of God and its brilliance was like that of a very precious jewel, like a jasper, clear as crystal. It had a great, high wall with twelve gates, and with twelve angels, one at each of the gates. There were three gates on the east, three on the north, three on the south and three on the west (Revelation 21: 11b-12a, 13).* At this sight, Melchizedek had fallen to his knees in worship. The angel, over the Eastern gate blew a trumpet and from within the city was heard a voice, like unto thunder which said, "King of Salem. See before you the glory of your city. Do not forbid my servant Abram from what his heart has told him he must do. For from him will come One who will be the very foundation and life of this city!"

Immediately the cloud was lifted from the Mount of the Olive Trees and came to settle over the rock of sacrifice on the Mount of God. Such a fog Melchizedek had never seen. It was cold and frightening. Thunder rolled from within her though the glory of sound's light could not be seen in the cloud. Then, as if rising from the rock was the form of a man stretched out. At first Melchizedek thought he was witnessing the horror of Abram's sacrifice of Isaac, but the form of suffering he did not understand. Never had he seen, even among the kings of the cities around him, such a horrific torture. Hanging by steaks of long formed rock cut into his hands and feet was one man, whom Melchizedek suddenly recognized in horror. He had met him only once, on this very mountain. He had come to him, as an angel, offering him bread and wine. The innocence of his spirit and wisdom of his words had captured Melchizedek's own heart and mind. He was like a god, only alive and filled with glory. This One, whom he had called LORD, after only a few minutes of conversation was being sacrificed.

Then the cloud enveloped the image of horror and lifted once again up into the sky and to the heavens from whence it came. Melchizedek awakened from his dream and made his way to Abram's room to give his permission.

And now in the soft gold of the mornings light, the King and Priest of Salem made his way up the mountain, anxious for his friend, the one from whose loins he now knew Salem's future was assured. His heart winced as he thought of the cost to God Most-High. Turning back to the north and looking up Melchizedek saw in the distance two images, one tall and the other, young. The form he had no doubt was that of Isaac, son of laughter. Picking up his steps and with the bounce that comes from a burdened relieved, Melchizedek moved toward the two distant figures excited to hear of the mornings drama; of the Story he knew was of God.

MY THOUGHTS 1—A PRE-STORY'S BIRTH

"Now after John was arrested,
Jesus came into Galilee,
preaching the Gospel of God, and saying,
'The time is fulfilled,
and the Kingdom of God is at hand;
repent, and believe in the Gospel."
(Mk 1: 14-15)

The coming of God's Kingdom in Jesus was called a gospel by the early writers. We have managed to mistranslate it as 'Good News,' although, to be sure the gospels are that; Good News. But Pope Benedict VI reminds us that the term when used by the writers was taken from a Roman context and *"figures in the vocabulary of the Roman emperors, who understood themselves as lords, saviors, and redeemers of the world. The message issued by the emperor were called in Latin 'evangelium', regardless of whether or not their content was particularly cheerful and pleasant. The idea was that what comes from the emperor is a saving message, that it is not just a piece of news, but a change of the world for the better."*

We get away with a shallower 'good news' because we have such limited ideas of what God is up to. As westerners we think in only personal terms—our personal salvation out of this world to another (eternal) place where time does not count—when God is thinking of us and our salvation it is in the context of place and time; of the whole universe bursting forth from Creation!

So when God envisions the restoration of Planet Earth and all whoever walked it's soil the gospel is still too small. *"God's purpose is now to show the rulers and powers in the heavens...the plan he had from the beginning of time that he accomplished through Christ Jesus our Lord"* (Ephesians 3: 10a,11b). The Gospel is really about the restoration of all things and Jerusalem is the city of earth that serves as the living sign of God's forever commitment to our Shalom— plentiful peace and justice and healing.

And so today's story reminds us that **from before Time, time was**. Time lived, hidden in the stories of the Father and Son. And the Spirit listened like a student hungry to discover a new idea. Inside one such moment the Word, his grin young and playful, exclaimed, "Yes, let us dream and create. Let the Holy One breath into our dreams beings like us and yet, unlike; Beings whose very existence gives meaning to Our eternal and unfolding dreams." And so, time was born. It began as a seedling inside the Father's heart and burst into life by the Word of the Son. But it was the breath of the Spirit hovering over the darkness that brought forth from the nothing, the light we call, time.

From such a genesis, God's Story emerges into the very Word of God we know today, the Gospel. John, the Revelator, declared that *"before the foundations of the world were laid, the lamb was slain"* (Revelation 13: 8). Surely, the foundations of Jerusalem were envisioned in the same breath, for from the very first pages of Genesis, (Jeru)-Salem is pictured. When we are introduced to the city it is already the community of peace, whose first citizen is both King and Priest.

God's Story, then, is born in time and within a city, whose *"architect and builder"* is God (Hebrews 11:10).

Quotes other than scripture above from "Jesus of Nazareth", by Pope Benedict XVI, page #46

Reflections on "A Pre-Story's Birth"

Q: Have you ever thought of Jerusalem as central and necessary to God's story?

Referring to Jesus the writer of Hebrews reflects:

> *"But God said to him,*
> *'You are my son; today I have become your Father.'*
> *And in another place,*
> *'You are a priest forever,*
> *in the order of Melchizedek'"*
>
> (Hebrews 5: 5b).

Q: Have you ever thought of Melchizedek and Abram's friendship as being a type of God's own friendship with us? ...How might that be?

In Salem of old, God is laying the pre-story, the foundation upon which he will build 'salvation' into human history.

Q: What is God's pre-story in your life? ...How did God come to you before you recognized him in Jesus? ...Write the scene out, like a drama.

Consider the place and time when you first met Jesus in faith and turn it to prayer.

Week-1: TUESDAY—GENESIS 22: 1-18

STORY 2—THE PRICE OF SACRIFICE

Imaginative Biblical Story as seen through Isaac's Eyes

"But Abba" (Daddy)? Isaac's voice broke into the troubled crowd of feelings that had overwhelmed Abraham since they had left their encampment three days earlier. Isaac knew why they were making this journey. He had watched as his Abba selected from among his collection of weapons and tools the one and only knife used for this sacred rite. He had seen the servants preparing for a journey of days, gather the skins and fruit, dates, nuts, wine flasks, together with the fine pottery and bag of precious coins. He had watched his mother bake her very best bread and wrap it in a pouch. Isaac had even guessed as to the destination. Probably, he thought, it would be Mount Moriah, near the King of Salem's residence. That would explain the number of animal skins and wine flasks, the fine pottery and the precious coins.

Once before he had traveled with his Abba to Salem and its king. After a day and night spent in feasting and laughter, Abraham had taken his son, high into this mountain of God, where his Abba had sacrificed a beautiful lamb. The memory brought sudden fear and pain to Isaac's heart. The lamb first chosen had been Isaac's favorite, a pet really. In horror Isaac had raised the knife over his very own lamb, the one he had given the name Jacob to, meaning to grasp or push. Isaac had watched Jacob's birth and seen how, as a little baby lamb, he had pushed and shoved the other members of his little family away in order to get to his mother's milk, or later, to eat of the feed. He had grown to love this little pusher who would nudge him when sleeping and lick his face. For just a moment, Isaac hesitated, knife in hand. His Abba had told him that God required a sacrifice of great value, one sufficient to cover the wounds of sin. So Isaac gathered his courage, closed his eyes and grabbing the handle with both hands he raised them above little Jacob, ready now to plunge the knife into the flesh of his very best friend. Suddenly from behind him the strong hand of his Abba captured Isaac's forearm and kept him from the horror of the act. Isaac opened his eyes and turned to see his Abba smiling with pride. "Enough, my son," Abraham spoke. "You have proved to me and to God your heart. You are ready to give up your very best. That is all God ever asks of us." And Isaac's Abba began to loosen Jacob free from the leather bindings that held him and slapped him on the buttocks so that the startled animal kicked and stumbled off the pile of wood and onto the ground. Then Abraham gathered up into his arms his very own and best lamb, one without blemish and showed Isaac the way of the sacrifice.

Now, three days into the journey, with Salem growing before them, with each passing hill, Isaac asked what had been in his mind from the first. "Abba," he began hesitantly, for his Abba had seemed in a dark and distant mood. "Abba, where is the lamb for the sacrifice?" Several moments went by before Abraham turned to his son, his heart heavy, his eyes sad and moist. "God will provide, my son."

Note: Written by Terry Mattson, though the original idea is from another source I cannot now remember.

Reflections on "The Price of Sacrifice"

In the Story of Genesis 22 we come to the heart of our journey in time. As it was for Abraham, so it is with all of his children. Only time, working through the circumstances that live inside our own stories, can bring, each and all of us, to the place where we open our hearts wide enough to receive the love of God, broken for us and wounded in our place.

God's Story unfolds on this mount. It is the Story of the Trinity of God who suffers for us, with us and in us. Jerusalem is the place of sacrifice. Our lives are the continuing and historic moment. On this mount the Father of All offered up his one and only Son and the Trinity's heart opened wide to receive back all the sheep who ever strayed.

Abraham's offering of love is both the living preview of this moment in time and the living representative of each of his sons/daughters as we open our own hearts, in our own time, wide to receive.

Q: Have you ever connected Abraham's story to Golgotha?

Q: How about Isaac's and his willing obedience to his father? ...What is the significance in the theme of 'sacrifice' being lived/re-lived through out The Story of God?

Q: Where are you in this story?

> ➤ Abraham brooding over the cost of the sacrifice?, or;
> ➤ Abraham offering his very best?, or;
> ➤ Isaac as a young learner, on his first trip to Salem, watching his father worship?, or;
> ➤ Isaac, in trust, offering up his life to his father?

Q: What would a sacrifice look like in your own life? …In your own family? …In your own Church?

Reflect on the price inside sacrifice and turn it to a prayer of confession or thanksgiving.

Week-1: WEDNESDAY—II CHRONICLES 36: 15-23

MY THOUGHTS 2—IT'S ABOUT TIME

"Imagine what it would be like to wear two wristwatches, each showing a different time. The watches wouldn't be set to different time zones, mind you; instead, each would measure time according to its own different pace and its own different rhythm. Some of the people around you would measure time according to the rhythm of one of the watches, and others according to the rhythm of the other watch. Does it sound confusing? Well, welcome to my world. More accurately, welcome to the world of the modern Jew."

From the Seattle Times faithpage@seattletimes.com, dated 09/22/07, an Article by Rabbi Mark S. Glickman

Our faith community bumps into time everywhere. About half of our congregation is tribal (Samoan, Native American) and the other half is from European descent.

Tribal communities value honor, title, relation; the individual is important as a significant member of a community much as in a family—where the dog, mother, father, sister, brother, aunt, cousin is important, essential even, but as defined by their relation. Time, as a function of the clock is irrelevant. Time is important and measured by communal events and celebrations. Whether they start at 6:00 pm or 6:13 pm is unimportant. Who is there and the honor accorded by presence is what makes 'time' important.

European descendants, on the other hand are highly individualistic. Our personal identity is the center of our universe and what matters is if we live into our sense of self—as measured by our values and character, our sense of justice. We measure our value by how well we do things or how much we have accumulated. Time is a function of ordering our lives so that we may accomplish more and thus actualize our self by creative and timely demonstrations that we are who we say we are. The clock matters as it measures our age, opportunities for accessing achievement (say 21 or college anyone?) and measures how well we have accomplished our potential as per norms.

Rabbi Mark Glickman, in the Seattle Times, has captured the essence of a tribal community (Israel) living within the American landscape by noting that *"today's Jews live in two different time systems.*

> *In one of those systems—let's call it Modern Time— days start at midnight, years start on Jan. 1 and workplaces close on Dec. 25. But in the other system—Jewish time—days start at sundown, years start sometime in September or October, and workplaces close for major Jewish festivals.*
>
> *Modern Time counts its years from the birth of a Jew who lived almost 2,000 years ago. Jewish time counts its years from when Jewish tradition says God created the world. It is now the year 2007 in Modern Time; but 10 days ago—last Thursday—was the Jewish New Year, Rosh Hashanah, the beginning of the year 5768 in Jewish time.*
>
> *Living in either one of these time systems can be perplexing; living in both simultaneously can often be a real challenge".*

Rabbi Glickman is writing on September the 22nd, 2007 on *"Yom Kippur, the Jewish Day of Atonement, Jewish Time's most solemn occasion".* He admonishes us; *"As you go about doing your errands or taking your kids to sports events, I encourage you to keep in mind that some of your neighbors, the Jewish ones, have gathered in their synagogues for atonement, fasting and worship".* He notes that this awareness of living with two watches, as he describes it, is felt every weekend as most Americans live for Saturday and Sunday—free of the rhythms of work—whereas Jewish persons live for Sabbath which starts at sundown on Friday and results in a day where the normal practices of the week become treasured because of Sabbath reflections re-centering life around eternal—timeless, if you will, values. He concludes:

> *"Living with two wristwatches can be difficult for us Jews, but it also provides us enormous and wonderful opportunities. Because nothing is more fundamental to a culture than the way it measures and lives time, the ability to live in each of these time systems allows us to participate simultaneously in two magnificent cultures".*
>
> *From the Seattle Times faithpage@seattletimes.com, dated 09/22/07, an Article by Rabbi Mark S. Glickman*

Reflections on "It's About Time"

"We'll be back on Modern Time tomorrow, but for today, we're living according to the rhythms of our Jewish lives". Rabbi Glickman

Time is essential to spiritual formation, precisely because it is a journey (pilgrimage is the old word, I think) that we are taking.

Q: How do you mark time? ...by the 24-hour clock, beginning at 12:00 AM or by the Story of God?

Q: Do you even have a sense of living in two time zones, two worlds? ...Which has the greater influence?

Q: How might you—your family—your Church better live The Story? ...What remembrances might help? ...What rhythms might help?

Consider the role of time in your life and turn it to prayer.

Week-1: THURSDAY—DANIEL 6: 1-28

Story 3—About Time & Place

Imaginative Personal Story from a devotional moment in Time

Introduction:

Water has always played a dance with me and Christ. Water has been present as an invitation/sign in the whole of my journey and continues to speak...

The Story:

It was 9:45 in the evening. I stood above the waters of the

mighty Columbia River. Across this gigantic expanse of water was the Portland Red Lion Inn with a perfectly round moon that seemed suspended in the sky above. To my right was an expansive bridge, across which the lights of the trucks and cars hurried on their way, unaware of the beauty or presence of the waters below. Except for an occasional homeless, couples aware only of each other and a few quiet and reflective persons, I was alone.

The river was almost perfectly still, the moon cast a silent light across its depth which seemed to come to me. The Holy Spirit gathered around me with what, at first, seemed an odd question.

"Terry, do you remember the first time you saw this river?"

Into my mind, almost uninvited, rushed the memory of a small boy, in the back seat, as my father paid the toll and we were crossing this same bridge—the biggest one I had ever seen.

Again, the Spirit...

"Terry, I AM the river of your life; quiet, still, faithful, holy and full of love. All that your life is, was and will be runs through the quiet power and presence that this mighty river represents.

Terry, look at those cars and trucks as they speed by, without seeing, noticing, enjoying my Presence. That was you, even as a child. I directed you to this very place, though you were yet unaware, as they are now."

My thoughts began to take in another time, when this very same body of water spoke into my soul. It was the time of God's silence.

It happened just after the deepest scare of my addiction. I came very close to acting out my fantasies and sought a purchased relationship (if it can be called that) with sexual intimacy. Something inside me backed away in horror. God spoke within me judgment and warning. That night I made an inner decision to get help.

Soon after, a home opened up for Joetta and I just above the Columbia River with a panoramic view of the river's moods and quiet power. Night after night, I watched in silence and was drawn into its quiet strength. I did not then connect the river's mysterious presence to the prevenient work of Christ, who in His time and mine was even then making room in me, for Him.

I had decided to move away from the rituals of sexual addiction and seek God. Still, God remained silent. God's silence seemed to distance me from the only source of help I knew of. The silence felt like punishment, but was actually forming in me a hunger for holiness that would become a reservoir of God's very Presence—not unlike the pockets that a salmon makes when it is preparing to spawn. It dives into the sand and rock and forms an impression underneath the rapid currents so that she may deposit her eggs in safety.

As I stood overlooking the Columbia on this October night I became aware that God had not been silent in those days long past. In me was a wall of sin, wounds, and addiction that could not hear God's Spirit. Even then Jesus spoke, but in sign, by water. In my journal that evening I wrote.

"I remembered when I first awakened to the beauty of the river, still… I would sit by the window and think of and dream of the peace that this river, strong and mighty could speak… And now, God has brought me home to the quiet of a soft night and the strength of a river, still.

Time unfolds and I feel like a child full of wonder—'What surprise is next, Father?'"

From "Confessional Holiness", the Chapter on "The Importance of Time", by Terry Mattson, pg #160-162

Reflections on "About Time & Place"

In this devotional, God seems to speak through a place and from a historical perspective, connecting the dots in Terry's life.

> *"Terry, I AM the river of your life; quiet, still, faithful, holy and full of love. All that your life is, was and will be runs through the quiet power and presence that this mighty river represents…"*
> Insight from Terry's Devotional.

Q: Looking back can you see a place that is 'sacred space' in your life?   …Where? …How so? …Why not?

On a piece of paper or computer, draw a time line of God's encounters with you; of your own journey. Mark off the important moments, including the 'silent spaces' and 'sacred spaces' as well.

Turn your reflections to prayer:

Week-1: FRIDAY—ISAIAH 40: 1-11

MY THOUGHTS 3—TIME'S PLACE

"That man is a being under way and that his way is not a fiction, but that something really happens to him in this life, and that he can seek, can find, but can also miss the mark."
From Salt of the Earth, page #41 by Pope Benedict XVI

Time is a gift of grace. The whole purpose of our journey is to see what will emerge in us, Christ or anti-Christ.

"You see, at just the right time, when we were still powerless, Christ died for the ungodly."
Romans 5: 6

Jesus, the Son of God—incarnate, enters into time as its creator, redeemer and fulfillment. In order to be our redeemer he must enter into our time as well.

"And Jesus grew in wisdom and stature, and in favor with God and men."
Luke 2: 52

Time allows for the unfolding of our humanity. We are not magically created, but born of both God and our human parents initiative, in time.

"Instead, speaking the truth in love we will in all things grow up into Him who is the Head, that is, Christ."
Ephesians 4: 15

Time is necessary to human/Divine interaction; at least as we understand life in this place. Time allows for the birth of the Holy Spirit in us and the growing up into Christ in all ways. We are not magically created spiritually; but born of both God's Spirit and shaped by the Church, in time.

" A saint is a sacramental personality."
From "the Complete Works of Oswald Chambers, Page #681

Time, together with faith give expression in holiness. Time and faith are both necessary to our coming to a place wherein we love God first as no other and our neighbor as our self (Entire Sanctification) as:

➢ Each moment we seek to fully respond, and;
➢ We become aware of the need for a deeper, profound and full surrender, beyond our initial confession(s), and;
➢ We hunger for Christ, his life to be fully formed in ours.

"My spiritual life is based on some word of God made living in me…The reception of the Holy Ghost depends entirely upon moral preparation.
I must abide in the light, which the Holy Ghost sheds and be obedient to the word of God; then when the power of God comes upon such obedience there will be the manifestation of a strong family likeness to Jesus.
'Tarry ye—until...' means concentration in order that the purpose of God may be developed in our lives… until ye be endued with power from on high…

*He does not expect us to carry on 'evangelical capers'
(or demonstrations) but to manifest the life of the Son
of God in our mortal flesh."*
From The Complete works of Oswald Chambers, pg 679— (or
demonstrations added for clarification).

Life is Sacramental in its essence. Everyone and
everything in the universe is created to live out the Glory
(Story) of God, unfolding. Both time (Story) and place
(Jerusalem) interact to create this 'sacramental' life we are
invited to share in.

These conclusions about time (with adaptations) are largely taken from
"Confessional Holiness", Chapter on "The Importance of Time" by Terry
Mattson, pg #163-164

Reflections on "Time's Place"

> ➤ **Time is a gift of grace.**
> ➤ **Jesus, the Son of God—incarnate, enters into
>   time as her creator, redeemer and fulfillment.**
> ➤ **Time allows for the unfolding of our humanity.**
> ➤ **Time is necessary to human/Divine interaction.**
> ➤ **Time, together with faith give expression in
>   holiness.**
> ➤ **Life is Sacramental in its essence.**

Q: Which of these strike you as most important? ...Why?
...How So?

Consider how you may cooperate with the 'gift of time',
instead of fighting it in the formation of Jesus within and
around you. Turn it to prayer.

Week-1: SATURDAY—JOHN 10: 1-16

STORY 4—WHERE TIME & ETERNITY INTERSECT

Biblical Imaginative Story—An Epilogue to God's Story based on Revelation 5.

"Lord Jesus Christ, Son of the Living God, have mercy on me a sinner." Over and again the prayer of Jesus ran through my mind/heart as I neared the moment when the fog of night overcame the dark stillness that was my bedroom, inviting me into the world of sleep. "Lord Jesus Christ, son of David, have mercy on me a sinner."…and my mind wandered, drifting toward the enflamed and burning sensation of my heart that often accompanies this prayer. "Lord Jesus Christ, son of Mary, have mercy… and eternity opened a window into my soul, by dream.

"Then I saw in the right hand of him who sat on the throne a scroll with writing on both sides and sealed with seven seals. And I saw a mighty angel proclaiming in a loud voice 'Who is worthy to break the seals and open the scroll?'" (Rev 5:1, 2) I looked around to my right and left. A vast and numberless ocean of women and men filled what appeared to be a stadium that sparkled in colors of the rainbow, with water pouring over falls in the furtherest edges of this spacious place producing a music unlike any I'd ever heard. I moved around and between the throngs of billions,

perhaps. I could not tell. Even so, I moved with ease, as though the only one present, watching their faces, hoping that someone would answer the angel's question; 'Who is worthy?' But each face turned away, some to the north, others to the south, the east and west; each with a faraway look, as though searching. I looked but could not see what they were all searching for. "If only I had more eyes, perhaps seven and could see beyond?" Then suddenly, I was directly in front of the angel who was asking, "Who is worthy to break the seals and open the scroll?" The entire stadium, filled with flesh, was now staring down upon me, searching into me. They could see with me every moment of my life; each breath and thought. "Oh, God!" I cried, for cast upon giant screens my life passed before me; Every lust filled moment, every passing curse, each jealous attempt to take center stage. I was exposed and naked and seen for who I was.

"Who is worthy...?" the angel continued, and waited. Time stood still. After what might have been a thousand years I gathered the courage to lift my eyes up and into the face of the angel whose question bore into the very center of my hunger. All my life I had longed to be holy, to simply be well and to love God, singularly as no other. But I could not. Inside the drama upon the moving screen before me were moments of selfless compassion, of child like and obedient response to Jesus. Yet each of these scenes were enveloped in scores of other moments where living color captured the greed and sensuality that too often overwhelmed. "I cannot," is all I said and fell before the angel and curled up into a ball of shame and tears.

"I wept and wept because no one was found who was worthy to open the scroll or look inside it. Then one of the elders said to me 'Do not weep! See the Lion of Judah, the Root of David, has triumphed. He is able to open the scroll and it's seven seals'" (Rev. 5: 4,5). Slowly my sobs turned into a rhythmic and gentle weeping, with tears gently flowing down the side of my face. Someone, whose face I could not quite make out, stepped out of the crowd with ease and reached

out his hand to touch my face and wipe away the tears. I sat up, encouraged and looked into the grand stands and felt the presence of tenderness looking down on me, each face now turned in my direction, none with judgment, each with a look of understanding, as though they, themselves saw something yet beyond me.

Suddenly, a sea as wide as time opened before me. The sea was perfectly still and shining, giving the appearance of glass. A rainbow shown from out of the sea. From within the sea and near the rainbow there emerged the figure of one whose robe was brilliant light. He was coming towards me. All eyes were now focused upon him, except for mine.

Looking to my right I noticed *"a lamb, looking as if it had been slain, standing in the center of the throne encircled by"* four living creatures and twenty four elders. The lamb had *"seven horns and seven eyes, which are the seven spirits of God sent out into all the earth"* (Selections from Rev. 5:6).

From within the lamb there flowed a continual river of blood making it's way out and into the sea of time, covering and touching all that lived within the sea. Taking courage and standing, I looked out and into the sea of time and saw that this was the scroll that could not be opened; the water falls on the edge of this place now falling back into the sea like the folds of living paper. Within the sea was the 'living mystery' inside each persons life, as the moving pictures were lived out. 'No wonder,' I thought to myself. 'No wonder there is no judgment in the faces of each person of billions in the stadium, for their own moving pictures were much the same as mine.' Some worse, some better. But each story was tragic, until touched by the blood which flowed from within the lamb and into the sea of time. In the center of the sea was this man of brilliant light whose movement was ever towards each of us. For we all, each one of us stood in the stands and also in the center of the stands next to lamb, as did I.

Fear and shame melted into 'awe' as I began to understand. *"Before time, the lamb was slain."* It was what I had always believed, but thought a metaphor.

Inside the sea of time was another and larger moving picture. It was different and filled with love beyond measure. There were no cursing or misdirected thoughts toward women. There was no ego, other than identity, simple and innocent, old and yet young.

My eyes turned away from my own 'moving picture' and onto this larger than life visual, growing with each passing wave of the sea. It was then that I noticed the reason that the sea looked as clear as glass. My story and all those in the stadium around me; All of our moving pictures were being taken up and into the Story of the One who was coming ever nearer, creating from a distance the visual of One life, One sea.

As I was taking all of this in, I found myself face to face with the One from within the sea. His face was not terribly handsome, but human and kind. His gentle eyes were like the stars and his hands were wounded. It was these hands, that only moments before had reached out from the crowd to wipe away my tears. Now they were lifted above my head. The One from within the sea spoke, a language I did not hear, but understood to be "LOVE ITSELF". Three times he spoke, or at least I heard it three times though the sound of each differed somehow. "Terry Vernon Mattson, son of the Living God, receive mercy." "Terry Vernon Mattson, son of Adam, receive mercy." "Terry Vernon Mattson, son of Eve, receive mercy." And, in that moment, all the prayers of the saints and Jesus own prayers and dreams, whispers and visions offered on my behalf while in the sea of time flowed from out of the rainbow and into my being, filling me with— well, Him, no me—no Him—no me—no Him, no—

My Thoughts 4—Where Time & Eternity Intersect

"So Christ was sacrificed once to take away the sins of many people; and he will appear a second time, not to bear sin, but to bring salvation to those who are waiting for him.

The law is only a shadow of the good things that are coming—not the realities themselves. ...But when this priest had offered for all time the sacrifice for sins, he sat down at the right hand of God. Since that time, he waits for his enemies to be made his footstool, because by one sacrifice he has made perfect forever those who are being made holy.

...Therefore, brothers, since we have confidence to enter the Most Holy Place by the blood of Jesus, by a new and living way opened for us through the curtain, that is, his body, and since we have a great priest over the house of God, let us draw near to God with a sincere heart in full assurance of faith, having our hearts sprinkled to cleanse us from a guilty conscience and having our bodies washed with pure water."   Hebrews 9: 28 & 10:1, 12-14, 19-22

"All inhabitants of the earth will worship the beast—all whose names have not been written in the book of life belonging to the Lamb that was slain from the creation of the world."   Revelation 13:8

Christ died, once for all. Protestants like to quote this verse from Hebrews to Catholics in order to undermine the heart/soul of the Mass. I would suggest, however, that we (and maybe a good deal of our Catholic friends with us) have missed the point of the Mass and need to look again.

Jesus death in time is singular. Christ died once. His sacrifice of death is given only once. His death is sufficient to reconcile "all" of us and "all" our sin(s) to the Father. He need not die again. But the living Mass (drama-unfolding mystery) is not about his sacrifice of death, but the ever present and living sacrifice in the heart of the Trinity of God for us and in us.

From before time, in eternity "the lamb was slain." What does that mean, if not an agreement between the three persons of the One God to open their fellowship of joy, peace and creativity to the pain, turmoil and deadly chaos, indeed boredom of our sinfulness. *"God made Him who had no sin to be sin for us, so that in him we might become the righteousness of God"* (II Cor. 5:21). In other words, in Jesus the Trinity of God changed and forever. God the Father— Son—Spirit opened themselves up to us. The mystery of love that saves and was poured out into time in Jesus, on that cross, lived eons before the moment.

This same lamb (sacrifice) is seen in John's vision as being present and slain in the very glory that is heaven. Do we then anticipate a bloody welcome in the Holy that is truly holy? No, of course not. Death has no more power. This last and real enemy of humankind is swallowed up. Yet the mystery of the sacrifice is forever present. A living stream of life (blood) flows from before/after time into time itself. In Jesus death, the Trinity of God grew in their experiential understanding of our sin/being. And Jesus, who is seated in the heavens at the right hand of the power of God ever intercedes (advocates—speaks a Living Word on our behalf).

Jesus, who was dead, now lives. He offers up to the Father his sacrifice as a sweet fragrance, the offering of perfect obedience. His is now a 'living sacrifice', that began before time and lives now in timelessness, but being poured out into our time—all time. For the Holy One of God, who lives in and between the Father and Son is given the ministry of taking this "living sacrifice", this mystery of God's perfect love and pouring out into Time and us its restorative and healing grace.

Reflections on "Where Time & Eternity Intersect"

"Jesus death in time is singular. Christ died once. His sacrifice of death is given only once. His death is sufficient to reconcile "all" of us and "all" our sin(s) to the Father. He need not die again. But the living Mass (drama-unfolding-mystery) is not about his sacrifice of death, but the ever present and living sacrifice in the heart of the Trinity of God for us and in us."
From Terry above

Q: Have you ever thought of the mystery within God's loving sacrifice as being anticipated and committed to before time?

Q: Have you ever thought of the Trinity of God growing from the experience of Jesus life—passion—death and resurrection...of now experiencing what had been anticipated only? ...Is that possible? ...If so, what does that mean in terms of our salvation?

Q: Have you ever thought of the sacrificial event in time now being experienced as a mystery—as an ever present sacrifice of love in the heavens as Christ speaks a living Word to the Father—Spirit on our behalf, continually?

Q: How would these ideas shape your own experience of Holy Communion? ...of life in the Spirit?

Reflect in silence.

Week-1: SUNDAY— EPHESIANS 1: 3-18, ROMANS 8: 15-28 REVELATION 5: 1-14 & 21: 9-14

MY THOUGHTS 5—TIME'S CENTER—HOLY COMMUNION

I am reading a wonderful six book series at this writing about Black Jack Gerry, a futuristic hero returned after a hundred years drifting in space and thought dead. It's a fun, fast action science fiction—a romp through the stars full of deceptions, the evil Syndics, betrayal in his battle fleet and all within the context of the near destruction of the Alliances (Earth) forces in deep space at the hand of Syndic deception, complete with a nearly fatal escape thanks to the resurrection of Captain Gerry and his 100-year-old and now forgotten ethics and strategies. The only problem is how to get home when deep in Syndic space and do the most damage to the enemy in the process of returning. It's all fun, a simple plot unfolding with everything pretty much on the table.

But what I really love is multi-layered mysteries or Sci-Fi's with multiple and seemingly unrelated plots that only come together at the end, their interlacing story lines barely perceptible even midway.

The evangelical Church has for far too long tried to read the Bible as a single layered plot (clear bad guys and clear good guys) with everything pretty much on the table. The only problem is God! It's not the way the Word was lived, told, written, gathered and finally evolved into its present library of

66 books (sub-plots) whose relation to the whole is often barely noticeable.

What we have forgotten is that The Word is an action centered story that emerges from:

> ➢ Original Events, and;
> ➢ As remembered by the People of God in a new worshiping context, and;
> ➢ Gathered in even newer worshiping historical settings that frame each book as finally written.

The Book is very much a Tom Clancy novel full of layered meanings; the same story reshaped for a new worshiping community and with an even bolder intent—to pour out into our time and shape the worlds living stories by the Story of the Trinity of God among us!

In Roman's eight Paul captures all these nuances inside a single idea: God fully present in us—reshaping our communal and personal futures.

> *"In the same way, the Spirit helps us in our weakness. We do not know what we ought to pray for, but the Spirit himself intercedes for us with groans that words cannot express. And he who searches our hearts knows the mind of the Spirit, because the Spirit intercedes for the saints in accordance with God's will...*
>
> *What, then shall we say in response to this? If God is for us, who can be against us? He who did not spare his own Son, but gave him up for us all—how will he not also, along with him, graciously give us all things... Christ Jesus, who died—more than that, who was raised to life—is at the right hand of God and is also interceding for us."*
> Romans 8: 26-27, 31, 32, 34b

This communion between the Trinity of God within humanity is the result of multi-layered plots coming together around holy communion. It's anticipated in a hundred sub-plots including:

➢ God's killing of an animal to cover Adam and Eve's sin, and;

➢ Adam's killing of an animal to cover Cain's sin, and;

➢ The three visitors who come to Abram's camp and Abram's offer of table fellowship and subsequent pleading for Sodom and Gomorrah, and;

➢ Abram's offer of his only son at Mount Moriah, and;

➢ The feeding of Israel in the exodus the bread of angels, and;

➢ The Tent of Meeting brought into the center of Israel's exodus encampment demonstrating God's close and forgiving Presence, and;

➢ The evolution of Jerusalem and the Holy Temple as a living—eternal sign of God's gracious Presence, and;

➢ The Psalms generally and Psalm 22 specifically turning David's and Israel's life, sins, triumphs and despair into Communal faith, and;

➢ The development of the Essene community and emphasis upon water and bread and renewal, and;

➢ The emergence of multiple mystery religions which foreshadow the real Story of God, and;

➢ John's gospel—telling the Story spiritually by means of water and bread, and;

On and On we could go. But what finally emerges is an invitation to the twelve (including Judas, per Luke's account) and through them to the whole world that this God seeks in communion—a re-enactment and renewal of bread fellowship lived out radically in the earth.

So in time the mystery is also renewed: Again, there is no continuing sacrifice of death (condemnation, guilt). These have been consumed by that the one sacrifice in time. But there is the continuing "mystery" (Perfect Love poured out) of God's sacrifice of the Father's own Son. Jesus is even now offering a *"living sacrifice"* in the heavens whose counterpart is played out by the Holy Spirit in God's Church. We are invited to become *"living sacrifices"* (Rom. 12: 1,2). And we are invited to eat of the mystery of His life and pour it out in sacrificial giving (John 13).

This work of the Holy Spirit in time has two aspects: Holiness and Love. In us the wholeness and holiness of the Trinity of God is being formed. We are partakers of the Divine Nature, even now. We are being changed. The language is ever clear.

> *"Since that time he waits for his enemies to be made his footstool, because by one sacrifice he has made perfect forever those who are being made holy*
> *...For this reason Christ is the mediator of a new covenant, that those who are called may receive the promised eternal inheritance—now that he has died as a ransom to set them free from the sins committed under the first covenant."*   Hebrews 10: 13, 14 & 9: 15

John echoes the same reality.

> *"How great is the love the*
> *Father has lavished on us...*
> *Dear friends, now we are children of God,*
> *and what we will be has not yet been made known.*
> *But we know that when he appears,*
> *we shall be like him,*
> *for we shall see him as he is.*
> *Everyone who has this hope in him purifies himself,*
> *just as he is pure."*
> I John 3: 1, 2-3

We are already made perfect forever, the writer of Hebrews says, yet we are being made holy. John says that we are to purify ourselves, just as we are pure. How can we be both pure and being made?

It is again to the mystery of the "once for all" we return. Paul says that we are seated with Christ in the heavenly realms (Col. 3:1-5). In Christ, who is our advocate the mystery is already complete. Our Father in the heavens sees us not with the blinders of the cross on, but with the full realization of earth made whole in eternity. The mystery of Christ's living sacrifice is this: We are complete and live before the Father, inside the very fellowship of the Trinity of God, even now. Only the now, for us must wait, till that day. **It's the best of science fiction made real.**

Adam's sin and the wounds which attend are really swallowed up by the 'birth, life, passion and death event' of Christ, in time. But Adam's sin and the wounds which attend are not healed as yet, in us. Not all of Christ's enemies, in time, have yet been made his footstool. In the Holy Spirit, by fellowship of the Church on earth and by means of the Eucharist we are invited to anticipate and increasingly (that's the 'being made perfect part') live out Jesus sacrifice— **Holiness anticipated and realized from before time, in time and into eternity** (Ephesians 1).

And now we come to the second half of the mystery. **Love perfected on earth.** Paul says that in one sense Jesus death is in fact incomplete. *"Now I rejoice in what was suffered for you, and I fill up in my flesh what is still lacking in regard to Christ's afflictions, for the sake of his body, which is the church"* (Col. 1: 24). He is not suggesting that we 'add' salvific grace to what Jesus did at Golgotha. Only that in and through us, the Church, the grace of Christ is extended to everyone.

That is why to the Galatians he writes, *"I have been crucified with Christ and I no longer live, but Christ lives in me. The life I live in the body, I live by faith in the Son of God, who loved me and gave himself for me"* (Gal. 2: 20). To the

Corinthians he affirmed, *"For we who are alive are always being given over to death for Jesus' sake, so that his life may be revealed in our mortal body. So then, death is at work in us, but life is at work in you"* (II Cor. 11, 12). And to the Philippians Paul counts his experience in jail and his concerns for them as *"being poured out like a drink offering on the sacrifice and service coming"* (Phil. 1: 17) from their faith, which—incidentally—references a pagan ritual offered to the gods before every meal, turned on its head; (Which is why we look even inside other faith traditions for the Spirit of God pre-figuring the Jesus Story).

We, who are the body of Christ, live out his sacrifice on earth, but in a living, creative and powerful way. We offer our lives as a 'sacrifice' so that others may know Christ, so that every enemy may be won over to Christ, including: death—sickness—suffering—hunger—war—addiction. We literally are the physical presence of Christ on earth. The life, he lived in time, is now poured out into the earth through us. The mystery (PERFECT LOVE) that was fully given on Golgotha is now poured out through His Church, until the day of Christ.

And so the Story reveals its center and the 'living drama' (Mass—Mystery) unfolds as eternity pours into time, restoring in time/eternity all things on heaven and earth.

Reflections on "Time's Center—Holy Communion"

"Therefore, I urge you, brothers, in view of God's mercy, to offer your bodies as living sacrifices, holy and pleasing to God—this is your spiritual worship."
Romans 12:1

"The mystery of Christ's living sacrifice is this: We are complete and live before the Father, inside the very fellowship of the Trinity of God, even now. Only the now, for us must wait, till that day."   From Terry above

Q: Have you ever felt/sensed God the Father say to you… "You are my son, in whom I am well pleased"?

Q: Understanding Holy Communion as the center of God's Story from before time, in time and after time—how will it affect the way you enter into Holy Communion?

"Adam's sin and the wounds which attend are really swallowed up by the 'death event' of Christ, in time. But Adam's sin and the wounds which attend are not healed as yet for/in us."   From Terry above

Q: Where do you see in you, Adam's wounds or sin? …Does the idea of the cross being sufficient, but needing to be lived out in you bring peace or fear? …Why?

Q: Do you see the significance of time—of story—of unfolding drama (mystery) in a new light? …If so, how will that affect the way you live Christ?

Turn your reflections to prayer.

Next:
The Person

2 THE PERSON

... The Sheep Gate

INVOCATION:

O LORD, YOU ARE MY SHEPHERD. I KNOW THAT I SHALL
NOT BE IN WANT AS LONG AS I AM WITH YOU. YOU, O
LORD, LEAD ME TO THE GREEN PASTURES WHERE THE
WATERS ARE STILL AND QUIET, AND FEED MY SOUL. YOU
WILL KEEP ME TO PATHS THAT ARE HEALTHY AND RIGHT, I
KNOW. I AM YOURS. I SHARE IN YOUR NAME. PLEASE,
WHEN DANGER COMES, EVEN TO THE POINT OF DEATH, HELP
ME TO NEVER FEAR. YOUR SHEPHERD'S STAFF BOTH
CORRECTS AND GUIDES ME. EVEN WHEN MY ENEMIES
SURROUND, YOUR PRESENCE GIVES ME COMFORT AND
IDENTITY. I KNOW THAT I WILL DISCOVER WHAT IS GOOD AS I
MAKE MY WAY HOME, TO YOUR HOME, IN THE HEAVENS AND
ON EARTH AND FOREVER. AMEN.

BASED ON PSALM 23

PSALM OF THE WEEK: PSALM 80

COMMANDMENT OF THE WEEK: I AM THE LORD YOUR GOD, WHO BROUGHT YOU OUT OF EGYPT, OUT OF THE LAND OF SLAVERY. YOU SHALL HAVE NO OTHER GODS BEFORE ME. DEUTERONOMY 5: 6, 7

DAILY SCRIPTURES:

MONDAY—JOHN 1: 1-18

TUESDAY—PSALM 78: 1-17, 38-39, 52-72

WEDNESDAY—EZEKIEL 34

THURSDAY—MATTHEW 11: 25-30 & 12: 1-14

FRIDAY—I KINGS 18: 21-39 & MARK 9: 2-8

SATURDAY—JOHN 1: 29-34, LUKE 1: 5-22

SUNDAY—LUKE 2: 8-20, JOHN 10: 1-16, MATTHEW 1: 1-4 & 9: 35-37, REVELATION 5: 11-14 & 7: 9-17

FROM
MATTHEW 21: 10

AND WHEN JESUS ENTERED JERUSALEM, THE WHOLE CITY WAS STIRRED UP. "WHO IS THIS?" THEY ASKED.

Week-2: MONDAY—JOHN 1: 1-18

MY THOUGHTS 6—IT'S PERSONAL

"Our tendency is to put truth into a dogma: Truth is a Person. "I am... The Truth," said Jesus."
From "The Complete Works of Oswald Chambers, under "Beginnings," pages #959-960

At the center of the Christian faith is a person, not dogma—nor world view. It is what is most unique about Christianity. Faith is not simply about believing a set of doctrines but living in relation with the Divine Presence.

Were that not radical enough **this person at the center is fully human—material—born of creation and still 'fully God'**...never born but begotten of the Father—Eternally the Word!

Oswald Chambers emphasizes the significance of God's incarnation; Getting down and dirty, into the mud is part of the Divine—the dust of the stars, if you will. He writes:

*"And the Lord God formed man
of the dust of the ground."*
(Genesis 2:7)

The first man is of the earth, earthy." (I Corinthians 15: 47)

...These two things, dust and Divinity, make up man. That he is made of the dust of the ground is man's glory, not his shame—it is only his shame in so far as he is a sinner, because in it he is to manifest the image of God.

We are apt to think that because we are "of the earth, earthy," that this is our humiliation, but it is not so; it is the very thing God's word makes most of. …If sin were in matter it would be untrue to say that Jesus Christ was 'without sin' because he took on Him our flesh and blood, 'becoming in the likeness of men.' Sin does not belong to human nature as God designed it, it is abnormal, therefore to speak of being 'eradicated,' rooted up, is nonsense, it never was planted in. I have no business to say, "in Christ I am all right but in myself I am all wrong"; I have to see to it that everything related to my physical life is lived in harmony with and perfect obedience to the life of the Son of God in me."

From "The Complete Works of Oswald Chambers, under "Beginnings," pages #959-960

Still, more radical is the nature of the personal human relation into which God's incarnation is borne—in humility, the dirty and thankless and lowly craft of caring for dumb sheep. It is no accident that shepherds are the first to see the Christ child—for they are the smelly, low economic and social outcasts that the Gospels use to identify the Person through whom God communicates acceptance, restoration and healing. Shepherds serve in many ancient cultures and especially in Israel a place of honor (even in their low station) for it is the shepherding, pastoral model that defines the purpose and mission of ancient Kings. Pope Benedict VI tells us that *"in the ancient near East, in royal inscriptions from both Sumer and the area of Babylonia and Assyria, the king refers to himself as the shepherd instituted by God…Of course In Israel,"* he writes, *"'the immediate precedents for Jesus' use of this image are found in the Old Testament, where God himself appears as the Shepherd of Israel. This image deeply shaped Israel's piety, and it was especially in times of need that Israel found a word of* *consolation and confidence in it…"* Benedict captures this when he says:

> *"… 'Pasturing sheep' is an image of his task as a ruler. This image implies that caring for the weak is one of the tasks of the just ruler. One could therefore say that, in view of its origins, this image of Christ the Good Shepherd is a Gospel of Christ the King, an image that sheds light upon the kingship of Christ.*
>
> *…Faced with the murmuring of the Pharisees and scribes over Jesus' table of fellowship with sinners, the Lord tells the parable of the ninety-nine sheep who remained in the fold and the one lost sheep. The shepherd goes after the lost sheep, lifts it joyfully upon his shoulders, and brings it home. Jesus puts this parable as a question to his adversaries: Have you not read God's word in Ezekiel? I am only doing what God the true Shepherd, foretold: I wish to seek out the sheep that are lost and bring the strayed back home."*
>
> From "Jesus of Nazareth", by Pope Benedict XVI, page #272-274"

Reflections on "It's Personal"

> *"That he (human kind) is made of the dust of the ground is man's glory, not his shame—"*
> From "The Complete Works of Oswald Chambers, pages #960

Q: Are you comfortable in your own skin? …How so? …Why not?

"Sin does not belong to human nature as God designed it, it is abnormal, therefore to speak of being "eradicated," rooted up, is nonsense, it never was planted in. I have no business to say, "in Christ I am all right but in myself I am all wrong."
From "The Complete Works of Oswald Chambers, under "Beginnings," pages #959-960

The Word of God is a person whose imaginative and creative Word will find expression or "actuality" in us only as we respond in obedience. This Christian thing is 'relational' to its core.
Q: Have you ever thought of 'salvation' as a restoration of God's original design or dream instead of as a 'new creation' or 'new start'? ...How does this understanding affect the way you see salvation? ...How about the way you see God? ...How about the way you see yourself?

Then consider how God wants to be formed in you—never less than inter-personal and human. Contemplate that thought and pray.

Week-2: TUESDAY—PSALM 78: 1-17, 38-39, 52-72

STORY 5—THE SHEPHERD BOY

An Imaginative Biblical Story based upon Psalm 78: 1-17, 38-39, 52-72

As David leaned over his knapsack gathering his papyrus he heard, in the distance, the sound of a familiar voice. Picking up the scroll upon which he had just written his most recent song, he turned to see his brother, Eliab, the eldest of his father, Jesse's sons running toward him. His body was slender and strong. He could run like the wind. "Come, quickly David! Your father wishes you in Bethlehem, now!" was all Eliab relayed. "I will care for the sheep."

Quickly David gathered his personal belongings and without hesitation matched his brother's urgency with the speed of a deer as he ran toward the town of his birth. 'What could be so important?' he wondered to himself. As he made a bend in the narrow path he spotted to his right the shelter where he had kept his lambs safe in the evening before. The song of his heart had been written there as he sat out under the stars, with his sheep between him and the cavern walls of

two hills as they together formed a natural sheepfold.

It was in the first watch of the night that his dog, Eli, had awoken him barking and growling. It was a growl David knew. It meant danger. He had chosen this place precisely because he could control the access to his lambs from both the north and south. The stream that ran along slowed into an open and still area just in front of the natural cavern as the spring made the bend in its direction, allowing for his sheep to drink. Along the east bank, up against the cavern walls was plenty of fresh green grass, fed by the bubbling waters of the stream. Only the gnats were a problem. But David always had plenty of oil and spices with which to anoint the heads of his black sheep. Most of the early evening he had labored, allowing his hands to feel the contour of their heads as he worked the oil into their soft woolen bodies. After the work and only when David knew his sheep were fed, watered and anointed did he allow himself the luxuries of a warm fire, a meal with some aged wine and time to think, pray and sing to the God of his love, the shepherd of Israel. In fact, it had been just that thought which had formed the first line of his new song, sung to a tune which flowed easily from the stringed instrument that he always carried.

"The LORD is my shepherd,"

he sang,

"I shall not want.
He makes me lie down
in green pastures,
he leads me beside quiet waters,
he restores my soul."

As the words and music merged from somewhere deep within this scene, David had remembered the path that he had chosen for his papa's lambs that day.

"He guides me in
paths of righteousness,
for his name's sake."

It was in this moment that his song was interrupted by the urgency of Ely's bark. David had swung into action, reaching for his leather knapsack, his eyes searching in the direction of his faithful Ely's growl, searching the hills above while his hands grasped for his sling and the smooth stones that he always kept at ready. Suddenly his eyes caught the movement in the rocks above. Its approach was stealth itself, the animal's paws made no sound to give away this predator. But the eyes, David caught. It was a mountain lion, perched above the helpless sheep below. The sheep, startled and in fear, had also moved away from the center and toward the walled hillside. All were frozen as they awaited the predator's next move. All, except David. Apparently, the lion was unaware of him, his focus on his dog. 'And that was good,' he thought to himself.

And Ely, now aware that his master's attention was fully awakened moved into the middle of the encampment and deepened his growl so that the predator's attention stayed with him. 'Good dog,' David thought. One rock was now firmly in the sling awaiting only for the right moment. Ely's aggressive attitude had allowed the shepherd boy to get his sling into full motion with the whir of his pouch unnoticed. At that moment the lion leapt from the rock high above and out toward Ely. In mid-flight, David released the rock into the night air so that it struck the lion's head just as she was landing on top of his trusted side-kick. The rock had found its target and the lion fell over the dog, rolling to the ground stunned, just long enough for David's shepherds crook to find it's mark, again and again, until the great cat at last lay tamed against the ground.

Only then did David stop and listen, as did every living animal whose breath filled the night air. Finally, David moved, satisfied there was no more attack coming and he checked his dog first, petting him and embracing him as one would a lost friend. After cleaning up the mess and cutting the lions carcass and only when the life of the camp had returned to her gentle norm did he take up his instrument to see if the words and music still flowed. They did and he played.

> *"Even though I walk through the valley*
> *of the shadow of death,*
> *I will fear no evil,*
> *for you are with me;*
> *your rod and your staff,*
> *they comfort me."*

That was last evening. As he made his way toward Bethlehem and the excitement of being able to see the holy man of God, Samuel, the music seemed to find him again. So, as he ran, he sang the last of the song as though the whole world were listening:

> *"You prepare a table before me*
> *in the presence of my enemies.*
> *You anoint my head with oil;*
> *my cup overflows.*
> *Surely goodness and love will follow me*
> *all the days of my life, and I will dwell in the*
> *house of the LORD forever."*
>
> (Psalm 23—in italics above)

Note: Inspired, in part, by stories of Jesus as a young man shepherding his uncles flock written by Marjorie Holmes in "Three From Galilee."

Reflections on "The Shepherd Boy"

"But now your kingdom will not endure; the LORD has sought out a man after his own heart and appointed him leader of his people, because you have not kept the LORD'S commands." I Samuel 13: 14

In this text, Samuel declares to Saul that God has turned away from him and to another, *"a man after his own heart"*.

Q: What might have God seen in this young shepherd's heart that was attractive?

Make a list of the quality or qualities that you imagine God seeing in David…

Q: Of these qualities, which are in you? …Why? …How did they get there? …Which are not in you? …Why not?

David's prayer, the prayer you have been praying this week, lies near the heart our journey in and to God. It is similar to another prayer Jesus taught us to pray.

Experiment: Match the phrases of the prayer Jesus taught with the phrases of David's prayer (in the Picture below).

Our Father who art in heaven,

Hallowed be Thy Name.

Thy Kingdom come, Thy will be done in earth as it is in heaven.

Give us this day our daily bread and forgive us our debts (sins) as we forgive our debtors (those who sin against us).

Lead us not into temptation, but deliver us from evil.

For Thine is the Kingdom and the Power and the Glory forever. Amen.

Davids Prayer

The Lord is my shepherd, I lack nothing.

He makes me lie down in green pastures, he leads me beside quiet waters, he refreshes my soul.

He guides me along the right paths for his name's sake.

Even though I walk through the darkest valley, I will fear no evil, for you are with me;

your rod and your staff, they comfort me.

You prepare a table before me in the presence of my enemies. You anoint my head with oil; my cup overflows.

Surely your goodness and love will follow me all the days of my life, and I will dwell in the house of the Lord forever.

Then select one of the phrases from each prayer; Meditate upon them and make them your prayer for today.

Week-2: WEDNESDAY—EZEKIEL 34

MY THOUGHTS 7—OUR SUPRA— SUPER—PERSONAL GOD

C.S. Lewis talks about the Trinity of God—the Three Persons of Eternity whose love makes them One in very essence, being—as existing in Personal Relations so complete that a hundred universes could not contain them.

Communal Personhood lies at the heart of our faith; we are not the sum total of our character, life experience, faith, traditions, beliefs, values—though we are certainly evolving and re-defining ourselves (repenting is the Biblical Word) in light of all. We are more than the combined parts of our experience because we are made in God's image. We are by nature personal and exist as human only in relationships. God is the Super—Supra—Personal One (Three) who is love and loving, holy in all!

> *"Our tendency is to put truth into a dogma: Truth is a Person. "I am... The Truth," said Jesus."*
> From "The Complete Works of Oswald Chambers, under "Beginnings," pages #959-960

Truth is a Person: It is this that Israel—in her devotion to Yahweh—did not grasp in the coming of Jesus.

Pope Benedict XVI explores with great feeling this central idea when writing of his Jewish friend, a Rabbi who respectfully gets the threat of Jesus to "Eternal Israel". Benedict turns to this friend and scholar, Jacob Neusner and his book "A Rabbi Talks with Jesus" to emphasize the essential nature of Jesus claim. Jacob Neusner invites his readers to sit with Jesus and listen to his sermon on the mount to identify what is so dangerous about him. Pope Benedict observes that his friend *"listens to Jesus and compares his words with those of the Old Testament and with the rabbinic traditions as set down in the Mishnah and Talmud… He compares, and he speaks with Jesus himself. He is touched by the greatness and the purity of what is said, and yet at the same time he is troubled by the ultimate incompatibility that he finds at the heart of the Sermon on the Mount…"* The Pope invites us into the Rabbi's story:

"Neusner has just spent the whole day following Jesus, and now he retires for prayer and Torah study with the Jews of a certain town, in order to discuss with the rabbi of that place… all that he has heard. The rabbi cites from the Babylonian Talmus: Rabbi Simelai expounded: 'Six hundred and thirteen commandments were given to Moses, three hundred and sixty-five negative ones, corresponding to the number of the days of the solar year, and two hundred forty-eight positive commandments, corresponding to the parts of man's body.
David came and reduced them to eleven… Isaiah came and reduced them to six… Isaiah again came and reduced them to two… Habakkuk further came and based them on one, as it is said: 'But the righteous shall live by his faith'.

Neusner then continues his book with the following dialogue:
'So,' the master (Rabbi Simelai) says, 'is this what the sage, Jesus had to say?'

I (Neusner): 'Not exactly, but close.'
He: 'What did he leave out?'
I: 'Nothing.'
He: 'Then what did he add?'
I: 'Himself.'

This is the central point where the believing Jew Neusner experiences alarm at Jesus' message, and this is the central reason why he does not wish to follow Jesus, but remains with the 'eternal Israel': the centrality of Jesus' 'I' in his Message."

Reflections on 'The Sermon on the Mount' By Pope Benedict XVI—requoting Rabbi Jacob Neusner from this Book "A Rabbi Talks with Jesus".

Note: (Neusner) added to text for clarification.

And here was the struggle for ancient and modern Israel— The Law, Sabbath and Holy Temple are the context which makes Israel real and eternal; even as people of exile. Jesus presence confronts Israel with God as supra—super Person; whose revelation in Israel transcends and thus fulfills both the Sabbath, the Law and the Temple. If his claim as God Present is true then Jesus is the reality upon which we "live and move and have our being" (Acts 17: 28). Jesus alone.

Reflections on "Our Supra—Super Personal God"

Imagine yourself seated with the thousands gathered at the Mount of Jesus teaching. (See Matthew 5, 6, 7)

Q: What would have grabbed you the most?

Q: Can you understand a little better a Jews' concern with a faith centered in a person rather than in the teaching or community?

> *"Neusner cites as evidence of this 'addition' Jesus' words to the rich young man: 'If you would be perfect, go, sell all you have and come, follow me' (Matt 19: 21). Perfection, the state of being holy as God is holy (cf Lev 19: 2, 11:44), as demanded by the Torah, now consists in following Jesus."*
> From Pope Benedict XVI

Q: Are you holy? ...How so? ...Why not?

Consider your own faith and if it is based in traditions, beliefs, actions, rituals or a person. Listen.

Week-2: THURSDAY—MATTHEW 11: 25-30 & 12: 1-14

STORY 6—GREATER THAN THE SABBATH

A Personal Story—A Sabbath Interrupted

I sat in my living room on the Lord's Day (our new Sabbath) with a good man (not so good right now) living on the streets. He felt called and knew he was anointed to preach. He knew his scripture and his Calvinist Theology. On this day he came by to seek help in turning his life around as he had fallen back into an addictive pattern that was consuming his days and making his night's eternal.

Our conversation turned to survival skills and he confessed that, in this state, he had stolen from grocers for food justifying it on the basis that, like David, when hungry had ate the Shew Bread from off the altar. "After all", my friend said, "am I not anointed as David was?"

Today he knew the sound of his own excuse for what it was—and laughed at himself for his dishonesty. We fed him, helped solve a lost Food Stamp Electronic Card issue, prayed with him and dropped him off at a Pentecostal church for their Sunday evening service that has good spiritually centered connections for getting men off the streets.

At this writing he is still on the streets but aware of his need to seek help and stops by occasionally.

MY THOUGHTS 8—GREATER THAN THE SABBATH

The Sabbath, the Torah (Law) and the Temple (or Tent of Meeting in Exodus) are the three realities upon which Eternal Israel rests. Shalom or Blessed Peace is the gift of God from which and to which the world is moving. After Creation God enjoyed a rest—A Sabbath of 'Blessed Peace'.

In the Exodus from Egypt these three centers in Israel (Sabbath & Torah & Tent of Meeting) were given to Israel as the means by which they would be formed as a people wholly different from the violent consumer—slave driven Empire—by:

> Holding Yahweh at center (No gods), and;
> Living out God's Name, and;
> Sabbath Rest, and;
> Keeping Human needs as sacred by:
> Respect for the aged who no longer give economic benefit (Honor your Fathers and Mothers), and;
> Value of Persons over Property (Do not steal or covet), and;
> Keeping faith in Word (Do not lie), and;
> Keeping in Relation (Do not kill).

In obeying these Israel would assure themselves a life very different than the powerful Empire from which God had rescued them. Indeed, God would make in Israel a new Sabbath community of Blessed Peace (Shalom).

And so, Benedict XVI once again brings us back to his Rabbinic friend who sees in the Gospels a creative and theologically driven emphasis upon Jesus as the new Moses with a renewed Torah delivered on a new mountain (Sermon on the Mount) and who in Matthew 11: 25-30 invites all Israel to come to him for Sabbath rest. The Rabbi focuses his rejection of Jesus through the story of Jesus allowing his disciples to eat wheat from a field on the Sabbath. When confronted by the Pharisees for their violation of Moses law Jesus responds by identifying himself with David who ate the Shew Bread from the altar; much like my homeless and anointed friend attempted to justify himself by this same story.

Rabbi Jacob Neusner writes:

> "Jesus begins his defense of the disciple's way of satisfying their hunger by pointing out the David and his companions entered the House of God and ate the holy bread, 'which it was not lawful for him to eat nor for those who were with him, but only for the priests' (mt 12: 4). Jesus then continues: 'Or have you not read in the law how on the Sabbath the priests in the temple profane the Sabbath, and are guiltless? I tell you, something greater than the temple is here. And if you had known what this means. 'I desire mercy, and not sacrifice' (cf. Hos 6a; 6; I Sam 15:22), you would not have condemned the guiltless. For the Son of man is lord of the Sabbath.' (Mt 12: 5-8). Neusner comments: 'He [Jesus] and his disciples may do on the Sabbath what they do because they stand in the place of the priests in the Temple; the holy place has

shifted, now being formed by the circle made up of the master and his disciples.'"

Reflections on 'The Sermon on the Mount' By Pope Benedict XVI—requoting Rabbi Jacob Neusner from his Book "A Rabbi Talks with Jesus"

Neusner does not see Jesus as simply giving a more liberal—relaxed version of the Sabbath laws. His concern is how Jesus makes himself Lord of the Sabbath, the law and the Temple. In doing so Jesus has replaced Israel's historic and social reliance on the Law, the Sabbath and the Temple with himself—so that according to the gospels *"Christ now stands on the mountain, he now takes the place of the Torah. The conversation between the practicing Jew and Jesus comes to the decisive point here. His noble reserve leads him to put the question to Jesus' disciple, rather than to Jesus himself: 'Is it really so that your master, the son of man, is lord of the Sabbath? ...I ask again—is your master God?'"*

And Benedict concludes: *"The issue that is really at the heart of the debate is thus finally laid bare. Jesus understands himself as the Torah—as the word of God in person..."*

Reflections on 'The Sermon on the Mount' By Pope Benedict XVI—requoting Rabbi Jacob Neusner from his Book "A Rabbi Talks with Jesus"

Reflections on "Greater than the Sabbath"

"'Christ now stands on the mountain, he now take the place of the Torah' (p.87). The conversation between the practicing Jew and Jesus comes to the decisive point here. His noble reserve leads him to put the

question to Jesus' disciple, rather than to Jesus himself: 'Is it really so that your master, the son of man, is lord of the Sabbath? I ask again— is your master God?'

From Pope Benedict XVI, re-quote of Rabbi Neusner, page #110"

Q: If this question were addressed to you, as a disciple, what would your honest answer be? ...Have you really come to the place where you recognize Jesus as LORD?

Q: What does it mean that Jesus is the Torah (law), the Temple and the Sabbath?

Q: Which do you need most in your life?

- ➢ Jesus as Torah (Law)?, or;
- ➢ Jesus as Temple?, or;
- ➢ Jesus as Sabbath?

...Why? ...How So?

Form you answer in a prayer of Repentance or Listening Silence.

Week-2: FRIDAY—I Kings 18: 21-39 & MARK 9: 2-8

STORY 7—VISIONS: GOD WITH US

Introduction: The Place of Transfiguration

From the crest of the mountains above Nazareth, Sepphoris or possibly Mt Eremos, all emerging from the west coast of the Sea of Galilee and looking across the plains of northern Galilee rises Mt. Carmel; the place of Elijah's confrontation with the 400 hundred priests of Baal, in ancient Israel. On that mount Elijah triumphed in a fiery display of God's power which ended in the annihilation of Baal's prophets. This imaginative story places John, following Jesus along with Peter and James to the crest of one of these hills taking in the grandeur of Israel's past, now in full view and just before Jesus is transfigured before them.

An Imaginative Biblical Story based upon Mark 9: 2-8 & I Kings 18:21-39 as seen through John's eyes...

Peter woke first. When fully awake, he reached over with his hands to shake me and my brother James awake. Slowly I emerged from a deep rest, as one does coming out of a thick fog into a clear sun filled day. I did not wish to wake up. I had fallen asleep thinking of Mt. Carmel in the distance and of Elijah's fearless challenge to the people before the four hundred priests of Baal. *"How long will you waver between two opinions? If the LORD is God, follow him; but if Baal is*

God, follow him," he had asked (I Kings 18: 21b). The fire had fallen from the heavens consuming the sacrifice, leaving only a steamy mist where once water had been. In my sleep, I had entered into the crowd as one of them. We fell as one to the ground, misty clouds rising from the fiery demonstration of God's power. We were all crying out... *"The LORD—he is God! The LORD—he is God!"* (I Kings 18: 39b).

"John!" I heard my name and in my dream state it felt as though the ground were shaking. "John, wake up!" I heard it again and again, the voice slowly pulling me away from my dream and into another moment no less intense. As the dream faded, filled as it was with fire and smoke and a mysterious rising cloud of steam, I became aware of another cloud just in front of Peter and James, both fixated upon it.

Inside were colors of the rainbow, swirling as if in a dance. From within the cloud appeared a man for whom the layered colors were dancing, gently caressing him, each touch a release of light. The reds, greens, yellows and blues were slowly coming to rest at his feet creating a single color of brilliant white light, which came to envelop him like clothes made of silk. I fell to my knees, as I had in my dream. Peter and James were already prostrate before the unfolding vision. I heard myself whispering again the words echoing from Mt. Carmel... *"The LORD—he is God! The LORD—he is God!"* (I Kings 18: 39b). I had the distinct sense that a great host were surrounding us, repeating the same words, though I could not hear them.

As my eyes adjusted to the dazzling light, I looked up and could make out the face of the one before me. It was my Master and Rabbi, Jeshua! I could now see into the cloud well enough to see two others, one to the right of Jeshua and one to the left. I do not know how I knew, but my spirit recognized one as Moses, the other as Elijah. It was the same Elijah as in my dream.

I trembled with fear, aware that my soul was shaking within. I could feel my heart racing. Next, I heard my cousin, Peter, crying out. "Rabbi!" Apparently, he also recognized Jeshua.

"Rabbi!", he again exclaimed, *"it is good for us to be here. Let us put up three shelters—one for you, one for Moses and one for Elijah"* (Mark 9:5). His idea, it seemed, was an appropriate response. Seized with fear, at least talking helped.

Suddenly, as if in response to Peter's suggestion, another cloud, filled with white lightening came from the heavens, enveloping Jeshua, Moses and Elijah and removing them from our sight. From within this second cloud a voice thundered. *"This is my Son, whom I love. Listen to him!"* (Mark 9:7c). At the sound of this voice I again fell prostrate to the ground and buried my face in absolute terror.

An eerie silence followed, around and within. There was no wind or signs of life; no birds singing or trees rustling. After what seemed minutes I felt his touch and heard his voice, soft, even playful. "John, Peter, James, sit up and follow." We did.

From: "Who Am I," Week 1—Saturday "Visions", by Terry Mattson, pg#33-34

MY THOUGHTS 9—VISIONS: GOD WITH US

At the very heart of Christianity is the person, Jesus; which means the word of God is narrative—a story before anything else. It also means that God is knowable and hungers for communion.

Our salvation stories need to reflect this truth. It's not about an angry God who wants to throw us in some kind of eternal prison called hell. It is about a person at the center of the universe who wants to take us out of our hellish environ— created only because God is removed.

**The Old Testament picture is Shalom—Sabbath rest.
The New Testament picture is the Communal Jesus.** It is
interesting to me that St. John's Gospel, while having no
specific account of the upper room Lord's supper, is all about
Holy Communion. The water and the bread motif runs
throughout the narrative. After the introduction of Jesus, it
begins with a wedding story and wine and ends with table
fellowship by the sea of Galilee where Jesus is cooking
breakfast for the eleven. Wow!

Reflections on "Visions: God with Us"

*"I am the way and the truth and the life. No one
comes to the Father except through me…"*
John 14: 6

The **Communal Jesus** is the fulfillment of God's promise to
Israel conveyed in the Law, Temple and Sabbath. **Jesus is
the way** (Temple), **the truth** (Law) **and the life** (Sabbath).

Q: How does this strike you?

Terry argues that a Person centered faith is narrative by
definition—The Story matters and by extension of love; so
do ours. He further suggests that if God seeks communion
then:

> "Our salvation stories need to reflect this truth. It's not
> about an angry God who wants to throw us in some
> kind of eternal prison called hell. It is about a person
> at the center of the universe who wants to take us out

of our hellish environ—created only because God is removed".

Q: Have you ever considered that a Person Centered gospel focused on God as communal will be different than gospel which focuses on God as Sovereign, as King? ...How so?

Q: How have you come to know God? ...as King? ...as One who seeks relation?

Consider the invitation of God to communion and turn it to prayer.

Week-2: SATURDAY—JOHN 1: 29-34, Luke 1: 5-22

STORY 8—THE LAMB

An Imaginative Biblical Story—on Zechariah's entrance into the Holy of Holies Based upon Luke 1: 5-22.

As the heavy iron doors opened before him, Zechariah could see into the Holy Place, a room he knew well. Stepping in and looking up and to his right and left he noticed the high colonnades reaching up into what appeared to be the heavens. In the early morning a cloud would sometimes fill the upper sanctuary giving it a mysterious feeling. Before him were men whose faces he knew, each adorned, as was he, in their very best temple gowns, perfectly white reflecting the purity of this place. The room seemed long and foreboding, the darkness interrupted only by the flickering of candle light on his left and right. Before him at the front was a single table of bronze, over laid with gold along the borders and fresh bread, baked early that morning in the Temple bakery. Incense mingled with the smell of blood from the lamb that was just slain for the sins of all the people. Zechariah's arms were outstretched so as to hold the bowl of blood as an offering to be given to Yahweh, God of Israel.

As Zechariah moved forward the bells around the bottom of his gown sounded their warning. Only Zechariah's robe, prepared a decade earlier for this very moment, had the bells. He was chosen from among brothers of Abijah for the honor of going into the very Holy of Holies, just beyond the table of showbread, behind the veil and into the very presence of God. The bells were the stark reminder that he might not return. The arrangement was simple. If the bells did not sound within one hour of his entry behind the curtain he would be pulled out from behind the veil by a rope, now being placed around him by the High Priest himself. As the High Priest gathered the rope into a tight and secure knot Zechariah's doubts began to force their way into his consciousness. His wife was without child. By law and tradition, the shame was borne by Elizabeth, his wife. But Zechariah knew better. How often had he, over the years, wrestled with his own feelings as he passed the daughters of Israel, their colorful robes tucked in such a way as to emphasize the contours of their own bodies? How often had he forced these thoughts away only to dream a more explicit version in his sleep? And what of his anger, that would surge when he considered Herod's tyrannies? Were it not for his Levitical calling, given by nature, he would gladly offer himself to the zealots, enemies of both Herod and Rome.

As the belt tightened firmly around his waist, Zechariah's attention was brought back to the moment. The high priest looked upon his priest with a kind of pride. He knew him to be an honorable man and was glad the chance had fallen by lot upon Zechariah. Zechariah saw into the High Priest the approval and knew it to be mistaken.

With each step toward the Holy of Holies, Zechariah's doubts seemed to rise. 'When, O LORD, when will you raise up a horn of salvation from David's loins, who will save us from our enemies? Who, O LORD, who is worthy to stand in your Presence? Who can bring to your people the salvation promised so long ago? LORD, the Holy One of Israel, is your hand too short to save?

You have spoken in the psalms that the blood of lambs does not really save. You are not pleased with this sacrifice? Why then have you chosen me? To kill me before all Israel? To expose my own inner shame?'

Zechariah's questions had never been felt so explicitly. Why now? Surely he would die the very moment he crossed behind the veil and moved from the world of time into the Eternal One's presence.

Letting go of the bowl of lamb's blood with one hand, Zechariah now reached out and with some effort pushed the three-inch curtain back and using his elbow and forearm prepared to enter in. Quickly he glanced back upon his friends, whose faces all reflected the hope that Zechariah's entrance gave.

In a motion almost slower than time, Zechariah's head now looked into and upon the Ark of God's Covenant. At once, from just above and to his right, above the altar of incense, a white and brilliant light appeared flooding his face with its warm embrace, so that he could see nothing beyond. At the same time the curtain closed behind him, allowing only a shadow of the brilliant light to escape the room. Then from within the light came a voice that seemed to Zechariah, from a place beyond. *"Do not be afraid, Zechariah; your prayer has been heard"* (Luke 1:13).

Inside Zechariah's mind, yet somehow more real than sight itself, he could see heaven's temple. It was huge, making Herod's seventh wonder of the world look like a model held in a child's hand. The doorway of this temple opened as they had for Zechariah, moments before. Only coming through the door was another, whose face looked beaten, whose appearance was not olive colored as his was, but instead covered in blood. In his hands he held a dove, pure and white. Looking closer, Zechariah could see that even these hands were wounded with blood gently falling to the ground below. The eyes of this one who was wounded were like lightening, yet somehow held within a gentle compassion, a tenderness without judgment.

Looking up, following the colonnades of the Temple, Zechariah could see thousands upon thousands of angels who sang a song he had never before heard and whose words burned into his doubts.

"Worthy is the Lamb,
who was slain,
to receive power and wealth and wisdom and strength
and honor and glory and praise!"
Rev 5: 12

Suddenly as the tender lightening of the one Zechariah now understood to be the very Lamb of God looked into Zechariah's soul the dove that he held lifted and came to light on Zechariah's hands instantly replacing the blood he had held.

Only then did Zechariah understand, as a deep peace enfolded him. All his questions and doubts, all his sins were atoned for and with him, all Israel. He knew.

And the angel continued, *"Your wife Elizabeth will bear you a son, and you are to give him the name John. He will be a joy and a delight to you, and many will rejoice because of his birth, for he will be great in the sight of the Lord… Many of the people of Israel will he bring back to the Lord their God. And he will go on before the Lord, in the spirit and power of Elijah, to turn the hearts of the parents to their children and the disobedient to the wisdom of the righteous—to make ready a people prepared for the Lord"* (Selections from Luke 1: 13-17).

Reflections on "The Lamb"

"Letting go of the bowl of lamb's blood with one hand,
Zechariah now reached out and with some effort
pushed the three-inch curtain back and using his
elbow and forearm prepared to enter in. Quickly he

glanced back upon his friends, whose faces all
reflected the hope that Zechariah's entrance gave."
From Terry Mattson above

Q: What is your favorite moment in a typical Sunday morning worship service? Why?

Q: Have you ever experienced a moment in worship when you knew God had spoken directly to you?

Experiment: If you have experienced a significant moment in worship when you knew God spoke to you, share it with someone this week. If not write God a letter and pour out your heart as Elizabeth and Zechariah must have on occasion.

Turn it all to prayer.

Week-2: SUNDAY— LUKE 2: 8-20, JOHN 10: 1-16, MATTHEW 1: 1-4 & 9: 35-37, REVELATION 5: 11-14 & 7: 9-17

STORY 9—THE SHEPHERD

An Imaginative Biblical Story as seen through Jesus eyes...

Based upon Matthew 5: 1-4 & 9: 35-37

'I must have fallen asleep,' I thought to no one. My eyes still refused to open to the bright sun of a new day and so I continued to rest my head against the side of the cave that had often become for me the very Sanctuary of my Heavenly

Father. It was about the 14th hour of the day (8 a.m.), the sun now making it's appearance above the hills on the opposite bank of the Sea of Galilee. From this sight on Mt Eremos, located just south of Capernum on the western side of the sea I could see the world I came of age in. 'See that is, if only my tired eyes would open...' I laughed a little. Bethesda, the little town from which five of my disciples came was across the lake, to the east and a little to the north; My own village of Nazareth not far and to the south.

The very thought of Nazareth brought back memories of having taken my uncles sheep up onto this very mount in search of green meadows to feed upon and near the brook which formed a ravine leading down and into the Sea. 'About a half an hours walk from here, I think…' I could still see in my minds eye the sheep gathered around the still waters I had formed at a turn in the ravine. 'As I had been taught by my uncle and his father before him, I would gather the rocks and create a dam carving out a little inlet to capture the water; "For sheep will not drink from a babbling stream. But lead them to still water and they will push and shove each other to quench their thirst!" I can still hear uncle Jacob's commanding voice. Always sounding angry, but rarely so.

And all this work would be done while keeping my head up watching for signs of danger or worse a stray sheep wandering off in search of wild berries or dates'. With that thought my mind raced to remeber 'how my dog, Jacovy, would run and bark and tend to the sheep as I would prepare them for their drink and later to bed down, their stomachs full for the day.

And they would be safe for, as always, I would use these curves in the ravine to form a kind of cavern, preferabbly one that rested against the walls of a cliff on three sides with the rock formation allowing an entrance much like a sheep's door. Here I would sleep, at the gate, watching and guarding just as shepherds had in these very sights for generations'. For a moment I let my eyes open, staring straight in front of me at the other side of the cave, the light at first blinding me a bit. Getting my bearings I closed them again and returned to my inner memories.

'Always I would take some of the scrolls loaned me by my good Rabbi… some containing the songs of David or one of the prophets or the teachings of the Mishna. …After the sheep were bathed with the pungent oils to guard against the bites of insects and working my leather like hands into their wool covered bodies clearing the brush and tangled webs of the day, I would talk to each of them as though a dear friend for I knew them all by name'. Laughing out loud my heart now raced ahead of my thoughts. 'And my sheep knew me by sight, yes, but mostly by smell; my own body now covered with cakes of dust and layers of oil and brush'… a smile now lingering.

'Then would come the quiet time as even Jacovy would lie down next to me, his master, facing the sheep now cuddled together for the night, all accounted for. And at last I would take a scroll and begin to read with the light of the fire bouncing off the cavern walls, the moon and the stars bathing and turning my little camp sight into a sacred place with the fire crackling and the air tingling, alive under the clear Galillean sky'.

Even as the memories came flooding in I felt my heart expand within as it did then, for I 'felt a connection with both the stories of old as witnessed in the scrolls and the very stars that were even older. I know; wiping a tear I could feel trickling down the side of my cheek…' Even then, at what? …the age of 15? I knew how Abraham must have felt as my Father showed him these very stars and promised him offspring that would outnumber them—and he, as a young man—I felt the expansion in my heart fade under the burden of hope within rising in me; Remember that 'even then I longed to make all Israel feel the air alive as I had, often, shepherding my uncles sheep'.

Suddenly a gust of air filled the cavern and a bit startled, I allowed my eyelids to open and begin to adjust to the light filtering in from the morning sun. My mind now awaked to the new day releasing the dream or memory—or whatever it was—that had awakened in me as I became awre of my current surroundings some 17 years in the future, now an Itenerant Rabbi.

Standing, I felt a pang of hunger, remembering that I had come up on Mt. Eremos in order to pray, at about the third hour (9 p.m.) of the day leaving my disciples and their fishing boats adjacent the sea. As I stepped out of the cave and looked out upon the sloping meadow before me I immediately realized my hunger must wait for a sea of sheep dressed in the gowns of men and women, boys and girls were making their way up the hill with Peter, James, and

John in front, leading the way. Seeing me they waved and I watched for a moment as they, with the other nine disciples, began working the crowd, maybe a thousand men, plus women and children and gathering them to form on three sides of the meadow a kind of ampi-theatre. Wisely they had used a rock emerging from the hill as a center point. So I stepped down from the small cliff and made my way through the throng, smiling, stoping to banter with a few—suddenly stoping; At some distance I noticed one older man seated alone—a man whose eyes and skin told of a story of rejection and disease. Walking up to him and without his permission, noting his eyes were filled with a kind of fear, I assume from rejection, I simply touched him and taking his hands brought him up to me. I could hear the gasp of some around. Looking into his tired and lonely eyes I simply asked, "What is your name?" He studied me for a moment, 'wondering', I think, 'if I was setting him up for one more pain filled encounter.' I just held him steady and waited, noticing his eyes now looking down at my two hands that held his disease ridden hands—he was evidently an untouchable. "Ephriam," he spoke. Placing my hands on his two shoulders and putting my face within inches of him, I spoke what I knew my Father would say. "Ephriam, son of Israel. Shalom. Be well." And I drew from my pouch, just under the fold in my garment, a little of the oil—the same I used with my sheep— and for the next five minutes just cleansed and rubbed, using my own outer garment as a kind of rag for cleaning. When done, Ephraim's eyes were wide with shock and joy…for his skin was like that of a child. "Now follow our Abba in the heavens and go, when this day is done, and present yourself to the Rabbi and offer what the law demands so that you may be pronounced, Clean!"

Turning to the crowd who by now were quiet, some standing, other's in front seated, all in awe and listening. How my heart once again expanded within. 'These are simply sheep who need a Shepherd'. Raising my voice I began the first sermon of the day…

"Blessed are you, my friends, who mourn—for you shall be comforted! Many of your families own sheep, do you not?" I could see on each face a knowing look, for either they or someone in their family or village knew the trade well. "If you had a hundred sheep…" I thought to myself… 'only those who are truly wealthy would have such a number' and continued. "If you had hundred sheep," I repeated. "And lost one. Would you not leave the ninety nine and search for the one who is lost and alone and frightened?" Walking now behind my new friend, Ephriam, I simply stroke his hair to embrace the point. "And having found the one, would you not place it upon your shoulders and bring it back joyfully to the safety of the fold where you would then pour oil on it's wounds and carefully rub it into it's wool cleansing and carressing that part of it's fleece that had become entangled in the brush and by fear?"

Making my way to the rock at the center of this hillside ampi-theatre I took a seat and lowered my voice for emphasis. "I tell you, that one daughter of Sarah or Son of Abraham who, being lost, is found and returns home brings great joy in our Father's Presence! For my Father will carry you upon his shoulder and tenderly heal what is broken, annointing you with the oil of His Spirit—and the angels surrounding will cry out in joy!" Then raising my voice, **"Blessed are you who mourn—for you shall be comforted!"**

Note: Inspired, in part, by stories of Jesus as a young man shepherding his uncles flock written by Marjorie Holmes in "Three From Galilee."

MY THOUGHTS 10—THE SHEPHERD

"My value to God is that in obedience to His spoken word I present to Him in actuality His idea in sending it forth, God's word expressed in me becomes its own witness to God."
From "The Complete Works of Oswald Chambers, page #959

God became a human. The Gate by which we enter into His rule is by a person, Jesus—our Good Shepherd. The priestly office wherein the life/Word of God is communicated is personal.

Pope Benedict drives this point home as he describes the necessity of the very Words of God, given on the Mount, being fleshed out in us, lived out. The Word of God is to be living in us, transforming our lives. God speaks a Living Word in His Son, but even this Living Word is to be valued, received and expressed in a human, personal response. For example, speaking of the 'poor in spirit', Pope Benedict writes:

> *"...It may be a good idea...to turn for a moment to the figure whom the history of faith offers us as the most intensely lived illustration of this Beatitude: Francis of Assisi. The saints are the true interpreters of Holy Scripture. The meaning of a given passage of the Bible becomes most intelligible in those human beings who have been totally transfixed by it and have lived it out. Interpretation of Scripture can never be a purely academic affair, and it cannot be relegated to the purely historical. Scripture is full of*

potential for the future, a potential that can only be opened up when someone 'lives through' and 'suffers through' the sacred text. Francis of Assisi was gripped in an utterly radical way by the promise of the first Beatitude, to the point that he even gave away his garments and let himself be clothed anew by the bishop, the representative of God's fatherly goodness, through which the lilies of the field were clad in robes finer than Solomon's" (cf. Mt 6: 28-29).

From "Jesus of Nazareth", under "Reflections on 'Living the Beatitudes' by Pope Benedict XVI, pages #78-79

Reflections on "The Shepherd"

Evidently, the Truth (Jesus) is ultimately personal and relational, and hence, must be 'lived' in personal and relational terms.

Q: How does this strike you?

Q: Does it bring a new light to the two-hundred-year old Protestant arguments over whether Scripture is primarily:

> ➢ 'Propositional' (about God's commands or instruction), or;
> ➢ 'Narrative' (about God's Presence among us)?

...How so?

"Francis of Assisi was gripped in an utterly radical way by the promise of the first Beatitude, to the point that he even gave away his garments and let himself

be clothed anew by the bishop, the representative of God's fatherly goodness."
From Pope Benedict XVI above

Q: What do you need to cast off, if you are to truly 'live the Word'?

Q: Do you have the faith to 'cast off' and 'be clothed' with Christ?

Write out your thoughts as a prayer or listen to the voice of God…

Next:
Trash in the City

3 TRASH IN THE CITY

... The Valley Gate

INVOCATION:

FATHER, CREATOR AND JUDGE. HELP ME TO RELEASE TO YOU MY FRIENDS AND ENEMIES; TO SEE THEM THROUGH THE EYES OF YOUR MERCY. ALLOW ME TO LOOK AWAY FROM THE SPECK OF SAWDUST IN THEIR EYES AND SEE CLEARLY THE TWO BY FOUR PLANK IN MY OWN.

ALLOW ME TO BE ONE IN WHOM YOUR TRUTH FINDS A HOME. MAY I HEAR AND OBEY. MAY I BUILD MY HOME UPON THE FOUNDATION OF YOUR WORDS, SO THAT WHEN THE STORMS OF LIFE COME, AS THEY WILL, I AM SECURE. LORD, WHEN MY HOME IS BUFFETED BY RELENTLESS WIND AND RAIN HELP ME TO REMEMBER HOW LOVING AND HOLY YOU ARE.

HELP ME TO REMEMBER THAT WHEN YOUR CHILDREN ASK, YOU GIVE. WHEN WE SEEK, WE ARE LED. WHEN THE DOOR OF LIFE SEEMS CLOSED, YOU OPEN IT AGAIN. AMEN.

BASED UPON MATTHEW 7: 1-27

PSALM OF THE WEEK: PSALM 143

COMMANDMENT OF THE WEEK: YOU SHALL NOT MAKE FOR YOURSELF AN IDOL IN THE FORM OF ANYTHING IN HEAVEN ABOVE OR ON THE EARTH BENEATH OR IN THE WATERS BELOW. YOU SHALL NOT BOW DOWN TO THEM OR WORSHIP THEM: FOR I, THE LORD YOUR GOD, AM A JEALOUS GOD.

DEUTERONOMY 5: 8-9A

DAILY SCRIPTURES:

MONDAY—EXODUS 3: 1-12

TUESDAY—II KINGS 23: 1-14, 21-27

WEDNESDAY—EPHESIANS 5: 3-14

THURSDAY—I JOHN 4: 16-18

FRIDAY—II TIMOTHY 2: 1-21

SATURDAY—PSALM 139

SUNDAY—ROMANS 8: 18-27, I JOHN 2: 9-17, II TIMOTHY 2: 20-21, I THESSALONIANS 2: 1-12

FROM
MARK 11: 15

THEY CAME INTO JERUSALEM. AFTER ENTERING THE TEMPLE, HE THREW OUT THOSE WHO WERE SELLING AND BUYING THERE. HE PUSHED OVER THE TABLES USED FOR CURRENCY EXCHANGE AND THE CHAIRS OF THOSE WHO SOLD DOVES.

Week-3: MONDAY—EXODUS 3: 1-12

MY THOUGHTS 11—WHY TRASH MATTERS

Reflections on Moses Encounter with a bush that does not burn up and so become trash... from Exodus 3: 1-12...

According to Pope Benedict XVI, what caught Moses attention was not that the bush was aflame. He had seen that often in the desert. What surprised him was that the bush was not consumed, left only with a black, weak and broken ember of what it once was, before the power of fire.

Fire was respected by the people of the desert. Fire ranked high in the fears of the ancients, right up there with water. Either could sweep down from the mountains; each reflecting the power of nature (gods). Each could destroy flocks and villages and leave in their wake only a dead memory of what once lived.

Moses had watched this fire from a distance and with respect but noticed, over time, that it did not consume. It left no trash in its wake. So he thought, *"I will go over and see this strange sight—why the bush does not burn up"* (Ex 3:3b). Suddenly Moses became aware that he was on holy ground, for from the fire came the voice of One whose presence had made this ground different, set apart, special. And YHWH spoke, addressing Moses' deepest fear, for he, Moses, had hid his face from looking upon the Fire in fear that he himself might be consumed.

What was Moses fear? What had kept him in the desert all these years, far removed from the city of his childhood and the center of earth's power? It was a trashy secret, still hidden within his soul. He was a murderer; one whose passion over injustice had flamed into an angry act that had left him, like garbage, a refuge and outside of the favor of the Pharaoh. He had run. Now, he hid his face.

And what did YHWH promise Moses? Nothing short of the removal of his people's status as trash, throwaways, garbage slaves. But Moses objected that this Fire did not understand. *"Who am I, that I should go to Pharaoh and bring the Israelites out of Egypt"* (Ex 3: 10b)? He wanted to confess, to tell this Fire that he carried a secret that makes him too trashy to carry out the request. Indeed, if caught, he would become a prisoner and treated like garbage, and properly so.

Then YHWH gave Moses the real secret, the purpose of all His work among humans. *"I will be with you"* (Ex 3: 12a). It is as if he said, **'Where I am even garbage is renewed. I am the Fire that does not consume, but restores.** The assurance of my presence is right here, on this mountain.' For he did say, *"And this will be the sign to you that it is I who have sent you: When you have brought the people out of Egypt, you will worship God on this mountain"* (Ex 3: 12b).

God gifted Moses—and through him Israel and us—with two additional gifts in the encounter on that holy mountain. Pope Benedict XVI, in "Jesus of Nazareth" captures them: A Name that is no Name and in the Name, relationship. Listen to him.

> *"...in the world of Moses' time there were many gods. Moses therefore asks the name of this God that will prove his special authority vis-a-vis the gods. In this respect, the idea of the divine name belongs first of all to the polytheistic world, in which this God, too, has to give himself a name. But the God who calls Moses is truly God, and God in the strict and true sense is not plural. God is by essence one. For this reason, he*

cannot enter into the world of the gods as one among many; he cannot have one name among others. God's answer to Moses is thus at once a refusal and a pledge. He says of himself simply, 'I am who I am' —he is without any qualification. This pledge is a name and a non—name at one and the same time. The Israelites were therefore perfectly right in refusing to utter this self-designation of God, expressed in the word YHWH, so as to avoid degrading it to the level of names of pagan deities...

If we want to understand this curious interplay between a name and non-name, we have to be clear about what a name actually is. We could put it very simply by saying that the name creates the possibility of address or invocation. It establishes relationship. When Adam names the animals…he fits them into his human world, puts them within reach of his call… We are now in a position to understand the positive meaning of the divine name: God establishes a relationship between himself and us. He puts himself within reach of our invocation. He enters into relationship with us and enables us to be in relationship with him… In some sense he hands himself over to our human world. He has made himself accessible and therefore, vulnerable as well. He assumes the risk of relationship, of communion, with us."

From "Jesus of Nazareth", by Pope Benedict XVI, page #142-144

Reflections on "Why Trash Matters"

Q: What is trash?

Seriously, think about what it is, where it comes from and what purpose it has. Take a moment and define... Trash.

> *"I will be with you"* (Ex 3: 12a). *It is as if he said, 'Where I am even garbage is renewed. I am the Fire that does not consume, but restores.'"* Terry Mattson above.

Q: Have you ever seen God take the 'worst' in you and use it?

Describe when and how...

Benedict points out that in understanding the Name of God—that is no name—we can begin to grasp why Jesus, in the Lord's Prayer begins with addressing God as Father and then adds; "May Your Name be Hallowed".

Q: Is Jesus petition that we keep God's Name as Holy something a whole lot more than—stop cussing? ...How so?

Q: Are you bringing honor to God's Name that is gifted to you and me in Jesus?

Write out your thoughts/feelings and turn it all to prayer.

Week-3: TUESDAY—II KINGS 23: 1-14, 21-27

Story 10—What to Do with Jerusalem's Trash

An Imaginative Biblical Story on King Josiah and the Garbage Dump Called Hell…

Introduction:

What a community does with its trash tells a lot about its life? Does she place it at the center, as in some third world countries allowing convenient access for everyone; Acknowledged and accepted as the price of being human? Or… perhaps, like many modern cities the trash is picked up, removed and hauled, barged or flown to distant landfills or even countries. In this way the smells and waste that flows through the city never seem to collect. They are out of sight, beyond our awareness, someone else's problem.

Jerusalem had an interesting solution.

The Story:

Suddenly and with great fear the king cried out and in a loud voice! His wife, lying in the state room reserved for her, just down the hallway of the Kings awoke to the strange cry coming from within the King's chamber. By the time she had gathered about her, her evening garments and made her way out into the hall and toward the king, the servants of young Josiah, King of Israel, were already ahead of her making their way into his chambers, but with quiet stealth.

The queen moved into the room, with little caution, for she knew her husband would receive her. The other attendants, upon her entrance, and seeing that everything was safe, turned and backed away from her and exited the doorway in which they had come.

The queen stopped and looked upon the body of the young king, not quite twenty-six years of age and saw in his eyes the terror which would not fade. This had been the third time in a week that she had made this trip. "Again?" Queen Rachel asked of her husband, her voice soothing and gentle, as she moved to his side and took a seat near his feet. A soft glow from the candle holders cast a warm light across his face. His eyes turned in her direction, but did not yet focus on her. The memory of the child's cry, still echoed in his feelings. The dream or vision or apparition, he could not tell, was the same each night.

Josiah could not be certain, but it seemed to him that his own eyes had witnessed the horror. It seemed like his own voice that cried out. But it was not the voice of the man he knew himself to be. It was not the eyes of the warrior he felt himself to be. It was a child's vision and child's cry.

Quietly a servant entered with a bowl of hot water, a towel and a glass of cool wine and stood just inside the king's bed chamber. When she saw the Queen, she had bowed her head gently and in respect waited. The Queen turned and with a nod and smile noticed. Quietly, the servant placed her offerings on the table just inside the King's Chambers and left, knowing there was no further need of her care.

"Grandfather?," the King spoke, his eyes now focused upon his queen, searching for understanding as a child who looks to his mother for comfort. Rachel moved from the foot of his chamber bed and up next to his side, removing the heavy quilts, now dampened by the sweat of the king's worry and pulling them aside slipped in next to her master. She did not lay, but formed with her lap a kind of pillow and drew the king sideways towards her so that she could listen and stroke his forehead. "Grandfather," the King again repeated as he lay down into the comfort of his wife's love. "Why?" In silence the king lay and in the security of his wife's arms he once again fell asleep.

As the sun's light cast her first rays into his chamber and illuminated with color the lining above his bed, he opened his eyes, aware that he was no longer alone. How he had come to be curled up in the arms of his young bride he could not remember, but the promise of a new day seemed good. But as he let himself free of her embrace, careful not to awaken her by his movement, he remembered. Hurriedly, quietly he put on his robe and walking out into the Hall of the Kings he ordered his servant to have Shaphan, his secretary to meet him this morning for breakfast.

At breakfast Josiah began to describe for his old and trusted adviser the dream or vision or apparition that had troubled him these last few nights. Now he could remember as though it were an event real to him. Yet he did not have sufficient knowledge and his dream was surrounded in the mystery of smell and shadows. Shaphan listened and with increasing fear knew exactly what troubled this young king, whose reign he had watched and nurtured since Josiah's eighth birthday, upon the death of his father, Amon.

Josiah described a great valley, huge and filled with the smell of animals as they were sacrificed. But the aroma also included a very different kind of smell which gave Josiah a shiver even as he described it. In the center of the valley was an altar, similar to Yahweh's in the temple, only bigger and crafted in gold covering with the figures of animals and snakes. In the center of the altar was a huge and hot fire. Josiah said that he was looking at some distance, above the altar and yet near. He was aware that thousands of Jerusalem's citizens were present, as were his own father and cousins. He remembered looking upon his mother and seeing in her a look of dismay, mingled with hate. But before him was a young man who was held bound upon the altar. This young man seemed to Josiah to be of the age of ascension, maybe twelve years of age. Josiah slowed his description as the horror of it took hold of him.

Shaphan wished the king had not called him to this breakfast. He had hoped that this small boy of three had been spared the memory of that morning, nearly twenty-three years before.

Shaphan did not need Josiah's account. He had been there at Topheth, in the valley of Bin Hinnom (Gehenna), just outside of Jerusalem's Valley gate. In the latter years of King Manasseh, as the wretched hunger of his flesh could no longer be satiated with the touch of his concubines and the wine which flowed freely in his court, he had turned to the spiritual for solace. But it was not to Yahweh he turned, but to the gods of the Assyrians, to the sorcerers with their drugs and to witchcraft.

That morning, the king had gathered all of his officials, including Shaphan, who worked even then in the King's service, a rising star, to see what the King had declared as his greatest 'sacrifice', that of his youngest son. He, together with some of the leading citizens of Jerusalem had determined to show Molech their loyalty in the offering of their children to the fires of this angry and ancient god.

It was that morning that Shaphan had determined in his heart that he would rediscover Yahweh, the God of Israel. It was that morning that had convinced him that his own sins, and they were many, would need to be atoned for. It was the guilt of that morning that allowed him to make contact with Hilkiah, the high priest over Yahweh's temple with the seditious purpose of planning for the death of King Manasseh.

Shaphan had never confessed, even to Josiah, his actions. The plans to overthrow King Manasseh never came to fruition, because this King had repented and began a period of renewal and restoration, late in his reign.

As Shaphan listened to his young king confess the torture in his soul, he realized that he had never even told his king that the seditious plans toward his grandfather had indeed been carried out upon his father, Amon, whose two-year reign had promised even worse than Manasseh's. "Never again," Shaphan, having been recently promoted to being the Secretary of the Affairs of the King's State, confided to the high priest. "Never again!" And together with many of the noblest families of Jerusalem they plotted Amon's demise and Josiah ascension to the throne of David. Some of the king's officials had given their life in order to hide from the people's courts the High Priest and Shaphan's involvement in the plot.

Shaphan's thoughts were suddenly interrupted by the silence that had come between them. Shaphan looked into Josiah's eyes and felt his own shame, from the event twenty-three years before. Slowly, carefully Shaman confirmed for the King that his dreams were real indeed. He described in greater detail than he had previously the depth of his grandfather and father's sin and the cost to the nation. It was then that Shaphan removed from his robe a scroll that had been given him by the High Priest the night before.

As Shaphan carefully pulled the leather bindings apart and exposed the scroll to the light of day, the King's eyes widened. He forgot his grief for a moment and gave Shaphan his full attention. "This scroll, my King," Shaphan began; "This scroll was found by the High Priest during the recent restoration projects you have ordered for the Holy Temple. Your majesty, this scroll is the books of Moses, given by Yahweh, the laws by which the people of Israel and their leaders are to live."

Over the next week Shaphan, the High Priest Hilkiah and their young King spent most of each day together, reading and discussing the meaning of Moses words. As they read of Israel's sin at Mt. Sinai, where the people turned back to Egypt's god, Ptah, and his consort, Hathor, the king stood tearing his King's robe from top to bottom and ordered his trusted Secretary for the Affairs of State and his High Priest to make a careful study of all that the Books of Moses command. As they left the King's presence, backing away, the King assured them. "We will have one more gathering of all the citizens of Jerusalem at Topheth, in the Valley of Ben Hinnom (Gehenna). But this time, it shall be the High Places of Judah, the Asherah Poles and all the devices of worship to the Baal's or to Molech that shall be burnt. From that day forward, the valley of Hinnom shall become a place forbidden. No worship or work or money shall ever again be exchanged in that place!"

Thus, this valley became a place deserted, useless—good only for garbage. And that is how the Valley of Ben Hinnom and known as Gehenna (Hell) in the time of Jesus, became the 'garbage dump' of Jerusalem!

Reflections on "What to Do with Jerusalem's Trash?"

Q: Your initial feelings? ...How does this story strike you?

"Neither before nor after Josiah was there a king like him who turned to the LORD as he did—with all his heart and with all his soul and with all his strength, in accordance with all the law of Moses."   II Kings 23: 25

Q: What would have to happen in your life, for this to be written of you?

Q: How would the trash in 'your life' be handled if you did love God with all of your soul and strength and heart?

Describe it and turn it all to Prayer.

Week-3: WEDNESDAY—EPHESIANS 5: 3-14

STORY 11—TAKING OUT THE TRASH

A Personal Story

The day is done. It was packed with activity, work, pastoral care, and contemplation.

I have just finished an hour of reading and prayer, preceded by another hour of television. Throughout the evening I ate too much, drank coffee too freely, laughed in the presence of "Everybody Loves Raymond" and read and worshiped in our sanctuary. The light of candles in our sanctuary seemed to flicker against the dark caverns of my soul.

I come home. My wife is asleep, a rest deserved from an equally demanding day.

I am restless and unable to sleep. Slowly, almost unconsciously at first, sexual desire, unfocused and unusually strong, awakens within me. I am surprised at the intensity of need awakened. I sit for a moment, frozen, between conflicting needs. Just two minutes before I was tired, relaxed and ready for sleep.

Now I feel trapped inside a race car, the doors locked and the engine running at full speed, rpm's racing, but in neutral, going nowhere fast. It is night and darkness has descended around me. My head lights peak out into the darkness, but there is no legitimate race track onto which I may direct this powerful force.

My wife is asleep. It seems unthinkable to awaken her and to what? ...sexual energy, unfocused? ...built up tension? Is this love? No. To go to bed and lie next to her is a struggle I do not wish to engage.

For five minutes or an hour I wrestle inwardly. TV is not an option, for then I would inevitably fall into channel surfing, probably landing nowhere (I don't have cable), but still, increasing exponentially the desire.

I look around the room for a sensual picture, perhaps in the newspaper. I am careful not to see, only to look. What an idiot! "Oh, God, please help me." Inward sin is now crouching at my heart's door.

By choice, my wife and I have long removed any pictures that might draw me in. Even this precaution is a cost to her. What to her is enjoyable and appropriate can, in me, awaken old memories and passion.

As the moment lingers (perhaps three minutes or thirty), I choose to read and divert attention. Failing that, I may just lay back in my recliner and like a drunk, dry but addicted, feel the convulsions until it is over. I am aware, that even in this, the adrenaline rush of sexual addiction is working through my being. There is no fantasy. None. Finally, I am free and make my way to bed, empty, tense, perhaps guilty, in heart, perhaps, not.

"Confessional Holiness", Chapter "Holy—A Little or a Lot?", by Terry Mattson, pg #26-27

STORY 11A—AN OLDER STORY

A Personal Story from a time, earlier; Decades before...

It was three o'clock in the afternoon. I turn the key of my truck off and make my way into a sexually explicit show. I am filled with powerful longings, no less addictive than crack cocaine. My eyes are the veins and guilt and shame is the rein forcer.

Those days, long dead now, both in fact and desire, alone, without fantasy, still, at some level, inform the empty re-run of psycho/social feelings pouring through me at the end of a busy day—keeping faith in behavior, but not in feeling. I realize again, that addiction runs deep.

"Confessional Holiness", Chapter "Holy—A Little or a Lot?", by Terry Mattson, pg #28

MY THOUGHTS 12—TAKING OUT THE TRASH

Heart Questions about Holiness

...or the lack of it!

What is this conflict I have just described?

> ➤ Is it an inter-generation, inter-personal expression of "conspicuence," ...that is the racial, generational, genetic and sociologically given wound/propensity toward sin that comes down to all of Adam's sons and daughters?
> ➤ Is it instead an infirmity, a wounded space in my life; the remains of my own personal history of sin (long forgiven and gone)?
> ➤ Is it the psycho/social environment in which my own sexual development took place?
> ➤ Is it all three?

What does it mean that I am in Christ?

What does this battle say about the quality of my relationship with Christ?

Reflections on "Taking out the Trash"

Q: So, after reflecting with Terry, what is the conflict he describes in the first story above ?

> Original sin?, or;
> A wounded/broken space?, or;
> Human nature?, or;
> All of the above?

How so?

Q: What does such a confession say about the 'Trash' in Terry's city?

Q: Does the trash need to be hauled away and buried or perhaps remain in his city, to be recycled?

Q: How about your city? ...Where is the trash found?

Reflect on the nature of 'trash' in your own life and turn it all to prayer.

Week-3: THURSDAY—I JOHN 4: 16-18

STORY 12—IS LOVE EVEN POSSIBLE IN A GARBAGE DUMP?

"God is love. No one but God could have revealed that to the world, for…we all indeed, see nothing but its contradiction in our own limited world of experience. It needs but little imagination to construe the life of hundreds of this great city's inhabitants into a vehement laughter at such a declaration as 'God is love'."

From "The Complete Works of Oswald Chambers", Article: "God is Love, not, God is loving," page #655

A Personal Story from the Projects…

Her name was Michelle, a friend from the streets who would drop by the office just to chat. She was often drunk but seemed to like the safety of our church.

She had called me at about midnight concerned for a Native American friend of hers from the Makah Nation. At this writing I don't even recall the issue—I think it was despair, possible suicide. When I arrived her friend was expressing his own hopelessness with living, both of them having drunk way too much.

He lived about six blocks from the church, up the hill and in one of the world war II barrack style housing in a place called High Point.

After about an hour's conversation and some prayer I stepped out on the porch and sat next to Michelle who was enjoying—well, having at least—a smoke. High Point is properly named. It is the highest point in Seattle and the view of the park and city is magnificent. Michelle was quiet and in the silence of the moment finally said, "Pastor, this is a God forsaken place."

Given the amount of un-natural highs that inflicted adults and children alike in that park and the associated destruction in violence, gangs, yelling—I could hardly dispute her observation. I think I muttered something about her being wrong, though, that God had neither forsaken High Point, her friend or her.

About 60% of our congregation lived or had lived in High Point. We, together with many faith traditions had poured time, resources, prayers and heart in this project. We had walked its streets praying, held multi-year Bible Schools, handed out the Jesus Movie to nearly all 700 units, enjoyed worship, potlucks and baseball games here. At this writing, May of 2016, we will be hosting a Pre-Teen choir from Nampa 1st Nazarene in concert in their park, this weekend.

Michelle died several years ago. She did not get to witness the transformation of High Point from one of the worst city housing projects in the nation to now, one of the very best! God continues to honor and unfold ours and many others

prayers for this sacred space—called High Point.

The story of High Point is told, in part, from a visual I created following a City of Seattle Council meeting entitled...

"Intersections: Watching God Weave all our stories into God's Story" …You can find it at:

https://www.youtube.com/watch?v=bI9F-JmrEuY

MY THOUGHTS 13—IS LOVE EVEN POSSIBLE IN A GARBAGE DUMP?

On: Is Love even Possible?

Oswald Chambers is an eighteenth century theologian/preacher who gets a 21st century idea. God is Love!

Oswald argues that this relation of love can only be discovered in the gift of God's Holy Spirit living inside the garbage dumps of our lives. He observes that a living faith is formed inside *"shattered, broken lives, from caverns of despair where fiends seem living rather than men"* and women. It is here, in *"the existing contradiction"* where *"murder and war and famine and lust and pestilence, and all the refinement of selfish cruelty is abroad in the earth"* that we need to declare and live 'God is love.'

Then Oswald Chambers underlines his premise by emphasizing the depth and nature of God's love. He writes:

> *"Consider this revelation, the eternal fact that God is Love, not, God is loving. God and love are synonymous. Love is not an attribute of God, it is God; whatever God is, love is. If your conception of love does not agree with justice and judgment and purity and holiness, then your idea of love is wrong. It is not love you conceive of in your mind, but some*

vague infinite foolishness, all tears and softness and of infinite weakness."
From "The Complete Works of Oswald Chambers", pages #655-656

Reflections on "Is Love even Possible in a Garbage Dump?"

"God is Love, not, God is loving."
From Oswald Chambers", above
Q: Is this distinction important? ...How So?

"It needs but little imagination to construe the life of hundreds of this great city's inhabitants into a vehement laughter at such a declaration as "God is love."   From Oswald Chambers", above
Q: How do you work out this dilemma?

Q: Is a Garbage dump really a place to declare the love of God? ...Why? ...Why not?

"Look back over your own history as revealed to you by grace, and you will see one central fact growing large—God is love."
From Oswald Chambers", above
Q: Is this true? ...How so?

Listen to the deepest spiritual—physical needs of your city and consider how and where God might place you to live "God is Love."

Story 13—Creative Use of Trash

A Personal Story with an entrepreneur in my Church...

Reflections based upon II Timothy 2: 1-12

We sat in our usual place of meeting, Starbucks. Over coffee and peppermint mocha we shared with each other our hopes, fears and needs as we prepared to pray.

I looked up and into the gentle face of my friend, a parishioner for whom I have great respect. He is a businessman with a priest's heart. He is one of several lay persons who is learning how to preach/teach the very Word of God. In character, better than most of us (including me), he lives what he preaches.

In the years I have known him, there has been a restless place in him. He has changed careers four times by my count, succeeding in each, as he looks for something that will fulfill the burning in his soul. It is a fire that does not consume him, as it burns slowly, pushing him ever forward. This fire will not be quenched and should not be until the fire has done its work in him.

Today's topic is twofold: First he confesses depression over the sermon he had preached on Sunday. Substantively, the sermon was excellent, speaking to one of the deepest needs of the Church.

Usually his sermons are devotional in nature. He takes a scripture and artfully tells a story or two applying the felt meaning of the text to our lives. This was the second time I have seen him stretch to discover the meaning of the text as written and heard two thousand years ago. His message was less artful, but certainly deeper.

Gently I suggest to him that the depression he feels is simply the awareness that the deeper the dig, the greater the work. In his busy schedule, he had not chosen to protect sufficient time to research the original textual meaning as written/heard and then make application, artfully and with current icons/stories. In light of today's text, he was putting away wood and clay in favor of gold and silver and forgetting that gold and silver take more time to refine.

Our conversation then turns to his current business interest. He is divesting himself of an old Fed-Ex business in order that he might get on the ground floor of a new bio-chemical business of some promise and with very credible investors in the northwest.

He describes for me the process wherein his company is taking the throwables (trash) from restaurants and beef butchering plants and using them to separate out and purify the natural oils in preparation for refining it into diesel. He observes that in the past these restaurants and butchering plants would have paid others to hall the throw away products away for dumping. "Now," he says, "we pay for the product and then separate out the oil and other bi-products." Evidently there is little waste because most of the bi-products can be resold for value and his company is left with the purified product from which to make fuel.

'Wow!,' I thought to myself. 'What a picture of what God does with the trash of our own lives when given back to Him.'

Nothing/No One ever created by God and given back to Him will fail to fulfill the purpose of his/her creation.

How often I've have preached that line. Now I realize that even trash (garbage) can be refined and separated out and used for creative purpose.

Note: Clarence no longer worships with us. He is now an elder at a local evangelical church—appreciative of what God is doing through him in his new faith community.

Reflections on "Creative Use of Trash"

"In the years I have known him, there has been a restless place in him. He has changed careers four times by my count, succeeding in each, as he looks for something that will fulfill the burning in his soul. It is a fire that does not consume him, as it burns slowly, pushing him ever forward. This fire will not be quenched and should not be until it has done its work in him."
                                                    Terry Mattson (above)

Q: Do you have a restless place with in? …What is the meaning of the 'restless place'?

Consider what the restlessness is pointing to:

- ➢ unfulfilled dreams? or;
- ➢ sin unresolved? or;
- ➢ broken spaces? or;
- ➢ creative potential? or;
- ➢ Adam's sinfulness within? or;
- ➢ longing unsatisfied? or;
- ➢ work of the Holy Spirit? or;
- ➢ Other: _____ ?

Q: Which one or two of the above seems relevant to your own restless spirit?

Reflect on it and listen for God's voice within and thus, turn it all to prayer.

Week-3: SATURDAY—Psalm 139

My Thoughts 14—Sifting through Trash

On: When Trash Matters

One person's trash is another person's survival! The citizens

of many third world countries pour through the city dumps for products to use or sell, for survival. Indeed, many cities are built around the garbage dump with some actually living within its perimeters.

It is also true that what may be a trash dump for us, today, becomes for an archeologist, a field of dreams.

Trash has a way of being recycled and reshaped. In the earth it slowly decays, being transformed by the Creator into another generations fertilizers or energy. As in the personal story of my friend's bio-diesel business, built upon the waste products of our food, we are constantly finding new uses for what once was thrown away.

God's love is forever and creatively doing the same with and in us. God is searching through the refuge of our lives with the purpose of 'redeeming' the time, finding within the open sores of our lost self:

> Our real purpose, and;
> A deeper love for Him, in restoration, than at the beginning, and;
> A place of 'compassion' for those who are still living inside the trash heaps of their lives, and;
> New and creative ways in which to explore life.

Imagine a world with no rebellion or broken spaces. **Is it possible that if our love for God were shaped only in an environment of perfect trust that we might have been stillborn?** Is that not what Paul is getting at when he writes: *"The whole creation waits breathless with anticipation for the revelation of God's sons and daughters. Creation was subjected to frustration, not by its own choice—it was the choice of the one who subjected it—but in the hope that the creation itself will be set free from slavery to decay and brought into the glorious freedom of God's children"* (Romans 8:19-21 CEB).

George MacDonald, mourning the loss of his children, echoes Paul's theme:

> *"Tis hard for us to rouse our spirits up—It is the human creative agony—Though but to hold the heart an empty cup, or tighten on the team the rigid rein.*
> *Many will rather lie among the slain:*
> *—Than creep through narrow ways the light to gain*
> *—Than wake the will, and be born bitterly."*
> From "Diary of an Old Soul, by George McDonald, page #52

There is something gained in the desolation of the valley of Gehennan (Garbage Dump for Jerusalem). As we walk through it listening to the Holy Spirit a wisdom and deepened love emerges in us. It is a love that would never have been, excepting for trash, re-stored.

Of this Julian of Norwich, a 13th century mystic who committed herself to living within the confines of the Church—with an open window to counsel and pray for those in her village who sought her out—writes:

> "I had often wondered why…the beginning of sin was not prevented…In this stark word 'sin' our Lord brought to my mind all things in general that are not good—and the shame, the despising and the utter stripping he accepted for us in this life, and his dying. He also brought to mind all the bodily and spiritual pains and passions of all his creatures.
>
> …And all this was shown in a moment and was quickly turned into comfort, for our Lord God does not want the soul to be frightened by this ugly sight. But I did not see sin. For I believe it has no kind of substance or manner of being and that it is only known through the pain it causes. And as for pain, as I see it, it is something temporary, for it cleanses us and makes us know ourselves and ask for forgiveness. And though out all this, the Passion of our Lord comforts us…saying: 'The cause of all pain is sin. **But all shall be well, and all shall be well, and all manner of thing shall be well.'**
>
> …So how unjust would it be for me to blame God for allowing me to sin, when he does not blame me for falling into it.
>
> …Also, God showed that sin shall not be a shame to man, but a glory. For just as every sin brings its own suffering, by truth, so every soul that sins earns a blessing by love… For the soul that comes to heaven is so precious to God, and the place so holy, that God in his goodness never allows a soul that reaches

heaven to sin without also seeing that those sins have their reward.

...In this showing my understanding was lifted up to heaven. And then God brought happily to my mind David and others without number from the Old law, and in the New Law he brought to my mind first Mary Magdalene, Peter and Paul, and those of India, and St John of Beverley—and also others without number. And he showed how the Church on earth knows of them and their sins, and it is no shame to them, but is all turned to their glory."

Reprinted from "The Joy of the Saints, edited by Robert Llewelyn (written by Ann Julian of Norwich), pages #167-168, 205

The garbage dump of Israel was declared by King Josiah to be a constant reminder of the emptiness and misery of their idolatry. Trash in us is the mine field through which the Holy Spirit walks, awakening in us, ever deepening sorrow; a Godly sorrow without condemnation, producing in us wholeness and love and joy.

Reflections on "Sifting through Trash"

"Only when we have come in touch with our own life experiences and have learned to listen to our inner cravings for liberation and new life can we realize that Jesus did not just speak, but that he reached out to us in our most personal needs..."

From Henri J. M. Nouwen in "Reaching Out", reprinted in "A Guide to Prayer for Ministers & Other Servants", page #262

Q So, what do you think of this view of trash? ...Is it true?

Take some time and consider if and in what way your own love for God has grown, as a result of 'trash' in your own life…

Turn it over in your heart—reflect, write about it and pray about it… Give thanks.

Week-3: SUNDAY—ROMANS 8: 18-27, I JOHN 2: 9-17, II TIMOTHY 2: 20-21, I THESSALONIANS 2: 1-12

STORY 14—RE-VISITING GARBAGE DUMPS

A Personal Story reflecting rituals of sin...

Based on Ephesians 5: 3-14

I remember turning off highway 12 and onto the single lane forested road that serviced our local garbage dump. I was very young, having just completed my third year in college. It was summer break. My father was dying of cancer. At least that is what the doctors had said. Before the end of the summer they were quite certain he would no longer be. I was asked by my father to serve our small local congregation as pastor, in his place. Given his immanent death I have no clue what possessed my father and his church board to entertain such an idea.

What I remember of that summer was the anxiety of living about a decade beyond my own identity, acting out the role, faithful to the trust afforded. In almost every Sunday evening service a nice old man, a bit of a mystic, would stand and testify, declaring that my father would not die. How did he know? God had told him. His confessions of faith were awkward for me, for when my dad died, I would have the responsibility of picking up what was left of the faith of these evangelical Christians who believed if God promised it—that settled it. I seemed to know intuitively that one of my responsibilities was to protect God's reputation. Huh?

Once or twice during the summer one of our older woman, Evelyn Springer, a nurse, would quietly take me aside and remind me that "your dad is dying and will likely die this summer." In a strange way this woman, three times my age, comforted me with this reality check. Her simple affirmation of what we both knew felt like a medication. As did this trip to the dump.

Upon arriving at the garbage dump I look carefully around and was relieved that no one was there. Quietly, quickly, I took from my car the book I had been devouring over the last twenty-four hours, filled as it was with word pictures of sensuality. I threw it in the trash, made my way back to my car and began to drive away, not knowing then that this moment was simply another kind of medication for my anxious, over worked and under nourished soul, trying desperately to act like I was more than I was.

This is the only struggle I recall while serving the church that summer. But it was enough. As I drove away from the dump, pulling back onto highway 12 and home, I cried out to God for forgiveness, wishing to somehow wash the memory of it away. And as I had in my adolescence, I pushed this failure deep into my sub-conscious, buried and forgotten. Forgotten, that is, until the moment God forced me to walk through it and other moments, again and again, for healing.

And my father? The old mystic was right. He lived.

My Thoughts 15—Revisiting Garbage Dumps

Reflections on the Story from my college years...

The days in which I ritually acted out my sexual hungers, emerging from the reservoir of my own garbage dump of lust, are past. Even the desire for those rituals have evaporated, most of the time. Still, the refuge remains. I no longer pretend (to myself) that this dump is an unwelcome and unreal self; another person who occasionally awakens, owns me in a moment and is then buried over and hidden under a mound of contrition and forgiveness.

Now, by the Holy Spirit, I am sometimes led back through the memories and into the still, at times, distorted and powerful hungers that attend. From these walks with God I have become aware that the healing/cleansing of my life is layered.

God really has given me a new heart and mind. My spirit seems to long for God alone. Yet, even now, at this writing, I have been taken by the Spirit into a season where we are again going through the trash, picking it up, turning it over. Now, it feels like the work of an archeologist. Each piece of trash and each memory awakened allow me to consider my life, all of it. This time, it is my body's memories and needs which seem to cry out for a deeper surrender and grace.

I sense that lust for food and sex are connected. God has chosen a moment when he has placed me with a personal trainer to develop new patterns of living and a counselor for my emotions. Early childhood memories, long suppressed, seem to have forced their way up and into my life. All I can do is listen and allow God to heal.

To this day I am aware that my view of women is effected by the sin of my past. I cannot with accuracy, separate out the natural and appropriate response from that which I ritually conditioned in an empty attempt to medicate myself. I am very grateful to God that there has always been a grace given which allows me freedom when I walk among the women (young and old members and friends) of the Church.

In seasons like the one I'm in, I find myself praying often, my own version of the Jesus prayer.

> ➤ *Jesus, Son of the Living God, have mercy on me a sinner.*
> ➤ *Jesus, Son of David, have mercy on me a sinner.*
> ➤ *Jesus, Son of Mary, have mercy on me a sinner.*

As I pray this prayer my heart is aflame, burning with a hunger for holiness. I often add to each phrase the following: Heal and cleanse my body and soul and spirit until I love You, Lord, singularly, as no other and my wife, as myself.

Reflections on "Re-visiting Garbage Dumps"

"And as I had in my adolescence, I pushed this failure deep into my sub-conscious, buried and forgotten. Forgotten, that is, until the moment God forced me to walk through it and other moments, again and again, for healing.

...Still, the refuge remains. I no longer pretend (to myself) that this dump is an unwelcome and unreal self; another person who occasionally awakens, owns me in a moment and is then buried over and hidden under a mound of contrition and forgiveness."
Terry Mattson (above)

Terry is suggesting that the 'evangelical' emphasis on "God forgiving and forgetting" may simply be a way of avoiding trash, delaying healing and cleansing grace...

Q: What do you think? ...Have you seen in yourself this tendency?

Spend some time, reflect—write—think—feel. Turn it all to prayer

Next:
Digging Deep

4 DIGGING DEEP

... The Well Gate

INVOCATION:

FATHER, ASSIST ME. DEEPEN BOTH MY HUNGER FOR AND ABILITY
TO BE A PLACE OF DWELLING FOR YOUR SPIRIT. GIVE ME A
WILLING SPIRIT THAT COOPERATES WITH YOUR TRUTH. LET ME
ACTIVELY SURRENDER ALL, KNOWING THAT MY ABILITY TO LIVE
OUT JESUS LIFE IS ALWAYS AND ENTIRELY DEPENDENT UPON THE
INITIATING LOVE OF THE SPIRIT OF CHRIST, IN ME. AMEN.

BASED UPON PHILIPPIANS 2: 13

PSALM OF THE WEEK: PSALM 24

COMMANDMENT OF THE WEEK: "YOU SHALL NOT MISUSE THE NAME OF THE LORD YOUR GOD, FOR THE LORD WILL NOT HOLD ANY ONE GUILTLESS WHO MISUSES HIS NAME."
DEUTERONOMY 5:11

DAILY SCRIPTURES:

MONDAY—II CHRONICLES 29: 1-5, 10-11, 35-36 & 30:1, 6-9, 13-15 & 31: 20, 21 & 32: 1-8

TUESDAY—EXODUS 13: 1-16

WEDNESDAY—I CHRONICLES 13: 1-14

THURSDAY—ISAIAH 59: 1-10, 15-21

FRIDAY—JOHN 4: 1-26

SATURDAY—EPHESIANS 3: 14-21

SUNDAY—ACTS 16: 23-34 , EXODUS 17: 1-7, PHILIPPIANS 2: 12-13, JUDGES 6: 1-22

FROM
MATTHEW 23:37

JERUSALEM, JERUSALEM! YOU WHO KILL THE PROPHETS AND STONE THOSE WHO WERE SENT TO YOU. HOW OFTEN I WANTED TO GATHER YOUR PEOPLE TOGETHER, JUST AS A HEN GATHERS HER CHICKS UNDER HER WINGS. BUT YOU DIDN'T WANT THAT.

Week-4: MONDAY—II Chronicles 29: 1-5, 10-11, 35-36 &
30:1, 6-9, 13-15 & 31: 20-21 & 32: 1-8

Story 15—Breaking Ground

Introduction

About the late 8th Century B.C., King Hezekiah of Judah
authorized the excavation of a new tunnel to access water
for Jerusalem from a spring further away from the original
source, store the supply in an underground pool, and hide
the entrance of the spring. In his attempt to thwart a possible
Assyrian siege of the city, the tunnel would become one of
the earliest examples of daring engineering feats.

It would take two teams of workers six to seven months to
literally inch their way through 765 feet of solid rock. Each
team chipped the way to the center from opposite sides of
the hill, extending an aqueduct south of Bethlehem to
Jerusalem. Evidently guided only by water fissure, they
laboriously dug out a tunnel about one yard in width, and
one to three yards in height. One man would methodically
and tediously hack and chip away, the others behind him
passing the broken stones out in baskets.

Chiseled in the rock at the point where the two teams met,
archaeologists have found a Hebrew inscription recounting
"the day of the tunnel" in which "the stone cutters made their
way towards one another ax-blow by ax-blow." The tunnel
diverted the exposed spring of Gihon to a concealed point
outside Jerusalem's western wall.

King Hezekiah, of Judah is one of the heroes of the faith. Like King David and like us, he was vulnerable to:

- ➢ The threat of enemies, near and far, and;
- ➢ Sickness and death, and;
- ➢ Excessive Compromise, and;
- ➢ The temptation to power, and;
- ➢ Arrogance.

Yet, in every vulnerable place to which he descends he faces his circumstance and turns his face toward God, in trust. His heart is always facing into Yahweh's and he is willing to risk everything in order to do what he knows to be God's will.

In "The LORD is my Song", author Lynn Austin portrays the wisdom of this king as he faces his enemies, within and around him. Of prime importance was King Hezekiah's project to tunnel beneath Jerusalem and into the Kidron Valley in search of a fresh water source for the city, soon to be under siege.

An Imaginative Biblical Story—written by Lynn Austin in "The Lord is My Song" with significant editing and re-writing to make explicit the multiple dramas of his reign, with brevity.

"May I bring you anything else, Your majesty?" Hezekiah's servant asked as he helped him remove his royal robes.

"No. I'm waiting for Eliakim to bring me some documents. Then I will be going to see my wife."

Hezekiah sank down onto the window seat and stretched his long legs. The day had been hot, and all the shutters in his private chambers now stood open to allow in the evening breezes. They carried with them the fragrance of the sacrifice from the Temple, and Hezekiah closed his eyes, trying to recall the Words of the evening prayers: "Find rest, O my soul, in God alone; my hope comes from him. He alone is my rock and my salvation; he is my fortress. I will not be shaken."

The words of David's psalms comforted him and he made an effort every night to read and memorize some of them. He picked up his Torah scroll and unrolled it.

"Lord Eliakim is here, Your Majesty," his servant announced. "Good," the King responded. "Send him in."

Eliakim entered, but hesitantly, for it was late in the evening to be intruding on the King. Even after so many years of faithful service as the King's chief engineer, he felt a little overawed in the presence of this King whom he trusted. Bowing slightly, Eliakim apologized, "I am sorry for interrupting your privacy, your Majesty. I've completed the itinerary, but it could have waited."

"No, I've been expecting you." The king laid down his scroll. "I am anxious for you and Jonadab to get an early start in the morning. Let me see it."

Hezekiah studied the list of cities the two men were scheduled to visit, scattered as they were along all the possible invasion routes that the King of Assyria might choose. The men had orders to inspect the fortifications and offer advice on reinforcing them. Jonadab, as his military commander would be looking to security issues while Eliakim would consider how to make stronger the protective walls and how to efficiently guarantee access to armaments, water and food as each 'defense' city came under siege. As usual Eliakim had taken care of every detail, and the document authorizing and enforcing the will of the King was ready for Hezekiah's seal.

"You think it will take about two months, then? "Two months at the very least, Your Majesty."

"It looks excellent, Eliakim." Hezekiah pressed his ring into the small lump of clay, then handed it back to his trusted engineer. Eliakim looked a bit tired. "You work too hard, my friend. You should learn to relax."

Since the day the King had ordered the construction of the tunnel to direct the waters of Gihon Spring into the walled city of Old Jerusalem, Eliakim had worked tirelessly. Eliakim's tunnel foreman had told the King that Eliakim rarely went home, staying in the tunnels almost day and night. 'Maybe traveling would be good for Eliakim', the King thought, knowing his engineer's exhausting efforts.

"My friend," the King continued, "I realize it's asking a lot of you to be away from the digging and fortifications of Jerusalem at this critical moment, but your project foremen are all capable men. You have chosen well." "Of course, my Lord." Eliakim responded. I am happy to do it."

Hezekiah smiled slightly. "I know you are anxious to finish your tunnel, but..." Before allowing him to finish, Eliakim startled himself with his own answer. "It's your tunnel, my lord, and it must be completed." And then catching himself for his rudeness and to the King, he added, "Forgive me, my Lord." Hezekiah's smile turned into laughter. "All I can say, is that I'm glad you are on my side, my friend."

As the King stood, indicating to Eliakim that the meeting's business was done, one of his servants hurried into the room. "Your Majesty, General Jonadab wishes to see you right away."

Eliakim was surprised, as was the king and wondered at what could be so urgent. When Jonadab entered he seemed deeply shaken. He was a battle-hardened soldier, but as he groped for words Hezekiah knew that this was something which troubled his commander in chief, personally. "I'm sorry to disturb you, Your Majesty," Jonadab hesitated as he noticed Eliakim and realized that his was not the only interruption the King had endured that evening.

Turning his thoughts back to the King he gathered himself and continued. "...but something terrible happened tonight, and..." "Sit down, Jonadab, take your time," the King interrupted and with a glance to his servant indicated the need for some wine. "Now tell me, what's wrong?"

"Your majesty, one of my watchmen at the valley gate saw a man and woman leave the city after sunset, carrying a bundle. They headed down toward the Hinnom Valley, and a few minutes later he saw what looked like a bonfire over by the cliffs—" An icy chill passed through Hezekiah. "Oh, no—" the king whispered, looking up and into the eyes of his friend, Eliakim and seeing in them, the same horror. Like the King, Eliakim could remember as a child witnessing in the valley of Hinnom the sacrifices approved by the King's father. In fact, he had been at the very sacrifice in which King Hezekiah's older brother, Eliab had been sacrificed by his own father, King Ahaz.

The general drew a shaky breath. "I'm sorry—but we were too late. By the time we arrived, the baby was dead. This is all that was left."

He handed Hezekiah a small funeral urn. Fine, charred bones lay on the bottom. Hezekiah's stomach turned as he read the inscription. The baby had been sacrificed to the goddess Asherah to fulfill a vow.

"Where is the couple now?" "Outside your throne room." "Let's go."

When Hezekiah was seated on his throne, Jonadab's soldiers brought in the prisoners. The handsome couple was dressed as if attending a lavish social function. The woman was adorned with expensive jewelry. But panic showed on their chalky faces as they cowered before the king, staring at the floor. The woman's shoulders quaked with silent sobs.

"Why did you do it?" Hezekiah asked, but they made no reply. "I asked why you sacrificed your child!" shouting, "Answer me!"

The husband finally looked up. His voice had the defiant tone of a man who knows he stands condemned and has nothing more to lose. "We made a vow to the goddess a year ago. She answered our prayers and granted me what I asked for, so we've kept our part of the vow in return."

135

Standing and moving toward the couple, Hezekiah asked. "You vowed to kill your own child?" "He's our son. Aren't we free to do whatever we want with him?" was the response, cold and calculating. Hezekiah gripped the urn until his knuckles turned white, controlling his anger only with great effort. He didn't need to consult the Levites. He knew what the Torah said. When he finally passed the tiny remains back to Jonadab, his hands shook.

"Give this little one a proper burial, then take his parents out of the city and stone them to death." "No!" the woman screamed, dropping to her knees. "Have mercy on us, please!" "Mercy"?, the king asked, turning away from her. "The same mercy you showed your own son?" With tears falling gently to his cheeks he turned once again to face this mother and spoke sadly. "You burned him alive, woman, and you're asking for mercy?" With that Hezekiah waved his hand in dismissal. "But, we have other children at home," she pleaded as the soldiers hauled her away. "Stone them both." was all the king spoke as they were taken away.

Gradually her cries faded as the soldiers hustled her away. Jonadab remained behind, clutching the urn. The room was silent as Hezekiah struggled to compose himself. Finally, after what seemed an eternity he spoke to his general. "Go home and go to bed, General. It's been a long night for all of us."

But as Jonadab turned to leave, Hezekiah stopped him. "Wait. See to it that their other children are cared for."

The incident left Hezekiah badly shaken. Eliakim turned slowly and without request, left with Jonadab, leaving the King in his throne room, alone with his feelings. He knew that his friend, the king, would feel no offence, if he even noticed. The King didn't notice, absorbed as he was with intense feelings. An hour later he was still trembling, and he debated whether or not he should go to see Hephzibah, his wife. He needed her to help him erase the events from his mind, but he didn't want to burden her with what had been a revolting duty.

As he left the throne room the King turned instead toward the privacy of his own bed chambers. Making his way down the hall he felt the stirrings of an old desire, long forgotten in the love of his wife and the commitment to follow all of Moses commands, including the one regarding many wives. How he longed for the comfort of one of her concubines.

He knew their passions could erase the memories of his own childhood and the day in the valley of Hinnom when his own brother was offered up to the fires of Molech.

In the sight of all the leading citizens of Jerusalem his own father had boasted of the great 'sacrifice' he was making in honor of the gods. How often he had watched his father wander these same halls, drunk with wine, looking for the Queens concubines.

It was from these memories that King Hezekiah had found the moral courage to reform the nation and place his own life under the authority of the Torah.

And so the king continued down the hall, troubled and alone. He did not wish to disturb the queen with his needy heart nor would he find in her concubines the escape he desired. Entering his chambers, he ordered his favorite wine and took again his seat near the window, allowing for the moons glow to work its charms and ease his spirit. Picking up the Torah he continued the quiet meditations he had begun before being interrupted and troubled by thoughts of enemies near or far.

Adapted from "The LORD is My Song" by Lynn N. Austin, pages #236-240

Reflections on "Breaking Ground"

"How is man's inner eye purified? How to remove the cataract that blurs his vision or even blinds it altogether?

...we meet the motif of purity of heart above all in Psalm 24, which reflects an ancient gate liturgy: "Who shall ascend the hill of the LORD? And who shall stand in his holy place? He who has clean hands and a pure heart, who does not lift up his soul to what is false, and does not swear deceitfully" (Ps 24: 3-4).
From "Jesus of Nazareth", by Pope Benedict XVI, page #93, 94

Q: What in your life is more vulnerable; Your heart or Your hands?

Q: In what ways can you identify with this story of a reforming King?

Q: With whom do you identify:

> ➤ The King? or;
> ➤ Eliakim? or;
> ➤ Jonadab? or;
> ➤ The couple?

Q: Identify the enemies in your own life?

Q: In what sense are they also found or even rooted in the larger culture?

Reflect and turn it all to your prayer.

Week-4: TUESDAY—Exodus 13: 1-16

Story 16—Striking Water: The Analogy of a Home

An Imaginative Story with a Wesleyan Motif... on Prevenient Grace

The following is not unique to me. It is drawn from memory and multiple sources. I have reworked it to incorporate (both in this story and its corollary later in this book) my own emphasis.

Imaginative Story: The Analogy of the Home

He was a king, I a poor and pretty pathetic picture of a man. He was refined. I, well, let's just say subtlety was not a practiced art with me. He was kind. I rude. He was aware. I was ignorant.

In his home servants attended his every need. Dust was not allowed, a left over fragment from a meal unheard of. If he was hungry a steward anticipated his need and wine and bread were available in abundance. His library was full of the knowledge of the finest minds of the kingdom; stories to fascinate a child's curiosity and an adult's imagination. He was the son of the King Most High, ruler of our lands.

When he came to my home—I still shutter at the thought of his coming into my little hut—my living room was cluttered with clothes and food half eaten. He came and spoke with me as though we were the best of friends. He sat among my cluttered living room pushing old food out of the way as though a trivial thing. I was embarrassed. He hardly noticed.

He laughed at my jokes; well, those he could and with quiet and charming grace suffered those too vulgar to mention.

That first afternoon we sat and talked and laughed like two old friends. I felt taken by him, alive in his presence. I realized, even that first afternoon that I had changed in his company. I felt like I was 'more' than I was; somehow connected to him, a prince myself and not a pauper.

On his second visit I was ready. I had worked all morning cleaning the living area, carrying out buckets of ash from the fireplace so that we could enjoy, together, a fire.

It was on his third visit that he expressed a desire for drink. I had not even thought of giving him so much as a cup. Without asking, as friends do, he made his way into my kitchen for a drink from the barrel of wine. I was horrified. I had never thought of cleaning out the kitchen. There were no clean goblets. He simply went to my sink, piled high, and cleaned one for himself and one for me as we continued our conversation. If he noticed I could not tell. On his next visit the kitchen was clean.

Each time he came he taught me something new about the kingdom of His father. Never had I felt so honored to be a citizen of our land. The books he brought me began to form a library.

Soon I was making and entertaining others in my little home, filled as it was with the fragrance of a king's son. I was the talk of our little village. Everyone noticed the difference in me. I was treated with respect.

One day, while walking by one of my very old friends home, I decided to stop by for a chat. It had been a year or two since we last spoke. I hardly recognized him. There in front of me stood the most repulsive excuse for a human being I had ever seen. His clothes smelled of his body. His hair was a mess. His language filled with the curses of an arrogant man who holds not his tongue in honor of his Majesty's name. I was repulsed. My former friend invited me in. Every part of me wanted to run. Evidently my eyes communicated what my soul felt for my friend looked down in shame. I turned to leave, in disgust. As I turned, a silent curse forming on my tongue, I heard it. From within the home of this disgusting man came the familiar voice of my King's Son.

Reflections

Q: How does this story picture grace?

Q: In what ways did the pauper change as a result of the King's Son's visits?

Q: What motivated the changes in his identity and lifestyle?

Q: What if he had not changed? How would the story have been affected?

Q: What still needed to change in the pauper?

Q: How does the King's visit to the home of the pauper's friend change the story?

Q: What happens if the pauper chooses not to accept his friend?

Q: When is prevenient grace no longer prevenient?

This writing with minor changes is also found in "Confessional Holiness: The Missing Piece of the Puzzle", chapter 1, "Toward a New Developmental Model" by Terry Mattson, pg #64-66

Reflections on "Striking Water: The Analogy of a Home"

"He was a king, I a poor and pretty pathetic picture of a man. He was refined. I, well, let's just say subtlety was not a practiced art with me. He was kind. I rude. He was aware. I was ignorant."

Terry Mattson (above)

The initiative in this story is always with the King's Son. It is his presence in the life of the peasant that initiates change.

Q: How did God first come to you?

Q: Did you recognize God's initiative? ...How did you respond? What changes came in your life as a result?

Consider how The Spirit of God is at work in your life... Give thanks or praise or respond, if you have not as yet.

Week-4: WEDNESDAY—I CHRONICLES 13: 1-14

MY THOUGHTS 16—ON DIGGING

One of John and Charles Wesley's significant contributions to the Protestant dialogue about salvation was to pay attention to how God, in the church of Christ and beyond, formed the life of Jesus, in us. John observed carefully his own spiritual journey and that of others and developed a 'way of salvation' for Methodist's to follow.

This developmental emphasis was not new, in and of itself. Wesley's subjective emphasis mirrored his understanding of salvation as a Divine/human relationship in which humanity was given the ability by God to respond to God's initiative in re-making us in the image of Christ.

In the Lutheran and Reformed traditions, the emphasis was upon the sovereign act of God in justifying us and giving us standing before God, who is King and Holy. We, who are mere peasants before a feudal Lord and deserving of banishment or worse were given pardon and acceptance in the Kingdom of our Lord. Ted Campbell and Michael Burns note how Ulrich Zwingli and John Calvin and their followers (including Congregationalist and Presbyterian churches) enlarged this tradition with an emphasis upon the human response to God's sovereign act of acceptance.

"According to this pattern, which Reformed teachers described as the 'order of salvation', Christians pass through the following stages or moments in the Christian life:

> **Effectual calling**—Usually accompanied by repentance and the recognition that one cannot save oneself;

> **Justification**—A Divinely given 'assurance' of 'adoption', ...that one is included among the elect;

> **Sanctification**—The believer is made progressively more holy by 'mortification' (death to sin) and 'vivification' (following the example of Christ), and;

> **Glorification**—after...death, the Christian enters into the blissful fellowship of Christ and the saints.

From "Wesleyan Essentials in a Multicultural Society", page #68, 69 by Ted A. Campbell and Michael T. Burns

What Wesley brought to this developmental model were two emphases: first, about the nature of the relationship and second, a developmental pattern in the human response.

In emphasis, **Wesley perceived that the real barrier to our relation with God was our inability to commune with One who is perfect and holy** and not the offence to Sovereign will. **God's gracious offering of His Son was a loving and holy Father's way of renewing communion. Holiness, in us, was necessary to this communion.** It had to be real, as well as legal. Our relation depended upon both God's gracious holiness and our participatory response. Hence, the work of Sanctification was his emphasis.

To Wesley, God is always the initiator. It is God who justifies and Sanctifies, but it is the human response of active, participatory faith that allows the Holy Spirit to make real in us, our relationship of acceptance (justification) and holy fellowship (sanctification). His developmental model included:

> ➢ **Prevenient Grace**—The movement of God in awakening us to our need of His holiness and love.
> ➢ **Justifying Grace**—The act of God in accepting us and by the new birth giving us the ability to respond fully to this new relation.
> ➢ **Sanctifying Grace**—The act of God, begun in our new birth and given full expression as Christ's life in us and our love for God becomes the central passion of our being. God enables ever deeper holiness in our behavior, service and devotion to God.

Wesley was Anglican and believed in the reality and security afforded in the sacraments of the Church. Wesley invited the Church into a process of spiritual formation by intentional worship, confessional small groups, missional service and mass evangelization, all designed to increase the believer's hunger to know and love God. He called this mature, realized state of grace, 'entire sanctification'. This process of Sanctification, Wesley taught, would inevitably lead to a perfect love for God and humanity.

This writing with minor changes is also found in "Confessional Holiness: The Missing Piece of the Puzzle", chapter 3, "Toward a New Developmental Model" by Terry Mattson, pg #67-68

Reflections on "On Digging"

Digging a well or tunnel is work. Hard work. Even so, the well or tunnel means nothing until water is struck. The dig is relatively unimportant, except that without the work of tunneling or the means to dig deep in the earth's surface the gift of life—water—would remain hidden, buried, unavailable. Water is everything!

In the same way, the means by which God moves us from darkness to light, from emptiness to fullness, from wounds to healing and from selfishness to love is also unimportant—though necessary. To that end we look upon the dig so that we may better work with the Trinity of God as we are drawn ever deeper through the 'trash heaps' of our lives and towards the 'living water'.

The Wesleyan model of spiritual formation emphasized:

> ➢ Prevenient grace, and;
> ➢ Justifying grace, and;
> ➢ Sanctifying grace.

Q: Which of these aspects of God's movement within us have played the greater role in your life; Prevenient, justifying or sanctifying grace? …How so?

Reflect and turn it all to prayer.

Week-4: THURSDAY—Isaiah 59: 1-10, 15-21

MY THOUGHTS 17—DIGGING DEEPER

On: Cultural influences on Spiritual Formation

Ted Campell and Michael Burns points to another change in cultural perceptions of salvation that needs to be noted. In the 17th, 18th and 19th century Protestant and western world the understanding of sin as real, personal and deserving of God's wrath was a given. A person coming into justification (God's acceptance), under any of the models of salvation would have understood the very earnest need for repentance over sin.

In the twentieth century, however, a reductionism has crept into both our Euro-American culture and the Church over the problem of sin. Hell as a place of deserving judgment and sin as an offence about which God has passionate feeling has been replaced by a theology of individual and personal enrichment and security. While conversion, as a point of decision and identity has been retained in evangelical circles, it has lost much of it's real, though sometimes misplaced, struggle with brokenness and sin. Initial confession/repentance, once devoted to the wrongness of a behavior or feeling pattern is now 'felt' as a loss of 'meaning or presence or identity'. They write:

> *"Divine grace, even for evangelical Christians, can become a casual relationship, a one night-stand with Jesus. The 'mourner's bench' so prominent in earlier camp meetings ...was largely forgotten.*

Revivals began to emphasize the urgency of conversion, but without the expectation that a person might spend a considerable amount of time in spiritual struggle prior to conversion.

Denying what had been a consistent part of Christian nurture impoverished evangelical spirituality."
From "Wesleyan Essentials In a Multicultural Society", page #68, 69 by Ted A. Campbell and Michael T. Burns

Dallas Willard, in "A Divine Conspiracy" develops a whole theology of holiness, centered in the Sermon on the Mount, that is intended to address this culturally and historically influenced failure to call for real change in relationship to both God and human kind that is shaped, in part, by character transformation.

On pages #367 and 368 Dallas Willard lays out five developmental stages in our relation to the Christ life. They are:

1. *Confidence in and reliance upon Jesus.*
2. *This confidence in the person of Jesus naturally leads to a desire to be his apprentice.*
3. *The abundance of life realized through apprenticeship to Jesus naturally leads to obedience.*
4. *Obedience leads to and issues from the pervasive inner transformation of the heart and soul.*
5. *There is power to work the works of the kingdom.*

From Dallas Willard's "Divine Conspiracy", Page #367-368

In Dallas Willard's "Renovation of the Heart", he explores the personal, identity, biological and social nature of 'spiritual formation'.

He describes the human self as a unity of person (soul) that takes shape in a multi-dimensional being. The six areas of personhood are:

> ➤ *Thoughts (images, concepts, judgements, inferences), and;*
> ➤ *Feeling (sensation, emotion), and;*
> ➤ *Choice (will, decision, character), and;*
> ➤ *Body (action, interaction with the physical world), and;*
> ➤ *Social contexts (personal and structural relations to others), and;*
> ➤ *Soul (the factor that integrates all the above to form one life).*

From Dallas Willard's "Renovation of the Heart", Page #30

With imagination, Dallas Willard has managed to give evangelicals a terminology commensurate with the psychological/ sociological language of western culture and still reflects the Biblical reality of our 'sinful' nature.

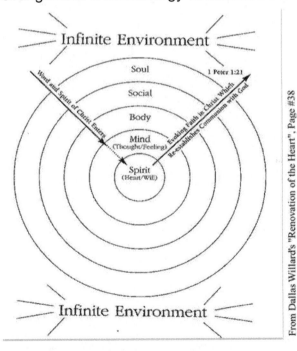

It is this gift of taking seriously human beings as having a nature (character or identity) rooted in social and personal history that is his greatest contribution. If we, as Wesleyans, in opting for relational language, fail to understand the 'reality of our social/ personal nature' formed outside of the holy—love of God, we will greatly diminish our ability to communicate the transformational power of knowing God.

This writing with minor changes is also found in "Confessional Holiness: The Missing Piece of the Puzzle", chapter 3, "Toward a New Developmental Model" by Terry Mattson, pg#84-85

Reflections on "Digging Deeper"

Consider Dallas Willard's developmental model below:

1. *Confidence in and reliance upon Jesus.*
2. *This confidence in the person of Jesus naturally leads to a desire to be his apprentice.*
3. *The abundance of life realized through apprenticeship to Jesus naturally leads to obedience.*
4. *Obedience leads to and issues from the pervasive inner transformation of the heart and soul.*
5. *There is power to work the works of the kingdom.*
From Dallas Willard (above).

Q: Where are you in this developmental model?

Q: Where does Jesus want to take you next? ...What needs to happen to move forward in Jesus?

Once again, consider how The Spirit of God is at work in your life... and cooperate.

Week-4: FRIDAY—JOHN 4: 1-26

MY THOUGHTS 18—DIFFERENT WELLS FOR DIFFERENT CULTURES

About: Culturally Sensitive understandings of Sin felt as anxiety—shame—guilt...

Cultures also communicate differing views of what it means for humans to be broken or wounded or sinful. In a communal society whose focus is on 'shame' the nature of sin/offence may be very different than for western cultures whose focus is in individual personality/identity formation and the role of 'guilt' in character formation.

For a 'shame centered' culture, character development is largely the result of external controls (Tribal, familial, Community) and a person's feeling of 'guilt' may have more to do with 'loosing face' or 'loss of relationship' with the community than any sense of 'wrong' felt as moral failure.

Augsburger, in "Pastoral Counseling Across Cultures" provides helpful models of the role of 'anxiety', 'shame, and 'guilt' in character formation as follows:

Anxiety—A loss of calm before a perceived threat. It is experienced as:

> ➤ Fear before real or fantasized dangers, or;
> ➤ Arousal before environmental demands, or;
> ➤ A primal emotion (powerlessness, fear of external powers, loss of being), or;
> ➤ As Paralyzing (panic, desire to run, fight or freeze).

Positive Power: Energizes, alerts, heightens perceptions, mobilizes defenses.

Negative Power: Distracts, disrupts rational perspective, reduces impulse control, overloads cognition.

Resolution: Anxiety must be released, discharged, ventilated or dissipated.

Shame—A loss face before significant persons or community. It is experienced as:

- ➢ Exposure before an audience, or;
- ➢ Failure before one's ideal, or;
- ➢ Embarrassed before social demands, or;
- ➢ An all-consuming emotion resulting in (rejection as a person, exclusion from community, with-drawl of love), or;
- ➢ As humiliating exposure, dishonor, self-negation (with impulse to hide, cover up or deny).

Positive Power: Can result in discretion motivation, energizes honor and disposition to virtue.

Negative Power: Feeling of disgrace can disrupt social life, disorient the self and leave one dishonored before community.

Resolution: Acted on can lead to earning place, recovering face, regaining honor.

Guilt—A loss of integrity before one's conscience. It is experienced as:

- ➢ Condemnation before an inner parent or judge, or;
- ➢ Pain under moral demands, or;
- ➢ A specific emotion resulting in (fear of judgment, correction of acts, with-drawl of trust), or;
- ➢ As humbling disclosure, discomfort, regretted acts; the impulse to justify or rationalize or excuse.

Positive Power: Can result in direct action toward better behavior, points to underlying values, a deep desire for integrity.

Negative Power: Feeling of pain due to internal incongruence—division, resenting failure, destruction of inner peace.

Resolution: Acted on can lead responsible behavior and character, expressing regrets, acting in repentance.

Interpreted from David Augsburger's "Pastoral Counseling Across Cultures", Figure 4-3, Comparison of Anxiety, Shame, and Guilt, page #122

Augsburger then goes on to visualize how three culture types experience Anxiety, Shame and Guilt in terms of conscious and unconscious motivation.

For: Tribal society with Animistic or cosmic fear traditions. 'Powers' and 'power structures' are the dominant control with guilt and shame largely unconscious and anxiety is

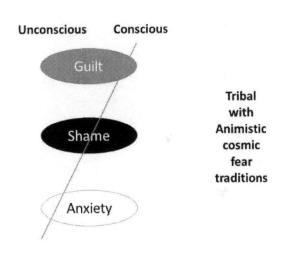

the consciously chosen motivator to either inhibit behavior or direct behavior to desired ends.

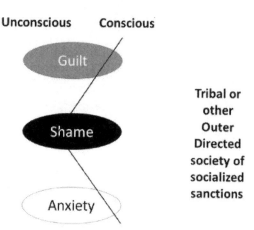

For: Tribal or other Outer Directed society of socialized sanctions for inclusion and exclusion. 'Shame' characterizes the major energy for inhibition or direction. The dominant controls are external and social. Anxiety and Guilt exist but work in largely unconscious ways.

For: An inner Directed Society of strongly individualized and internalized controls. 'Guilt' characterizes the major psychic structure of a conscience that is a 'parental judge', with shame and anxiety largely repressed and unconscious.

Interpreted from David Augsburger's "Pastoral Counseling Across Cultures", Figure 4-2, The Distinction between conscious and unconscious controls, page #125

A doctrine of 'holiness' that relies heavily on 'internalized' values and develops models of spiritual formation centered on the Work of the Holy Spirit within individual persons may have little relevance to a community who cares only about 'community identity' centered around ritual/role consciousness, with little concern for personal identity or personal guilt. 'Guilt' of course is still present, but is felt in relation to 'failing—shaming' the whole society, the elders or the family rather than an inability to keep faith with an internalized view of the self before God.

At the heart of Old/New Testament holiness is a communal understanding and presence that we in the Western (especially American) experience simply do not see. We see in Pentecost the 'fire' which purified the 120 individual participants in the upper room. A socially centered culture may miss entirely that part of the story while being fully impressed with the 'gift of languages' and repentance that is the result of 'shame' or 'loss of face'.

> *"Therefore let all Israel be assured of this: God has made this Jesus, whom you* (note: communal you) *crucified both Lord and Christ. When the people heard this, they were cut to the heart and said to Peter and the other apostles, "Brother, what shall we do?"* Acts 21: 36-37

In my father and grand-father's generation it was enough to 'preach against sin' for the shared cultural expectations (individualized-guilt centered) meant that almost everyone knew that facing sin and stepping into Christian faith was a step up. The revivalism that permeated much of North American Christianity said 'repent so that you can step in and up'—be accepted—saved —in.

In this new post-modern world where every communal story is heard and honored and emphasis is placed upon acceptance as the highest expression of 'the communal good,' the Christianity of my father and grandfathers vintage is seen as a step down and away from what is virtuous. 'Why would anyone want to carry bigoted baggage just to know God?

It is not hard to imagine then that the Camp Meeting emphasis upon personal guilt and repentance so prevalent in North American revivalism would look like nothing more than the caricature in Neil Diamond's song, "Brother Love's Travel'n Salvation Show" to a Millennial, not to mention Native American or Samoan or African.

> *"Room gets suddenly still*
> *and when you'd almost bet*
> *You could hear yourself sweat—*
> *he walks in*
> *Eyes black as coal*
> *and when he lifts his face*
> *Every ear in the place is on him.*
> *Startin' soft and slow,*
> *like a small earthquake*
> *And when he lets go,*
> *half the valley shakes."*

In the multi-cultural context of our modern—post-modern world, it is restoration, healing and communal salvation that will connect. The Trinity of God, as a Community of Persons of Holy—Love and the unique work of Jesus must first be developed as Story before individuals and communities can begin to grasp the depth of human need including sin and broken spaces (personal and communal). Only in relationship with the Trinity of God and the body of Christ can our wounded/broken spaces be healed and cleansed. In short, it is the arms of God wide in Jesus—acceptance—that defines faith; We are in the Story of God, saved, accepted and as part of this new community begin to experience God's ideal communion—holiness.

Any Spiritual Formation model in which the God Story in Christ takes hold must take notice of the felt needs or wounds of the culture—its own sense of fear or shame or guilt—it's vision of what 'the ideal' human being or community should look like.

This writing with minor changes is also found in "Confessional Holiness: The Missing Piece of the Puzzle", chapter 3, "Toward a New Developmental Model" by Terry Mattson, pg #76-78

Reflections on "Different Wells for Different Cultures"

The Old and New Testament knew very little of 'individual' religious experience so prevalent in the American Church. While faith was personally experienced it found its source and expression in the community of Israel and of the Church. God always came in community and to communities.

Q: How has the 'body of Christ' shaped your own experience of Jesus?

Review the table above that provides positive and negative effects of:

> Anxiety, and;
> Shame, and;
> Guilt.

Q: Which do you feel the most? ...Why?

Q: What is the positive and negative effects or affect of this primary 'emotion' in your own life? ...in the life of the 'faith community' of which you are a part?

Reflect and turn it all to prayer.

Week-4: SATURDAY—EPHESIANS 3: 14-21

MY THOUGHTS 19—A NEW MODEL FOR DIGGING

On: The Holy—Love of the Trinity of God reaching deeply into our broken world

In my unpublished book, "Confessional Holiness" I suggest four developmental stages for Christian growth. They are:

> ➢ **Pre-Christian**, and;
> ➢ **Rooted in the love/story of Christ**, and;
> ➢ **Ability to Explore fully our new life in Christ**, and;
> ➢ **Fully given over to the Love of the Trinity of God**.

1) Pre-Christian

As Pre-Christians we live outside of the conscious and inner presence of Christ. Our life is largely centered around the emotional/psycho-personal and sexual needs of our identity and bodies. Our personal identity is largely molded by the social, political and cultural ethos given to us. Multiple and layered addictive patterns inform our decisions and relationships. Our personal story evolves from this chaos.

In this context Christ is fully present, but largely unseen. God, in Christ begins inter-acting with us to capture our attention, inform our conscience about sin and draw us into a world of Jesus choosing. God acts both in the western world of science and its materially formed awareness and also within the rich religious experience and traditions of communal societies.

It is in this context that other religious, spiritual, material, sexual or psychological-social pursuits become, for us, the beginning of our encounter with the living God, as hunger is fully formed.

Example: From St. Augustine's Confessions.

"Ask the beauty of the earth, the beauty of the sky. Question the order of the stars, the sun whose brightness lights the day, the moon whose splendor softens the gloom of night. Ask of the living creatures that move in the waves that roam the earth, that fly in the heavens.

...Question all these and they will answer, 'Yes, we are beautiful'. Their very loveliness is their confession of God: For who made these lovely mutable things, but he who is himself unchangeable beauty?

Too late have I loved you, O beauty ever ancient, ever new, too late have I loved you. I sought for you abroad, but you were within me though I was far from you. Then you touched me, and I longed for your peace, and now all my hope is only in your great mercy...You have made us for yourself, and our heart is restless till it rests in you."

2) Rooted in the love/story of Christ

Christ, His plans and dreams enter into our life, first by nature (the church, teaching, visuals) and then in the presence of the Holy Spirit as we become aware of, intrigued with and captured by Christ.

For most people there are two clearly defined stages in becoming rooted in the story of Christ.

The first is the work of the Holy Spirit in drawing us to faith in Christ and convincing us of the necessity to follow Jesus.

➤ **Individually Centered/Internalized Control:** The Word of God comes alive, worship and fellowship in His body captures our sense of awe and the intuited need for holy love is consciously felt and defined.

➤ **Socially Centered/Externalized Control:** In communal societies this often takes place in a familial or tribal setting in which a whole community comes to faith in Christ, the elder (King, Chief, Grandfather, Father) declaring for the community, their loyalty to Christ.

The second is when the need for forgiveness and the holiness of God grieves our own spirit or community and we are conscious of God as a loving Sovereign—Creator desiring relationship, blocked by our own inner dispositions and lack of trust. In this/these moment(s), the birth of the Spirit takes place.

Example: From Oswald Chambers.

> "The early disciples were honest, sincere, zealous men; they had given up everything to follow Jesus; their sense of the heroic was grand, but where did it all end?
>
> 'They all forsook Him, and fled.' They came to realize that no human earnestness or sincerity on earth can ever begin to fulfill what Jesus demands of a disciple.
>
> ...The bedrock in Jesus Christ's Kingdom is not sincerity, not deciding for Christ, not a determination to serve Him, but a complete and entire recognition that we cannot begin to do it."
>
> From "The Complete Works of Oswald Chambers", page #676-677

3) Ability to Explore fully our new life in Christ

Inner transformation takes on reality as we desire his likeness. In this stage of development, we become keenly aware of our contradictions and wounds and of our inability to fulfill, in our own strength, the call too Holy—Love.

Putting off the old-self and putting on our new-self become the story of our journey, but only in response to our deepening awareness of the love of God and our own inner tension about God.

The Church, and her human weaknesses, become the context for working through and beyond our wounds and the 'sin' which so easily entangles. The Church of Christ is the broken space in which Christ's love is felt and the contradictions about Christ are exposed.

> ➤ **Individually Centered/Internalized Control:** The issue of 'sin' as a pride centered disposition or an ingrained cultural/personal attitude of independence is exposed. Our faithlessness is deeply felt as drift or rebellion or lack of faith or addiction, even as our desire to love Christ is increased. The *"cravings of sinful mankind, the lust of the eyes and the boasting of what he has and does"* (I John 2:16b, NIV) are exposed both personally and culturally, guilt fully released and our life is transformed.
>
> ➤ **Socially Centered/Externalized Control:** In shame centered cultures the 'pride of Adam' may be externally communicated in the rituals of the tribe/family with healing/cleansing taking the form of:
> > o Social/family restoration as community values and relations are seen in light of Christ's Kingdom, and/or;
> > o A reverent spirit seeking righteous relationship within the familial/tribal community, and/or;
> > o The spiritual Disciplines of worship, prayer, confession, communion and service become the living context for Christ's Spirit to form in us, Christ's death, resurrection and life, lived.

Example: From Oswald Chambers.

"The Holy Spirit at work in our personal lives enables us to make the ideal and the actual one, and we begin slowly to discern that we have been brought into the place where Christ Jesus dwells."
From "The Complete Works of Oswald Chambers", page #677

4) Fully given over to the Love of the Trinity of God

In this developmental stage we become aware of the Trinity, as never before; Three Unique Persons, Co-Eternal and so interwoven in Love as to exist as One in real Essence.

We begin to get a glimpse of the Father as Holy—Love, of Holy—Communion in whom the cross, before time is formed. The Father's goodness and awesome holiness fully engages our imagination in prayer and longing. Christ is the Father, fully present, perfect, sinless and in Jesus we are invited to know the Father. His loving relation with the Father becomes an open invitation to us. The Holy Spirit is no longer an abstraction, but is the Father and Son poured out into the broken spaces of our own story. A new human being is being formed in us, in Christ. We become aware of intimacy that is beyond feeling; Presence.

The church becomes a mystical communion, centered in the sacraments and in the speaking and hearing of worship, informed around the Word of God.

It is in this Christ filled life that Love increasingly calls us out of our wounds and into Love's wholeness. We are given an increasing ability to imitate the love of Christ. Guilt, shame and fear are transcended as the fully developed 'surrender' and 'trust' take hold in our lives, Churches and communities.

Missional presence in the community becomes, not a means of influencing the culture or empowering the Church, but simply and fully as the Love/Presence of the Trinity of God, incarnated in the Church. We live to serve the community, in Christ's place.

This writing with minor changes is also found in "Confessional Holiness: The Missing Piece of the Puzzle", chapter 3, "Toward a New Developmental Model" by Terry Mattson, pg # 93-100

Reflections on "A New Model for Digging"

Reflect and allow the Holy Spirit to help you identify where you are in your own spiritual pilgrimage. They are:

> ➢ **Pre-Christian**, and;
> ➢ **Rooted in the love/story of Christ**, and;
> ➢ **Ability to Explore fully our new life in Christ**, and;
> ➢ **Fully given over to the Love of the Trinity of God**.

Q What Developmental Stage captures your present experience?

Q: What Developmental Stage captures you own faith community? ...Your family?

Reflect and turn it all to prayer.

Week-4: SUNDAY— ROMANS 8: 18-27, I JOHN 2: 9-17, II
TIMOTHY 2: 20-21, I THESSALONIANS 2: 1-12

STORY 17—SWIMMING IN WATER: A SECOND RESPONSE TO A KING'S VISIT!

The analogy of the home—Part II

An Imaginative Story with A Wesleyan Motif...on Sanctifying Grace

It has now been many years since the King's Son first entered my home. The first two rooms he entered were the living room and kitchen.

For many months I was happy to entertain him there. Our conversations were always filled with the wonder of discovery... that is until I made that fateful visit to my friend's home, to visit him as the King's son had me, so long ago.

At first I was enraged. I swore, something I had not done in such a long time. "By all the King holds dear", I said, "how could his son even think of going there?" To myself I thought, "What would the villagers think of him, of me?"

Slowly the anger subsided as I made my way back home and a new feeling began to enter... guilt over my response to my friend, earlier that day. I thought to myself, "Why should I care who this future King visited? And why was I repulsed by the condition of his home? Had not mine looked much the same? Had not I looked, well, repulsive?"

Night had already fallen as I entered the courtyard door of my hut. I quickly glanced into the living area and was struck by its warmth, filled as it was with the light of dancing flames from the fire hearth. It looked so inviting. I wanted to go in and weep; to admit to the fire and to myself what a fool I had been; to run back to my friend's house and beg his forgiveness and somehow apologize to the King's Son, himself.

Instead I just leaned back against the courtyard wall, sliding down the wall till I was seated on the cobble stones which formed a kind of patio opening to the living area, kitchen, bedroom and library.

It was then, only then, I realized that all the changes in my life were the direct result of the King's Son and his presence in my life. Before him my library was just a dust filled room, empty of life. Before him my kitchen existed only as an extension of my hunger. I drank only to get drunk. Before him my living room was cold and empty of warmth, human or other.

As I explored my feelings I realized another thing. Before the King's Son came I could pretty much do as I like... but I never really liked what I did. Now everything in my home was new. To enjoy the pleasures my new home afforded required a good deal of discipline and work. all of which I was happy to do, because after all, the son of the King might come, that very day!

Until that moment it had never occurred to me that the King's Son visited anyone else. I never took with me, out of my little hut, the changes he had made inside my home. Sure I bragged, all the time about our visits, the things we talked about and the joy we shared. On occasion, I even invited my friends into my home to dine with the son of the King Most High…But never had I thought that the Son of the King Most High might just be interested in my old friend as well.

And now that thought troubled me. Knowing him as I did, I knew what it meant. I could no longer live to myself, for myself in the village square. Where ever I went, the spirit of the King's Son would have to go. His graceful demeanor, his gentle laughter, his helpful way of working and playing all at the same time would need to become my demeanor, my laughter, my helpful way of working and playing.

As I looked up to the starry sky the crackling sound of the fire in the room next to me lulled me into a peaceful sleep. When I awoke he stood in front of me, a twinkle in his eye. "Come," he said, "let's go!"

I followed and did not ask where we were going. I knew. We were going to visit me, before Him. We were going to chat in my old friend's front room.

Reflections

Q: How does this story's picture of grace different from the first?

Q: What changes had the pauper made up to that point?

Q: What was about to change next?

Q: Was this a crises or critical moment of transformation? If so, in what way?

Q: If the Church's weaknesses and the struggles that attend is one of the methods by which God forms in us an awareness of holiness, how should that transform the way we respond to conflict in the church?

This writing with minor changes is also found in "Confessional Holiness: The Missing Piece of the Puzzle", chapter 3, "Toward a New Developmental Model" by Terry Mattson, pg #101-103

Reflections on "Swimming in Water: A Second Response to a King's Visit?

Q: In your journey in Christ have you ever noticed a moment (or series of moments) when your focus changed from inward transformation to simply receiving and giving love? ...If so, can you describe that moment? ...What changes took place in you and in your world as a result? ...If not, should you look for such moments?

Consider your own need to seek and be fully given over to the hallowing Presence of the Holy Spirit... and turn it all to prayer.

Next:

Fresh Water

5 FRESH WATER

... The Water Gate

INVOCATION:

HOLY SPIRIT OF MY FATHER. MY SOUL IS BROKEN.

MY THOUGHTS ARE TROUBLED AND EMPTY. THEY ARE FED
FROM THE WATERS OF MY LIFE; WHICH ARE LUKE WARM AND
DEAD. ONCE THEY FLOWED AND BUBBLED WITHIN AS LIVING
WATER. PLEASE, SPIRIT, COME AND STIR UP THE WATER.
TROUBLE ME AS YOU WILL. ONLY LET ME THIRST AND DRINK
AGAIN FROM THE LIVING STREAM OF YOUR SON, JESUS.
AMEN.

PSALM OF THE WEEK: PSALM 42

COMMANDMENT OF THE WEEK: "OBSERVE THE SABBATH DAY BY
KEEPING IT HOLY, AS THE LORD YOUR GOD HAS COMMANDED
YOU. SIX DAYS YOU SHALL LABOR AND DO ALL YOUR WORK, BUT
THE SEVENTH DAY IS A SABBATH TO THE LORD YOUR GOD."
DEUTERONOMY 5:11

DAILY SCRIPTURES:

MONDAY—JOHN 1: 19-36 & 3:5 & 19: 28-30

TUESDAY—JOHN 5: 1-15

WEDNESDAY—JOHN 2: 1-11

THURSDAY—JOHN 7: 37-39, PHILIPPIANS 2: 14-17

FRIDAY—REVELATION 3: 14-21

SATURDAY—JOHN 3: 1-21

SUNDAY—JOHN 1: 1-18 & 16: 5-16 & 9: 1-41

FROM
HEBREWS 12: 22,23A

BUT YOU HAVE DRAWN NEAR TO MOUNT ZION, THE CITY OF THE LIVING GOD, HEAVENLY JERUSALEM, TO COUNTLESS ANGELS IN A FESTIVAL GATHERING, TO THE ASSEMBLY OF GOD'S FIRSTBORN CHILDREN WHO ARE REGISTERED IN HEAVEN, TO GOD THE JUDGE OF ALL, TO THE SPIRITS OF THE RIGHTEOUS WHO HAVE BEEN MADE PERFECT…

Week-5: MONDAY—JOHN 1: 19-36 & 3:5 & 19: 28-30

STORY 18—WATER'S FASCINATION

Introduction: In Jewish custom at the time of Jesus, the thirtieth birthday was critical. For after that day a Jewish Rabbi was considered old enough to teach others.

An Imaginative Biblical Story—as seen through Jesus eyes...

The Sea sparkled as droplets of the sun seemed to bounce off the gentle waves of Galilee. It was a bright, warm day, a gentle breeze making it comfortable as well. Jesus smiled, to know one, for he was alone and walking north toward Capernaum and eventually Bethesda, to the home of Salome, his aunt, with details from Mary regarding the upcoming wedding at Cana for Salome's youngest daughter. Mary was to serve as hostess for what would be a three to five-day event for all the people of Cana and guests from Nazareth and Bethesda—home to Jesus cousins John and James.

Looking up to his left toward Mt. Eremos Jesus smile broadened as memories of shepherding his uncle's sheep up in these hills flooded his mind. 'It was right over that cleft, just beyond the place of three hills that form a kind of amphitheater with a flat rock at center'—his thoughts now running away—'that I first seriously entertained what is now a crisis in my own sense of my calling'. His rabbi's voice echoed within like the sounds of his uncle's sheep bleating against the cavern walls he had found for them near a cool

and running stream. 'What a wonderful pain sheep are!'
Jesus was thinking of how he would gather rocks and form a
kind of dam to still the water as David of old must have done,
for sheep, as his uncle often impressed upon him, '"will only
drink from still waters."' Jesus laughed at the thought,
realizing that his uncles voice had interrupted that of his
Rabbi.

Jesus brief laughter turned back toward serious thought
hearing once again his Rabbi clearly, '"Jeshua, I tell you,
you cannot offer yourself up to the Baptist in baptism. I
understand your heart and love for the Essene's mission.
I myself agree with the need for all Israel to repent as we
require of the pagans. But you..."' Jesus was interrupted for
just a moment by a dove fluttering and flying away from a
bush, hidden from view by the foliage. '"But you are thirty
and now of age to teach others—even as a S'mikhah; One
having authority to make new interpretations given your
heart and understanding of YHWH's Story, if only..."' Jesus
thoughts finished what his Rabbi would not. '...if only he had
finished his Talmud studies formally and been recognized as
a S'mikhah in Jerusalem.' Jesus smile returned as he was
enveloped with memories of his villages good Rabbi, also a
man in whom the ability, though not the recognition, to
understand and draw meaning from scripture was
extraordinary.

Seeing a shaded place for rest Jesus stopped along Galilee
and pulled out his knap sack filled with the dates, cheeses,
grapes and bread that Mary had prepared. 'This good man,'
Jesus thoughts returning to his beloved teacher, 'had—when
Jesus was 15 years of age' and following graduation from
Torah at ten and the Mishnah (Oral Torah interpretations) at
thirteen—Rabbi Ben Jacob had 'urged Mary and Joseph to
allow Jesus to study the Talmud.' Only the very brightest
students are invited to begin training for a career as Rabbi.

Popping a date into his mouth Jesus mulled over his Rabi's
influence upon him. His mother, ever conscious of the
Angelic visit had wanted Joseph to allow this investment. But

Joseph, believing Jesus would benefit as much from a work ethic and the skills of a masonry and carpenter trade craft had said no. 'Well, partly no...' The taste of mama's bread now filled his senses mingling with the warm remembrances of late hour visits to his Rabbi for just such teachings—but only after his father's work and instructions were complete. A tinge of sorrow filled Jeshua as he thought of his loving papa— 'May his name be ever remembered and beloved'— his death not a decade old.

Jesus put down his food, laying it on a rock nearby and turned to face the Sea of Galilee to pray and listen, his thoughts now bearing down on the one question that had increasingly enveloped his life from the teachings of Rabbi Ben Jacob. 'Was he the very Son of Man in Daniels vision and who, according to some Rabbinic traditions would become the Presence of YHWH who seeks and saves the lost of Israel according to Ezekiel 34?'

His Rabbi's voice returned in thought '"Jeshua, I tell you, you cannot offer yourself up to the Baptist..."' Jesus remembered his own response. '"Good teacher"—His Rabbi had placed a hand over Jesus mouth at the offering, saying, "Ever remember, there is no one who is truly good, except our Heavenly Father—YHWH Himself!"' Jesus memory now vivid and moved by his Rabbi's humility had responded. ' "Yes, Master, but that is exactly why I must be baptized, can you not see. All of us, sons of Israel and the pagans are among the sheep who are lost. Should we not fulfill all righteousness and acknowledge with Isaiah that our own righteous acts are as filthy rags in comparison? And does not the water of the Baptist represent not only the cleansing of YHWH but also the fiery deep wherein all of God's enemies reside?"'

With that conversation and following his thirtieth birthday Jesus had set out for his aunt's house to convey his mother's message about the coming wedding. But he had also confided in his mother that he would not be coming back—not soon anyway—until he had found John, Son of

Thunder and John the Baptist, his cousins. He remembered his mama's dismayed look until he had added. "'Woman, do you not know I must be about my Father's work?'" And with that Mary had relented, except to say. "'Yes, but you must also be about your mamas work and that means you will be home within three months for the wedding at Cana.'" With that memory Jesus smile returned to full bloom, for he had responded as only a good son, could. "'Yes, mama.'"

MY THOUGHTS 20—WATER'S FASCINATION

The shower ritual has become the delight of the modern world. Every day our life is renewed under the pulsating power of hot water pouring over our bodies. This pleasure, once reserved only for kings, now marks the ordinary beginning of each new day for millions.

Under the warmth of water's embrace we turn into music stars, our vibrato filling the steamy room with magical places of the mind. The promise of living water requires only the turning of the knob. Tired muscles relax and tensions are released in the message of her liberal tingles. Even the dark thoughts and shadows of the mind find a respite within her cleansing touch.

No one among the ancients could have understood, much less imagined, the modern's fascination with running water. For them water represented want and fear. Water was life, but it took a lot of living to ensure the supply. Water was scarce. Water was work. Usually it was dead (still) and accessed by means of deep wells. When water was living (flowing) danger was present. The danger of a sudden flood pouring in from the mountains destroying everyone and everything in its wake. Or the deep of the ocean, the place of demons, ghosts, behemoths and hell. The gods (at least the scary ones) were at home in the deep.

Even so living water, fresh as a mountain stream, was the promise of God to His people. A stream that would one day be poured out on all people. This promise, easy for moderns to appreciate, held out a promise that, for the ancients, only the imagination could grasp. It was a promise reserved for kings. Perhaps that is part of the reason that the Water Gate in Jerusalem was only used occasionally and by the priests of God, during the festival times.

As you walk through this gate draw from both the fears and needs of the ancients and your own real understanding of what it is to drink and bathe in 'living' water.

Let us hear anew the Eastern Church's fascination with the meaning inside Jesus Baptism but through the eyes of the Western Church in Pope Benedict XVI. Speaking of the Church, the Pope says:

> *"She sees Jesus' remark to John that 'it is fitting for us to fulfill all righteousness' (Mt 3:15) as the anticipation of his prayer to the Father in Gethsemane: "My Father...not as I will, but as thou wilt" (Mt 26:39).*
> *...The icon of Jesus' Baptism depicts the water as a liquid tomb having the form of a dark cavern, which is in turn the iconographic sign of Hades, the underworld, or hell. Jesus' descent into this watery tomb, into this inferno that envelops him from every side, is thus an anticipation of his act of descending into the underworld: "When he went down into the waters, he bound the strong man" (cf. Lk 11: 22)...as repetition of the whole of history, which both recapitulates the past and anticipates the future. His entering into the sin of others is a descent into the "inferno." ...he goes down in the role of one whose*

suffering—with—others is a transforming suffering that turns the underworld around, knocking down and flinging open the gates of the abyss. His Baptism is a descent into the house of the evil one, combat with the "strong man" (cf. Lk 11:22) *who holds men captive (and the truth is that we are all very much captive to powers that autonomously manipulate us!)".*
From "Jesus of Nazareth", by Pope Benedict XVI, page #19,20".

Reflections on "Water's Fascination"

Q: What is your own relationship with water? ...Fascinated or dread or both?

Q: When you shower are your thoughts usually dark or happy? ...how about when you're done?

Experiment: When you shower this week, consider praying; With prayers of confession, praise, petition and intercession.

Q: How might this simple change affect your start or end of the day?

Reflect and turn it all to prayer.

Week-5: TUESDAY—JOHN 5: 1-15

STORY 19—WATER'S HEALING POWER

Introduction: According to Jewish tradition at the time of Jesus, the waters in the pool of Bethesda near Solomon's Porch in the Holy Temple were able to heal, but only when stirred by an angel and then for only the first person to jump in—after the waters were stirred.

An Imaginative Biblical Story—from within the Holy Temple near Solomon's Porch...

As best he could, Jacob slowly gathered up the wine skin and pieces of bread, dates and curds that he had collected from those who took pity on him. Extending his tired and crooked arm was hard enough, but it was always his mangled and deformed hand which had the most difficulty.

He simply could not close his fingers enough to grasp the smallest pieces of bread or fruit. Jacob always looked helpless at day's end. His legs were stretched out under him, resting flat against the marble flooring and side ways to his crippled body.

When at last he finished gathering his gifts of mercy, dropped by worshipers coming into and out of Jerusalem's Holy Temple, he would begin the painful and difficult process of lifting himself so that, with the help of his walking stick, he might make the two-hour journey home.

What took him two hours would have taken any of the worshipers who were gathered near a few minutes to walk from the Temple Mount to his home just inside David's city.

Today was Sabbath and so any help he might have received, by way of a lift on a cart could not be expected. It would have been considered by the Temple authorities as work. Jacob understood. Fortunately, there was no rule, as yet, prohibiting the use of walking sticks. That was some small comfort. So long as Jacob carried nothing that could be seen he could walk through the Dung Gate and home without violating Sabbath protocols.

As Jacob's arm strained awkwardly his hand finally fell on the nuts that had been contributed. As he focused his attention, trying to command his hand to close sufficiently, the perfectly formed hand of another touched his, gently. Jacob looked up into the soft and tender smile of a man, younger than himself by decades. "Friend," the stranger spoke, "may I help?" Thinking he would receive something from him, Jacob stared back, though cautiously. His left hand began searching for his walking cane, just in case.

The stranger continued, "Your friends tell me that you have been coming to this pool of healing for some years now." Now Jacob was curious. 'Who,' he wondered, 'had been gossiping to this northerner,' for he could see that this stranger was a Galilean. Still, he saw no reason to deny the obvious. "Yes, for thirty-eight years, longer than you are old, I would guess."

The stranger released Jacob's hand and quickly gathered the rest of his bread and fruit, carefully enclosing it in his gathering cloth. "You guess right, my friend." Jacob wondered at the familial sound in the stranger's voice and the natural laugh that followed. He stopped reaching for the walking stick and relaxed again on the comfort of his mangled legs.

The stranger continued, "Yes, you guessed right. I have not experienced so much as you. Still, I was wondering, do you truly wish to be healed?"

Anger rose quickly with in Jacob's chest. What kind of question was that to ask a poor beggar and from a younger man than he? Had he not been coming to this very pool all these years, hoping that when a gust of wind or angels, as tradition taught, stirred the waters he might be the first into the pool and thus receive the healing that Yahweh promised.

Every son and daughter in Israel believed that when the angel of the LORD stirred the waters of the pool of Bethesda the first person into the water would be healed and perhaps receive the longing of his heart.

"Sir," Jacob replied, deciding to assume that his questioner's intent was honest, "I have no one to help me into the pool when the water is stirred. While I am trying to get in, someone else goes down ahead of me."

Jacob lowered his eyes, expecting that the next thing from this Galileans mouth would be a sharp word of condemnation or worse, contempt. Experience had taught him to feel numb towards the worst men could say about him, for within him were already enough feelings of disgust and darkness formed by years of just such judgment. These feelings had also hardened from the years of knowing himself to be a sinner whose appearance was the very judgment of God.

Silence followed. Finally, the stranger knelt down beside Jacob and took his two mangled hands into his own. He looked deeply into his eyes. Jacob felt an acceptance which both surprised and disarmed him. Suddenly a gust of wind with some strength burst into the temple leaving a whirring sound as it made its way around the colonnades. The waters of the pool moved and the gathered cripple, blind, deaf, mute and simply depressed moved quickly, trying to outpace each other in an effort to reach the water's edge. Only Jacob sat still, gazing into the eyes of one in whom no judgment shown, only love. It seemed as though everyone and everything around him was at a distance. All he could see was the eyes of the stranger. All he could hear was the command, "Get up! Pick up your matt and walk!"

Immediately a warm sensation poured through Jacob and with the help of this man younger than himself, he stood. As he was lifted up he felt his arm stretch out, fully. His hands, in the hands of this one, grasped onto the stranger and with strength. His fingers closed. His legs became strong and straight. He looked and felt like every other son of Adam. Excitedly, he obeyed the stranger, picking up his matt, he hurried out into the court of the gentiles and toward home. He could not wait to tell his friends and family of this special day's gift.

As Jacob moved across the court of the Gentiles and entered into the covered area opposite the Holy Place, from which he would find the Dung Gate he heard the familiar sound of a staff against the marble stone moving in his direction. He knew exactly whose staff it was for he had heard its sound often. It was the sound of authority. With a loud voice the administrator of the Temple grounds, Zerah, spoke out. "Old man!" for he knew him by sight, though not by name. He had seen him often over the years, a pathetic picture of a man. A beggar. One of those to be tolerated as the law demanded. Zerah had even given him a coin or two over the years. For the first time in his life, Jacob knew he could ignore Zerah and even outrun him, if he wished. He did not wish to. Jacob stopped, frozen by the sound of judgment that ringed throughout the colonnade. It was a sound that still echoed in the frozen chambers of his soul. Zerah continued. "What do you mean by desecrating this Holy place, by working on the Sabbath!?"

Jacob turned toward the old priest, afraid and inattentive of the priest's failure to acknowledge the obvious change in his appearance. "It is the Sabbath. The law forbids you to carry your matt." Jacob knew the law, for one does not live near the Temple, visiting her sanctuary daily, without knowing. Defensively and without fore thought he replied. "The man who made me well said to me, 'Pick up your matt and walk.'"

Upon hearing this, the priest's attention turned from Jacob and a darker mood, something beyond authority appeared in his eyes. "Who is this fellow who told you to pick it up and walk? the old priest demanded. Looking around Jacob could not see the stranger who had healed him. "I don't know. I did not ask him his name. I was so relieved at his gift that I did not think to ask." With that explanation the formerly lame man laid down his matt near a colonnade and promised that he would come back tomorrow and remove it.

In disgust, seeing that Jacob was no threat and of little use Zerah turned to leave. "See to it!" And with those words he walked away from Jacob.

Slowly and thoughtfully Jacob also turned again toward the Dung Gate and home. The joy of his healing was now overshadowed by the feelings of disgust and judgment he had grown up with. To himself he thought, 'I am an outcast and will always be one.' The closer he got to the gate leading to David's city the deeper was the fear that owned him. 'What if Zerah were to cast him out of the temple and so declare him pagan, with no faith in Israel?' Such an outcome would surely be worse than being crippled, Jacob reflected.

As he near the Dung Gate he once again heard the voice of the stranger call to him, "Jacob." Jacob stopped and again looked into the eyes of this one who still seemed to reach out to him. "Jacob," he continued. "See, Yahweh has stirred the waters for you." Jacob was amazed at the ease with which the unpronounceable name of YHWH rolled from his tongue. "You are well," the stranger continued. "Only let the Spirit of Yahweh stir your heart too. Let him heal your wounded soul. With the LORD you are accepted. Trust Him or something worse may yet happen to you."

Jacob heard the words and yet didn't. A fog of fear still surrounded him. Finally, he found his tongue and thanked the stranger and began to move away again, still lost in his troubled thoughts over his encounter with the chief administrator of Yahweh's Temple. Just inside the gate he remembered and turned back and in a loud voice called out. "What did you say your name was, sir?" Jacob noticed a subtle sadness come over the strangers face as he answered. "Jeshua, of Nazareth," was all he said. "Thank you, Jeshua." Jacob responded. "Thank you, again."

As Jacob turned once again toward home he thought to himself. 'Tomorrow, I will go to Zerah and let him know the name of this man. After all, why should I be cast out? Why should I be made to suffer for the ill-considered advice of this Galilean?'

Reflections on "Water's Healing Power"

This encounter with Jesus, as written by John in the memory of the Church is one of the saddest of all Jesus miracles. This cripple betrays Jesus.

Q: Why? …Of what was he really afraid? …What caused this fear?

Q: Of what was this cripple not healed? …In what way did he remain wounded or crippled?

Q: Why do you suppose Jesus came back to warn him?

Q: Of what do you need to be healed? Do you really want healing?

Consider your own broken spaces and turn it all to prayer.

Week-5: WEDNESDAY—JOHN 2: 1-11

MY THOUGHTS 21—AT WATER'S EDGE

On: The Jesus Attraction

Millennials have been called 'Therapeutic Deists'—it's all good if it works, if it feels good. It's an apt description. **This is a generation committed to inclusion, acceptance and healing.** Everyone's in—no one left out! All Stories are equal in significance, if not in what they reveal, for they are 'our' communal world view. Who is to question that? Any action or voice that disturbs inclusion or acceptance is inherently evil and should not be at our table. So much for the first amendment of the American Constitution.

What this generation knows of Jesus they like, for isn't he the dude that kept talking about love and breaking down barriers that keep us apart? He is! Jesus fits the therapeutic-—it's all good—model.

It's the Church that is problematic for it argues that the Jesus Story is God's ultimate story and inherently claims stuff about Jesus which calls into question every world-view, every story.

Jesus own mission as experienced in the memory of the Church is defined by two supporting themes. They are:

1) **Jesus is human and connected with us, and;**
2) **Jesus breaks down every wall of division, leaving no one beyond the reach of the Father's love and mercy.**

Indeed, the Church has a vivid memory of Jesus being angry with the Jewish Community (God's People) precisely because they kept trying to keep people out. So far, so good.

The problem in our time starts when we, who are Jesus followers, press the exclusive claims of the Jesus Story, like:

> ➢ Jesus is God's Story—God's way of receiving all humanity, or;
> ➢ Jesus violent death expresses God's passionate, deliberate and wresting choice of each/all of us because—at great cost—this Communal God chose to enter into our violence (lust, greed, pride, judgments, sensual misuse of each other) in order to redeem us, or;
> ➢ God requires us to emerge from our violence (lust, greed, pride, judgments, sensual misuse of each other) if we are to know intimately the Trinity of God, or;
> ➢ While God is active within each/all personal and communal stories longing to find common ground, it is God's Story which establishes the possibility of and fullness of (loving/holy) relation—God's Story alone.

Stated differently, our communal and personal sin is a wall that separates us from God. Arrogance, pride, unwillingness to commit to covenantal relationships, greed, materialism, lack of concern with social and personal justice, and abusive actions create in themselves distance from one another and from a Communal God who is both offended by and will not co-participate in creating these broken spaces.

The extraordinary thing about the Jesus Story is that God, in Jesus life, teachings, passion, death and resurrection has chosen to enter deeply into these broken spaces in order to find communal ground and give us a larger world view and heart in which to enjoy God's purposeful Creation—a re-creation of Love in and among us. God has chosen us over the Divine's passionate hatred of much that makes up our human stories!

Oswald Chambers—a brilliant pastoral theologian of the 1800's—picks up on this same tension inside the early Jewish followers of Jesus. They saw themselves as saved by their cultural God-Story and loved Jesus take on all things Jewish. Jesus was the life of the party, evidenced in John's memory with the story of his turning water into wine at a multi-day wedding celebration. Jesus teachings down by the lake where fisherman were cleaning their nets and hundreds of villagers gathered in was captivating—his stories coming from the agricultural and fishing images they were used to. None of the Rabbis could make God seem so close. It was all so therapeutic, until… Peter allowed Jesus to fish with him. Suddenly the Holy of God and the Love of God collided and the infatuation with God became real and personal. Peter asked Jesus to *"Go away from me, Lord; I am a sinful man!"* (Luke 5:8).

And what did Jesus do? Give him the four spiritual laws and ask him if his troubled awareness of sin was real? No, he simply said *"Don't be afraid; from now on you will fish for people"* (Luke 5:10b).

Reflecting on the Jesus invitation to follow, Oswald Chambers says that ***"the call of God is never articulate, it is always implicit"***. Describing what captured the disciples interest he writes:

> *The dominating sentiment which attracted the early disciples to Jesus was not a sense of conviction of sin; they had no violent sin to turn from, and consequently no conscious need of salvation. They were not sinners in the ordinary accepted sense of the term, but honest, sincere men, and they were attracted to Jesus by something more… The spell of Jesus was on them, and when He said, "Follow Me," they followed at once…*
> *There was in the disciples the 'one fact more' which put them in one kingdom and Jesus Christ in another*

kingdom. Our Lord was never impatient. He simply planted seed thoughts in their minds and surrounded them with the atmosphere of His own life. He did not attempt to convince them, but left mistakes to correct themselves, because He knew that eventually the truth would bear fruit in their lives. How differently we would have acted! We get impatient and take men by the scruff of the neck and say: "You must believe this and that." You cannot make a man see moral truth by persuading his intellect. "When He, the Spirit of truth, is come, He shall guide you into all the truth."
From "The Complete Works of Oswald Chambers", by Oswald Chambers, page #676

Today's generation stands with the disciples by the water's edge. They do not see themselves as sinners and within the limited world view of 'therapeutic Deism' are correct. The Church, like Jesus, should find common ground and plant seeds and watch the Holy Spirit water it.

Reflections on "At Water's Edge"

"The dominating sentiment which attracted the early disciples to Jesus was not a sense of conviction of sin; they had no violent sin to turn from, and consequently no conscious need of salvation."
From "The Complete Works of Oswald Chambers", by Oswald Chambers, page #676

Q: What is the primary motive of most people who 'first' become Christian today? ...Are we like or unlike Chamber's description of early Christians? ...How so?

Q: What role does a 'deep sense of sin' play in most people's conversions now? ...Did you have a 'deep sense of your own sin' when you came to Christ? ...When did you begin to really feel sorrow over sin? ...Have you?

> *"The call of God is never articulate; it is always implicit."*
> *From "The Complete Works of Oswald Chambers", by Oswald Chambers, page #676*

Q: What does this statement mean? ...Has God's awakening in you been 'articulate' (In your face—dramatic—clear) or 'implicit' (subtle, implied, intuited)? ...Is that a good thing?

Q: Are you able to 'articulate' even now why you follow?

Consider your own life as one who 'follows' in the footsteps of Jesus and turn it to prayer.

Week-5: THURSDAY—John 7: 37-39, Philippians 2: 14-17

The Water Gate

Shaar Hamayim - Water Gate, and its adjacent chambers

During the festival of Sukkot, the Kohanim drew water from the Shiloach Brook, and brought it through this gateway. The water gate was open only during the festival.

Mikvah - The Ritual Bath
Above the water gate was a mikvah. It was used only once a year, by the High Priest on Yom Kippur.

On that Holy Day, the High Priest immersed himself five times in a mikvah. The first immersion was done here. This mikvah above the water gate, may also have contributed to the Gate's name.

The water gate took its name as well from the narrow stream of water that flowed from beneath the foundations of the Heichal, across the courtyard, and out through the Water Gate.

STORY 20—LIVING WATER

An Imaginative Early Church Story taken from traditions surrounding Mary & the texts for this day...

Mary put down the scroll, tears poured gently down her face. She prayed, "Oh my Son, Emmanuel and Papa, my beloved creator and LORD... Please comfort your servant Paul. May the offering of his life truly be a wine poured out to all the broken of Your world."

One more time Mary strained to read the words of Paul, a letter addressed to *"All the saints in Christ Jesus at Philippi, together with the overseers and deacons"* (Philippians 1:1). The moist of her eyes cleared, allowing her to focus again upon these words of life. *"Do everything without complaining or arguing, so that you may become blameless and pure, children of God"* (Philippians 2: 14,15a). Mary smiled to herself. 'He writes as he talks, sentences without end.' A chuckle forced itself into a laugh until she again came upon the words that had brought a tear. *"But even if I am being poured out like a drink offering..."* (Philippians 2: 17)

Mary lay the scroll down and lay back against the wall of her cozy little home in Ephesus. John, the beloved of Jesus would be home soon and she would then be busy preparing the evening meal. But for now she would listen for Papa's voice or that of her son and the love they shared, felt in Mary as The Spirit.

Her thoughts turned again to Paul's letter, that had been copied by Epaphroditus and delivered to the churches in Ephesus and Asia Minor, to John the Beloved and to Mary. 'Only Paul...' Mary thought to herself, 'Only Paul could take a pagan rite, that of pouring wine before a meal in thanksgiving to the gods, and turn into a sign of Christ.' Although she had never liked Paul much, by way of personal presence, as she enjoyed John, still she loved him for his love of her son. She respected his gift of finding her son present in all of life. She continued reading aloud, *"...poured out like a drink offering on the sacrifice and service coming from your faith"* (Philippians 2: 17b). 'Well written, Paul!'

With that her thoughts turned to the first of Jesus' miracles, the one that she had committed her son to perform. She had often regretted how she had misused Jesus' gift for her own personal needs. 'Not hers,' her mind quietly defended, 'but her sister's.' She was the manager of her sister's wedding and it was the third day. Theirs was a poor family and they had run out of wine. It would be an embarrassment that her sister and brother-in-law would never live beyond.

She had gone to her son and implored him to assist. She remembered his response. '*"Dear woman, why do you involve me? ...My time has not yet come"'* (John 2: 4). Mary remembered her response as well. '"Your time has not come? Did you not confide in me that you just returned from the Baptist's affirmation and the forty days of testing by Lucifer? And now you are home with what? Ten students, whom I have fed and whose clothes I have washed? If not now, when?"' A smile, admittedly proud, formed as she relived the moment. With that she had turned to the steward and instructed him to '*"do whatever he tells you"'* (John 2: 5b).

Mary's feelings were now racing. 'That was a drink offering poured out on the whole village!' She smiled sensing even now something of the arrogance of her demand of Jeshua. Still, a feeling of deep love and presence surrounded her. '"Mary... Mary, you have done well. Even then your love showed itself as a sweet tasting wine, poured out."' Mary turned her intuited thoughts over in her mind. She knew that Voice. It was Papa's and so she received His comfort and smiled freely. But it was smile short lived for an earlier memory now rushed in as her stomach tightened.

It was following the last Passover Jesus had celebrated in Jerusalem...as a spear buried deep within her memory forced it's way anew into her heart. She was standing before her son, John's strong arms holding her steady, as her shaken body took in Jesus last breath. She could still hear the voice, muffled by her pain sounding as if it were a Jerusalem block away—and interrupted momentarily as she thought of the city's fall not two years earlier—her mind returned to Golgotha and the Centurion's voice, '"Here, take this spear and finish him! The coward died before his time so do not bother with his legs. It appears there is no breath left in him! Just make sure the criminal is dead"' ...'dead,' Mary's thoughts froze as her mind took in the water and blood flowing from his side... '"

Mary did not notice that Paul's letter, his parchment scroll now lay in her lap—Just as Jesus did so long ago as the heavens opened wide with thunderous waters pouring over her son's dead body now lowered and laid out in her arms— Mary now resting against the wooden frames upon which the cross-beam had been raised. 'Poured out' her thoughts now mingled in sadness and hope. '...Does not Paul tells us that we are to be poured out into the whole world? ...offering freely the water and blood which flows even now from my son's side in waters of Baptism and the wine of Holy Communion?'

Mary spent a few more moments feeling and thinking, listening to her Papa in the Heavens and to His Spirit. Too seldom in all these years had she felt her son's voice in this communion. How she longed to see him again!

As Mary stood and with care put away the scroll her memories recalled one more scene from the Holy City—The last day of the Feast of Tabernacles earlier in that same Jewish cycle.

On the last day of the festival and standing above her and maybe a thousand others just outside the Water Gate, the High Priest had lifted high the golden and now empty pitcher—his face clearly reflecting the joy of this moment— commemorating the waters that gushed out from within the rocks of Sinai when Israel was in the desert. Mary had lost track of her son in the crowd and did not really care, so taken she was with the power of the processional as they all followed the High Priest down the winding cobble streets to the Pool of Shalom—where the waters of Mt. Olivet poured into the city by Hezekiah's underground water duct. Once there the High Priest would fill the jar and lead the crowd back up to the Water Gate as the younger women danced and all sang the songs of Israel.

'Such a moment!' Mary remembered...taking her own simple and poor jar, she began to fill John's cup and hers...knowing he would soon walk through the door. Then Mary froze abruptly as, once again, the memory of that moment in the festival poured over her anew. Just as the High Priest lifted the pitcher prior to pouring the waters of Shalom over the porch of the Water Gate—the sun's rays glistening off it's polished gold—a voice she knew well cried out from near the very back of this vast sea of people. Mary's son exclaimed, ' *"Let anyone who is thirsty come to me and drink. Whoever believes in me, as Scripture has said, rivers of living water will flow from within them"'* (John 7: 37b). Mary was suddenly brought back to the present and startled by the sound of her own simple and poor jar breaking over her hard and compacted dirt floor. But she had not forgotten—not then nor now—the look on the High Priest's face at her son's cry. It was at that moment so long ago that Simeon's prophecy had flooded her mind with anxiety for her son. '"And a sword will pierce your own soul too"' (Luke 2: 35b).

This story is a creative compilation inspired by two writings: My own in an e-published book "The Advent of God Through Mary—A Narrative & Devotional Journey through Advent", chapter 5, Sunday and "Parable of Joy" by Michael Card, pages #96-98.

Reflections on "Living Water"

The water motif runs throughout John's gospel. It is present in the Baptist, at the wedding of Cana, the woman at Jacob's well, the story of Nicodemus meeting with Jesus, the paralytic at the pool of Bethesda, Jesus walking on water, the washing of the disciples, the teachings on the Spirit, at the crucifixion, and of course, the fishing stories.

This story is near the heart of John's gospel. In Jewish writings the most important information is to be found in the center. On the last day of the Festival of Tabernacles Jesus identified himself as the Messiah... as the *"streams of living water"*—the new Moses! (John 7:38b)

The Church and her theologians have wondered of 'whom' this promise refers. Do the streams flow from within the believer (the Church) or from the Messiah (the Lord of the

Church)? Surely, whatever the immediate meaning attributed by John, the salvific meaning is BOTH! Jesus is the 'river of life' in the New Jerusalem and from Jesus and the Father the Holy Spirit is given, a living stream within each of us.

Q: Does the Jesus stream flow from within you?

Q: Do you know anyone in whom the Holy Spirit is evident? ...How so?

Action Item: Send that person a test or tweet or Facebook message, a card, an email or verbally communicate your appreciation of their life and story.

Week-5: FRIDAY—Revelation 3: 14-21

MY THOUGHTS 22—MAKING JESUS REAL IN US

There are many today who are sincere, but they are not real; they are not hypocrites, but perfectly honest and earnest and desirous of fulfilling what Jesus wants of them, but they really cannot do it, the reason being that they have not received the Holy Spirit who will make them real...

From "The Complete Works of Oswald Chambers", "The Making of a Disciple" by Oswald Chambers, page #677

On: Facing the impossible

All of my ministry I have wondered at the vast number of believers in our Lord, who are committed to Christ and his Church but who do not yet show sensitivity to the Person of the Holy Spirit. In the 'sacrament of communion' I have served many whom I believe are authentic followers but not yet 'born of God', who are Christian in their soul (identity) but do not reveal a mystical—spiritual (spirit) knowing of God in Jesus. These are disciples whose spiritual formation seems to be exclusively within the rhythms of the Church and in the Sacraments.

Oswald Chambers is the first evangelical I have read from within the heart of my own tradition who took seriously these followers. When he says the are 'not real' he is referring not to 'the status of their heart or identity' but to their inability to 'enter into' the life of Jesus in any transformational way. They are not counterfeit, but sincere. Still they hold Christ as 'a faith' rather than in a personal and communal sense.

Especially I have noticed this among some First Nations Communities where the identity as Christian is held in communion with the elder—King or tribe; deeply held so that this faith is alive within the community and in each individual of the village. In Samoa at 6 pm each evening an hour of prayer is observed and the head of each family leads it. When the village bell or siren sounds if a child is not home and ready she/he must sit down and meditate where they are, waiting for a final bell/siren to announce family worship is done. Only God knows what happens to the child who then makes their way home after failing to participate within the family.

Oswald goes on to describe this disciple as follows:

> The bedrock in Jesus Christ's Kingdom is not sincerity, not deciding for Christ, not a determination to serve Him, but a complete and entire recognition that we cannot begin to do it; then, says Jesus, "Blessed are you." Jesus Christ can do wonderful things for the man who enters into His Kingdom through the moral frontier of need.
>
> Decisions for Christ fail not because men are not in earnest, but because the bedrock of Christianity is ignored. The bedrock of Christianity does not lie in vowing or in strength of will; to begin with it is not ethical at all, but simply the recognition of the fact that I have not the power within me to do what my spirit longs to do. "Come unto Me," said Jesus, not "Decide for Me." When I realize my inability to be what the New Testament tells me I should be, I have to come to Jesus "just as I am." I realize that I am an abject pauper, morally and spiritually; if ever I am going to

*be what Jesus wants me to be, He must come in and
do it…*

*The first thing a man needs is to be born into the
Kingdom of God by receiving the Holy Spirit, and then
slowly and surely be turned into a disciple. The
entrance into the Kingdom of God is always through
the moral frontier of need. At any turn of the road the
touch may come...*

From "The Complete Works of Oswald Chambers", "The Making
of a Disciple" by Oswald Chambers, page #677

Reflections on "Making Jesus Real in Us"

*"The modern phrase we hear so often, 'Decide for
Christ,' is most misleading, because it puts the
emphasis on the wrong thing, and is apt to present
Jesus Christ in a false way as Someone in need of
our allegiance. A decision cannot hold forever,
because a man is the same after making it as before,
and there will be a reaction sooner or later. Whenever
a man fails in personal experience it is because he
has never received anything. There is always a
positive difference in a man when he has received
something—new powers begin to manifest
themselves..."*

From "The Complete Works of Oswald Chambers", "The Making
of a Disciple" by Oswald Chambers, page #677

Q: What do you think about this emphasis upon 'the Holy
Spirit' and God needing to add something (someone, really)
in us if we are to make real our 'faith' in Jesus?

Q: Are you born of God?

At different times in my life, such as this writing, I have found myself struggling once again with sin within my spirit (heart—affections), soul (identity), or body and come running once again to my Father for renewal of 'being real' in the Presence of God's Spirit.

Q: Can you relate with Terry's confession?

Turn it all to Prayer and confession.

Week-5: SATURDAY—John 3: 1-21

Story 21—Awakening!

The following imaginary story takes place immediately after the conversation between Nicodemus and Jesus as recorded in John 3.

An Imaginative Biblical Story based upon Nicodemus encounter with Jesus as seen through his own eyes…

As he descended the hill a gust of strong wind swept around Him. His heart echoed the chill of it's cold breath.

Moments earlier, as he sat in the presence of the Nazarene, his heart had felt strangely warm, drawn as he was to Jeshua's words. He thought to himself, 'How did this rabbi know the cry of my own heart?' "Nicodemus," Jesus had said, placing his hand gently on his shoulder and looking deep in his eyes, "You must be born again, from above. Born of water and the wind of God." 'But baptism,' Nicodemus now continued his argument with Jesus inside his again chilly soul. 'Baptism is for sinners, not the righteous, for those outside of God's covenant with Israel.'

Suddenly the wind caught Nicodemus breath. The blast was fierce. He stopped, a little dizzy and leaned against a tree catching himself, silent, frozen in time. The words of Ezekiel, which he had committed to memory, came to Him. *"I will sprinkle clean water on you and you will be clean. I will give you a new heart and put a new spirit in you. I will put my Spirit in you and move you to follow my decrees and be careful to keep my laws"* (Ezekiel 36: 25-26). Nicodemus body seemed to shutter within him, as if forcing the still, breathless moment to end. Gasping and coughing, he took in a deep breath. The wind was not cold as before. It seemed to fill his whole being. Relaxing, he let his back slide down the tree to the ground.

His thought turned to the Baptist, John. He had led a delegation of Pharisees about three weeks earlier to witness John's ministry of baptism to the Jews. The words John had then spoken had stung. But now he felt as though Yahweh, God Himself were speaking them. There was no condemnation as they now echoed within.

"Nicodemus, my son, do not think you can say to yourself 'We have Abraham as our father. Produce fruit in keeping with repentance.'" The wind around him stirred again, its warmth seemed to cushion his cold and troubled spirit. Sitting, he leaned forward rocking back and forth. He felt his heart break within. Nicodemus, for the first time in his life, felt his sinfulness. How he longed to find a priest, to secure a lamb and offer it. Never before had he thought of himself as a sinner. Oh, yes, as one who occasionally sinned, as everyone does, but not as an unrighteous man, a sinner. Wasn't he better than the masses who waded into the water weeping over their evil ways? So he had thought.

"You brood of vipers!", John had declared. And he was. Now he understood. We all were. All of Nicodemus' righteousness; his clothes, his prayer shawl, his tassels, his pious teachings, now seemed like the filthy rags of the Baptist—John. Like the rags the prophet of old, Isaiah, spoke about. His envy and pride and his secret lust now gripped him. If only he could seek out the Baptist, not in the secret of the night, but in the clear of the day. What he needed was light.

Nicodemus began to groan. He rolled to the ground, falling against it, lying flat, face down. His hands reached for dirt which he lifted over his head and poured. Before God he cried the words of David. *"Wash me completely clean of my guilt; purify me from my sin! Because I know my wrongdoings, my sin is always right in front of me. I've sinned against you—you alone. I've committed evil in your sight"* (Psalm 51: 2-4a). After what seemed like hours he sighed and his breath escaped him. It reminded him of the sound given when one dies. Exhausted, he rolled over and onto his back, looking up into the heavens.

It was only then he remembered what else John had said. The words that had begun his private journey up this mount. Upon seeing Jesus, John had declared, "Behold, the lamb of God!" Nicodemus understood then that John was declaring Jesus as the One, but what had astonished him was Jesus next act. Moving out into the water and kneeling before John, Jesus was baptized, identifying himself with all these sinners.

That was what had troubled Nicodemus so badly. He had been listening for months to Jesus teachings when he could find the time and when Jesus was near. But this single act had made him question all the positive feelings that he had with regard to this one from Nazareth.

Now Nicodemus understood what Jesus had said. *"No one can see the kingdom of God unless he is born again. Born of water and of the Spirit"* (John 3: 8).

As Nicodemus stood, the gentle wind once again turned to a gust, this time warm and powerful, filling his robes and sifting through his dirty hair. Nicodemus breathed of its warmth deeply and smiled. Tomorrow, he would find the Baptist.

Reflections on "Awakening!"

"The conception of new birth in the New Testament is not a conception of something that springs out of us, but of something that enters into us. Just as our Lord

came into human history from without, so He must come into us from without. Our new birth is the birth of the life of the Son of God into our old human nature, and our human nature has to be transfigured by the indwelling life of the Son of God. Have I allowed my personal human life to become a 'Bethlehem' for the Son of God?"

From "The Complete Works of Oswald Chambers", "The Making of a Disciple" by Oswald Chambers, page #677

Q: Are you born of God? ...Are you living in an active relationship with God through God's indwelling Holy Spirit?

Consider your own journey. Write out your thoughts and feelings, or; Perhaps allow God to write in you...

Week-5: SUNDAY—JOHN 1: 1-18 & 16: 5-16 & 9: 1-41

STORY 22—BAPTISM

Introduction:

Water plays a dance with ancient tribal communities; desperately needed, especially living (running) water and yet the source of deepest fears. From within the mountainous runoff a flood could destroy whole villages or the crops of life that surround. In the waters of the sea all the mysteries; the gods, monsters—fate itself were thought to dwell.

All of the gospel accounts include reference to Jesus baptism by John. In this moment God and waters fear meet; an epic struggle within each of us and all of us together is the result. The following imaginary story is taken from Matthew three; the Baptism of Jesus

An Imaginative Biblical Story based upon Jesus Baptism as seen through Jesus eyes...

As he descended the hill above the Jordan river his eyes swept over the vast crowd who looked like sheep moving in step with its shepherd, this one covered in camel's hair with a leather belt around his waist, his body rugged with the strength of the desert, his skin dark brown under the heat of the sun and his beard like Moses of old. Each person—save those finely dressed, their prayer tassels flowing to the ground around them with their elegant robes ruffling in the air and looking as out of place as their hardened and distant faces evidenced—all the others; prostitutes, shop owners, tradesman, farmers, even a Roman soldier or two and the occasional tax collector all gently pushed and shoved into the waters of the Jordan to come into the presence of the Baptist and through him YHWH.

Having descended the hill, Jeshua suddenly found his cousins face and took his own first step into the water as the memory of his own Rabbi's warning that he, as knowledgeable as any authoritative scholar, should not go to the Baptist. "'Jeshua," Jesus remembered, "I tell you, you cannot offer yourself up to the Baptist...'" As he had just days before, Jesus remembered his own response. "'Good teacher"—His Rabbi had placed a hand over Jesus mouth at the offering, saying, "Ever remember, there is no one who is truly good, except our Heavenly Father—YHWH Himself!'"

How Jesus loved this good pastor and priest and learned from his humility and teachings that all in Israel are among the sheep who are lost, together with the pagans, and as Isaiah had said, *"Like sheep, we had all wandered away, each going its own way"* (Isaiah 53: 6).

The waters of the muddy Jordan now enveloped him to the waste as Jesus finally stood before the Baptist. The memory of his and John's three-day journey into the wilderness during the Feast of Tabernacles flooded over him. They were each fifteen and as they sat in a cave overlooking the Jordan with a small fire burning and enjoying a meal of roasted locusts, honey, dates and grapes together with the milk of goats, John had first raised the question which often burned inside Jeshua's breast. "'Tell me cousin," John had asked, "is it true what my mama and papa—may God ever honor Zechariah's service—say of you?" Jesus knew of what his cousin spoke, for his own mama and papa had on very few occasions spoken of the same and told him the nature of his birth and the mysteries surrounding. Still he had asked John, "And what do they say, cousin?" John affirmed, "That you are the one chosen of God, the Messiah who will renew Israel as David and Solomon of old."'

Jesus noticed that John was suddenly still, saying nothing as the Nazarene stood before him. 'Perhaps,' Jesus thought, 'he is remembering as I am of our last meeting.' "Jeshua, my cousin..." John finally spoke. *"I need to be baptized by you, yet you come to me?"* (Matthew 3: 14b).

Jeshua smiled at his cousin. 'He remembers.' "Allow it John. For it is necessary to fulfill all the promises of YHWH—all the righteousness envisioned by Isaiah's suffering servant." With that John relented and stepping back directed his cousin to kneel and embrace the muddy waters.

As Jesus knelt and the waters began to envelop his chest a fear suddenly seized him. 'Am I truly the One whom God, my Father, has chosen or am I?' His head suddenly went under the waters, his breath stopped and from a place deeper than sheol, the place of the dead, images filled the tender and impressionable mind of Jesus. Only in his dreams had he encountered them—each vivid and nightmarish—a mixture of snakes and demons, of brilliant light in the heavens imploding and in its wake a mushroom cloud of enormous power rising in the earth; the heavenly city of Jerusalem felt the quake as whole cities in the earth suddenly vanished now enveloped in the memory of 1/3rd of the heavenly creatures following the beauty of Lucifer of old from within the city of God, falling to earth as victors!

As Jeshua's body began to demand attention to his growing need of oxygen Jeshua felt an overwhelming doubt emerge within the dirt of the Jordan washing over him. "Am I truly the One?"

And then it was over. Jeshua's head was lifted from the water and the cloud of heaviness that had surrounded seemed to vanish in the bright Judean sun. Suddenly, on Jeshua's shoulder he felt an impression and the flutter of wings—looking to his right, he noticed a perfectly formed and beautiful white dove. As his cousin helped him stand and gather himself, Jesus felt the strong arms of John steady him, a hand on each shoulder and heard from his lips and within his own spirit the echo of these words. "I see heaven opened. I hear your voice, Father." And looking straight into Jesus eyes, he continued. *"This is my Son whom I dearly love; I find happiness in him"* (Matthew 3: 17).

Reflections on "Baptism"

Terry emphasizes in his interpretation of the God/man Jesus the very human qualities of identity, hope and doubt that is common to us all.

Q Have you ever thought of Jesus struggling within his own identity? …How does that strike you?

Q: Does the power and import of the Baptismal waters of the Jordan change or increase if Jesus experiences human doubt? …How so?

> *"On the basis of the Redemption God expects us to erect characters' worthy of the sons of God. He does not expect us to carry on "evangelical capers," but to manifest the life of the Son of God in our mortal flesh.*
> *From "The Complete Works of Oswald Chambers", by Oswald Chambers, page #679"*

Q: Why do you suppose God uses water—which historically incorporates our deepest human fears—as a primary means of communicating grace in Baptism?

Q: If that is true, how will this affect the way you value or remember your own Baptism?

Reflect and turn it all to prayer.

Next:

Life in the City

6 LIFE IN THE CITY

... The Fish Gate

INVOCATION:

FATHER OF MY HOME, FATHER OF MY NEIGHBORS, FATHER OF OUR CITY, FATHER OF OUR NATION AND FATHER OF OUR WORLD; ETERNAL AND SOVEREIGN, LIVING IN A WORLD LOST FROM YOU.

PLEASE HELP ME TO SEE MY HOME AND NEIGHBOR, OUR CITIES, ETHNIC COMMUNITIES, OUR NATION, AND OUR WORLD THROUGH YOUR LOVING AND HOLY EYES, NOT MINE. PLEASE HELP ME THIS DAY TO STAND INSIDE THE CITY GATE, LIVING JESUS.

I PRAY THIS IN THE NAME OF YOUR SON, WHO EMPTIED HIMSELF AND BECAME FULLY PRESENT TO ME AND OUR WORLD. AMEN.

PSALM OF THE WEEK: PSALM 49

COMMANDMENT OF THE WEEK: "HONOR YOUR FATHER AND YOUR MOTHER, AS THE LORD YOUR GOD HAS COMMANDED YOU, SO THAT YOU MAY LIVE LONG AND THAT IT MAY GO WELL WITH YOU IN THE LAND THE LORD YOUR GOD IS GIVING YOU."
DEUTERONOMY 5:16

DAILY SCRIPTURES:

MONDAY—MARK 3: 13-19, LUKE 6: 12-16

TUESDAY—JONAH 1

WEDNESDAY—JONAH 4

THURSDAY—JONAH 2, LUKE 11: 29-32

FRIDAY—LUKE 5: 1-11

SATURDAY—ACTS 10: 27-48 & 16: 25-34

SUNDAY—LUKE 5: 12-16, LUKE 16: 19-31, REV 21: 9-14

Rev. Terry Mattson

FROM
ACTS 2: 5,6

THERE WERE PIOUS JEWS FROM EVERY NATION UNDER HEAVEN LIVING IN JERUSALEM. WHEN THEY HEARD THIS SOUND, A CROWD GATHERED. THEY WERE MYSTIFIED BECAUSE EVERYONE HEARD THEM SPEAKING IN THEIR NATIVE LANGUAGES.

Week-6: MONDAY—MARK 3: 13-19, LUKE 6: 12-16

MY THOUGHTS 23—THE SHOPPING MALL

"In all the stages of Jesus' activity that we have considered so far, it has become evident that Jesus is closely connected with the 'we' of the new family that he gathers by his proclamation and his action. ...This 'we' is in principle intended to be universal: It no longer rests on birth, but on communion with Jesus, who is himself God's living Torah.

...Jesus calls an inner core of people specially chosen by him, who are to carry on his mission and give this family order and shape. That was why Jesus formed the group of the Twelve... Mark 3: 13-19 begins by saying that Jesus 'went up on the mountain, and called to him those whom he desired; and they came to him' (Mk 3:13).

...The calling of the Twelve, far from being purely functional, take on a deeply theological meaning: Their calling emerges from the Son's dialogue with the Father and is anchored there...Twelve—the number of the tribes—is at the same time a cosmic number that expresses the comprehensiveness of the newly reborn People of God. The Twelve stand as the patriarchs of this universal people founded on the Apostles. In the vision of the New Jerusalem found in the Apocalypse, the symbolism of the Twelve is

elaborated into an image of splendor (cf. Rev 21: 9-14) that helps the pilgrim People of God understand its present in the light of its future and illumines it with the spirit of hope: Past, present, and future intermingle when viewed in terms of the Twelve.
From "Jesus of Nazareth", by Pope Benedict XVI, page #169-171

The Fish Gate

"At this gate the fish for the local market were brought into the city. Jesus said He would make us fishers of men and challenged us in 'the Great Commission' (Matt. 28: 18-20) to reach every tribe and nation. During David's time, this gate was called the Gate of Ephraim. Ephraim means "double portion" and represents the blessing of God upon our lives and ministries. "Instead of your shame you will have a double portion" (Isaiah 61: 7). May God give us a double portion as we fish for men with all of our evangelistic efforts."
From "Can You Feel the Mountains Tremble?", by Dr. Suuqiina, page #82

On: Discovering Familial Disciples

Pike Place Market, lying in the heart of downtown Seattle, is full of sounds and smells, unique. "20 lb. Salmon, coming up!" is yelled out by the man behind the counter and immediately echoed by all the employees of this fish market. Another employee immediately picks up a salmon, slippery and with eyes bulging, from the ice filled chest and apparently without looking, tosses the fish through the air in the direction of the original caller. "Fish flying!" echoes throughout the open market, again by all the employees. Amazingly the fish finds its new home and is quickly wrapped into the awaiting newspaper. The cash register rings, money is exchanged and the banter of two strangers, cashier and buyer, finish the drama being acted out. Their conversation sounds as if they were lifelong friends, but all present know; they are just intimate strangers. Retailer and customer both play their parts as the public looks on with a smile in our eyes and on our faces.

In this city Pike Place Market beckons back to another time and place. It is the village square where the retailers and customers know each other and engage one another in an easy and playful spirit, bread of hundreds of years of shared experience.

In the ancient village of Capernaum, the town that ignites Jesus mission, there is no play acting. The smell of fish and sea, of wine press and donkeys rolling large stones all mingle as friends gather to do business and share in communal life. It is an urban village of the first century, a crossroads for the economic life of Galilee, but it retains its familial setting.

The gospel accounts of the calling of the twelve seem at first glance to be mysterious, strangers chosen of prayer. A closer look reveals, however, that the small village market place was the real context of the call. Jesus ministry was based in the town of Capernaum. Remnants of the village synagogue still witness to the personal and intimate setting of this public square. Several of the twelve were all from an even smaller village nearby, called Bethesda, a town of maybe a hundred. Most of the disciples knew each other in person or by reputation. Some were cousins and in business together. Others friends. At least one was an enemy. The exception was Judas Iscariot. Some of the disciples had clearly gathered around Jesus for some time, listening with interest to his compelling teachings. And yet, from the intimate setting of a Palestinian village, twelve were chosen to live out the call of Christ to go into the 'fish markets' of the whole world.

Jerusalem's Fish Gate opened into the noisy traffic of an urban market. The citizens of the world gathered here as intimate strangers. Few knew each other, but the smells and bantering of retailers and customers allowed for the illusion of intimacy, much like the Pike Place Market of Seattle. And it is here that Jesus calls us to go.

The tragedy of the modern Church is that we have opted for a ministry of 'intimate strangers' instead of an authentic ministry of friends to 'intimate strangers'. We have tried, through our own ministries and in our worship to replicate the Pike Place Market. We have surrounded it with the mystery of sign and the rhythm of music and attempted to hallow it by prayer. Sometimes, even all night prayer. Yet, we have forgotten the most important lesson inside the calling of the twelve. Jesus called a community of brothers and enemies into a new and holy fellowship. He lived inside their own story long enough to capture their heart and patiently show them a different kind of communion. His message of love lived reconciled a busy and pious fisherman (Peter) with the local and hated tax collector (Matthew) before sending them out into the more public village squares of the Galilean country side. These twelve lived inside the story of the Prodigal Son and of the paralytic man lowered through Peter's roof. They learned the story as a living sign before communicating its message to intimate strangers.

The Church, today, too often rushes into the village square as actors performing, throwing fish and bantering easily, but without the relationship with Jesus and each other that is the 'transformational' Story. The people inside the "Fish Gate" of your city can tell the difference between the real and fake.

Reflections on "The Shopping Mall"

Terry seems to be suggesting that 'relationally' centered ministry has to be something more than a group of people meeting in an intimate setting.

Q: What do you think?

Q: Do we really have to be in intimate relation with both Jesus and each other in order to make disciples in modern times? ...Is that even possible? ...Describe what it might look like.

Consider your own church. Give thanks to God for the Community of faith or pray that it might become intimately related to both Jesus and each other.

Week-6: TUESDAY—JONAH 1

STORY 23—JONAH'S STORY

**An Imaginative Biblical Story based upon Jonah 1...
from the Captain's Perspective**

'By the gods' I had lived, honorably and with a faithful love of life and the sea. I never left our home port of Joppa without buying a sacrifice for a safe journey. It was the least I could do for my passengers.

I had done the same on the day that Jonah boarded my old sea worn and sturdy vessel. His beard was long, his hair unkept. But what captured me was the look in his eyes; Revealing the empty and lonely soul of one on the run.

From the first I had kept my eyes on him for fear that his intentions might displease the gods or worse curse our voyage. I was also concerned that whatever chased him might capture us all. My fear of him grew as I listened to him that first night speak of that from which he ran. Apparently, he was a leader, honored among his own people. He spoke as one appointed by his god from childhood, the result of some holy man whose name I had heard, though I could not be certain where. Elijah, Jonah called him. He even claimed to have been raised from the dead by this prophet as a boy. "All this is the stuff of myth", I thought to myself. "But dangerous myth, nonetheless." Then, I distinctly remember Jonah's spirit darkening. His eyes once again seemed like an empty grave, the home of a demon. He spoke of his country's enemy, Nineveh. He told us that his god had called him to go to his enemy with a message of judgment. He had pulled his cloak tightly around him, as if the thought frightened him. My first mate spoke up and asked him, "So, you were afraid to obey your god and speak a word of judgment upon your enemy?"

Jonah's eyes suddenly filled with fire at the suggestion of cowardice. He barked at my first mate. "Afraid?! Yes, but not of the Ninevites." And then he spoke of his god in terms I had never before heard; Not about a god anyway. In a breathy, almost dark voice he said, "It is my god I fear. He is Creator of all you see, of every people and nation. Even of this sea. He is holy and good and filled with love." Then Jonah grew quiet and withdrawn as he finished in a breathy whisper. "My God does not send his prophets and priests out with a message of judgment except to warn a people he loves, so that they may change their ways and turn and be saved!" Then he said nothing for a long time, until at last standing and gathering his blanket, he said "What I fear is that my enemy, my people's greatest enemy might be saved through the message I have been given!" He was no longer whispering, but at a near scream. With that he left us and headed for the lower bunks and fell into a deep sleep.

It was at that same moment when a great wind stirred the waters of the sea!

Reflections on "Jonah's Story"

Q: What strikes you in this story?

Q: Does it surprise you that even in Jonah's disobedience these who had never heard of YHWH respond in worship? …How does it strike you?

Experiment: Go for a walk around your neighborhood each day this week. On the first walk or two, go in silence asking God to help you see them as God does. Than on the 3rd or 4th or 7th time began to put words to the prayer that emerges in your heart.

Week-6: WEDNESDAY—JONAH 4

MY THOUGHTS 24—DIVING DEEPER INTO JONAH'S STORY

Reflections on Chapters 1 & 4 of Jonah

What is striking in the first and fourth chapter of Jonah is the apparent and maturing faith of the Captain and passengers in contrast with Jonah's deeper knowledge of the God who is and Jonah's faithlessness.

Both crew and passengers were certain that the cause of the distress was spiritual, not natural. That in and of itself is of no surprise. All men were believers in one god or another and the sea held the deepest spiritual fascination for ancients. It represented the depths from which all human fears and addictions (demons) might rise. What is unique in this story is the way the faith of these sea voyagers were transformed by the life and testimony of Jonah. As their rituals dictated, they cast lots to determine who among them was responsible, who had angered his god? When the lot fell to Jonah, they did not immediately seize Jonah and throw him over.

Instead they went to him for council; to test their theology by experience. *"Tell us, who is responsible for making all this trouble for us? What do you do? Where do you come from? What is your country? From what people are you?"* (Jonah 1: 8b). And in the midst of a life-threatening adventure they were told of the *"God of heaven, who made the sea and the land"* (Jonah 1: 9b). This knowledge terrified them further for, if true, then this God could destroy them or save them. *"The sea was getting rougher and rougher. So they asked him, "What should we do to you to make the sea calm down"* (Jonah 1:11). And even after Jonah instructed them to throw him over they sought another way out of their predicament. Finding none, they threw Jonah over and then sacrificed to God, "The Almighty One", and made covenantal vows to him.

In contrast, in chapter four, Jonah gets it, but doesn't like it. His theology is excellent throughout the story. What he cannot abide is his enemy's relief and salvation.

So what is amazing in this story is the very universal picture of salvation. It is the picture of God who works even in pre-Christian/pre-Jewish faith to redeem all. This little ship is the first redemptive act in the story of Jonah. It is not the last.

Reflections on "Diving Deeper into Jonah's Story"

"So what is amazing in this story is the very universal picture of salvation. It is the picture of God who works even in pre-Christian and pre-Jewish faith; to redeem all. This little ship is the first redemptive act in the story of Jonah. It is not the last."

From Terry (above)

Q: Have you ever considered the 'salvation' of the passengers in this story? ...If their salvation is part of the narrative's purpose, what is the significance? ...What would that say about God's inter-action with other faith traditions? ...What does it say about God's ability to use our own rebellion to honor God's Name?

Q: What do you encounter more of when you are with pre-Christians?

> ➢ Nominal faith
> ➢ No faith
> ➢ Other religious faith
> ➢ Significant faith

Reflect and pray.

Week-6: THURSDAY—JONAH 2, LUKE 11: 29-32

MY THOUGHTS 25—OUT OF HIS DEPTH—JONAH'S STORY

On: Jesus Baptism

"The icon of Jesus' Baptism depicts the water as a liquid tomb having the form of a dark cavern, which is in turn the iconographic sign of Hades, the underworld, or hell. Jesus' descent into this water tomb, into this inferno that envelops him from every side, is thus an anticipation of his act of descending into the underworld: 'When he went down into the waters, he bound the strong man' (cf Lk 11: 22), says Cyril of Jerusalem. John Chrysostom writes: 'Going down into the water and emerging again are the image of the descent into hell and the Resurrection.'"
From "Jesus of Nazareth, by Pope Benedict XVI, page #19.

Reflections on Chapters 2 of Jonah

"This is a wicked generation. It asks for a miraculous sign, but none will be given it except the sign of Jonah."
Luke 11: 29b, Jesus

In this ancient story of a reluctant prophet, afraid of success, we see into the very center of human fear.

Sheol, the place of the dead, still grips us no matter how much we protest and try to convince our modern selves that death is simply another phase of life. To the modern, life without bio-chemical reaction is fantasy. We are stuck in our nothingness.

However, to the ancients the sea was representative of the dark abyss, the dwelling place of demons and angry gods, who occasionally emerge from the deep in the form of floods and torrential rains whose power can destroy everything in its wake. It was into this very abyss that Jonah's disobedience threw him.

What is unique in this story was Jonah's encounter with God; who saves! This is the central truth that captures our heart and transforms this story from myth to reality. Jonah experienced what King David only sang of: *"If I make my bed in the depths, you are there... If I say, 'Surely the darkness will hide me and the light become night around me, 'even the darkness will not be dark to you"* (Psalm 139: 8b, 11, 12a). Jonah's refusal to follow Israel's God into holy—love led him into the very center of human fear and what he discovered there was, God!

In this, Jonah is a (negative) type of Christ! Jonah ran from sacrificial love, as do we all, and fell into the pull and power of hell. Jesus obeyed and followed the way of love into the center of human disease and fear. Jesus and Jonah were both redeemed from this un-holy place by the hand of the Father, one saved from disobedience and the other by obedience.

For Jonah and Jesus the resurrection was earthy. *"And the LORD commanded the fish, and it vomited Jonah onto dry ground"* (Jonah 2: 10).

So, for the modern and ancient alike the hope inside this story is universal. God is ever present, even in our darkest night. It is a costly presence and should be lived out in the city of humankind.

Jonah was sent to the market place of Nineveh. Even today, it is the Fish Gate or market place that is the setting for telling God's story. The shopping Malls of America remain an empty abyss, spiritually. It is an abyss of debt and the longing for 'things' that do not satisfy. It is here that the gothic young, the metro-sexual, the lonely and stressed house wife mingle. It is here we encounter the diversity that is the city. We are indeed intimate strangers. We walk past each other with ease and spend ourselves into another kind of pit. We live on the verge of the 'coming abyss' (redemptive judgment).

Reflections on "Out of His Depth— Jonah's Story"

In my congregation is an older man who tells a story of losing his teenage daughter. She ran away. He had heard a rumor that she might be in southern California. So he drove from Seattle to California in search of his lost daughter. As he was in a mall, looking into the face of each young woman, the thought suddenly struck him: "Ralph, you know how deeply hurt you are and how you long to see in the face of each child, your daughter? Imagine my own suffering as I am calling home all my children, who are lost."

Q: How does this story reflect your ow purpose in telling other about Christ? Is your motive the same as God's? ...Or, like Jonah, does another concern motivate you? ...Fear, perhaps?

Experiment: Go to any mall or city center and sit, watch, listen for an extended time.

Q: What do you see? ...What does God see?

Reflect and turn it to prayer.

Week-6: FRIDAY—LUKE 5: 1-11

MY THOUGHTS 26—ON CASTING YOUR NET

On: Casting your Net…

Learning your craft as reflected in Luke 5: 1-11

At first glance the setting seems so casual and easy. The story feels fanciful. Peter and his business partner's response appear impulsive. However, a closer look is warranted. What emerges from inside this story is Jesus sense of mission, his knowledge of his followers and their world.

Jesus began his ministry in Capernaum, a village on the edge of everywhere. Capernaum was connected to the whole world because of the Appian Way, a Roman highway running through its Provinces. Even so, Capernaum remained uniquely Jewish. Fishing was one of the city's exports. Another was olive oil, whose texture and quality was known throughout the province.

We enter the story with Jesus. He is comfortable with his followers. He knew them and they him. It is not hard to hear him bantering with Simon about the night's empty catch. Mid-morning finds them surrounded by a crowd of people who have caught up with Jesus. Apparently, they knew where to find him.

Jesus familiarity is seen in the text. *"He (Jesus) got into one of the boats, the one belonging to Simon, and asked him to put out a little from shore. Then he sat down and taught the people from the boat"* (Luke 5: 3). Peter must have been familiar with Jesus as well. His brother Andrew had introduced Simon to him and had become one of Jesus close disciples.

Jesus knew his hearers needs as well. *"When he had finished speaking he said to Simon, 'Put out into deep water, and let down the nets for a catch'"* (Luke 5:4).

It is very likely that Jesus, while sitting in Peter's boat teaching, saw a shoal of fish at some small distance away. It is the kind of thing that would naturally happen on Galilee when the light and distance come together for the trained eye. Peter's trust in Jesus speak of something more than spiritual respect. *"Simon answered, 'Master, we've worked hard all night and haven't caught anything. But because you say so, I will let down the nets'"* (Luke 3: 5).

For Jesus, none of this is casual. All of this happened because of a consistently present and curious interest in his hearers. The miracle is inside the natural and unfolding story, not above or beneath the water. These very human relationships led to the most significant of spiritual discoveries. Jesus holy-love was compelling not because he is magical, but because he is so ordinary. The hunger to be holy lived inside Simon's life and the light of Jesus message penetrated this fisherman's heart. He was captured by the net of Jesus presence in the place of Simon's occupation. *"When Simon Peter saw this, he fell at Jesus' knees and said, 'go away from me, Lord; I am a sinful man!'* (Luke 3:8a).

And what was Jesus response? Ritual? An invitation to visit with him at the next Sabbath service? Absolution? Hardly. His response was earthy and fitting. *"Then Jesus said to Simon, 'Don't be afraid; from now on you will catch men'* (Luke 5: 10b).

Only in the last verse do we leave the ordinary and enter mystery. *"So they pulled their boats up on shore and left everything and followed him"* (Luke 5: 11).

As it was with Jesus mission, so it should be with us today. Jesus disciples are called to live inside the human story, not apart from it.

Reflections on "On Casting Your Net"

Considering Jesus example:

Q: What is the most appropriate place for telling/living the Story of Christ?

> ➤ At Church?
> ➤ At the Mall?
> ➤ At Work?
> ➤ At Home?
> ➤ In another cultural context near or far away?
> ➤ In a communal context with persons who are marginalized by society?

Q: Where are you currently most gifted in telling/living the Story of God?

> ➤ At Church?
> ➤ At the Mall?
> ➤ At Work?
> ➤ At Home?
> ➤ In another cultural context near or far away?
> ➤ In a communal context with persons who are marginalized by society?

Q: Why is that?

Reflect and turn it to prayer.

Week-6: SATURDAY—ACTS 10: 27-48 & 16: 25-34

MY THOUGHTS 27—CASTING THE NET WIDE?

Salvation: A culturally framed and Divinely Inspired Mystery

At this writing the world was informed of what only a few of us inside the story were aware. My daughter, Nicole and son in law, Dennis are about to have another child. I no longer have to keep an inside secret, anxiously watching my every word afraid I might let the cat out of the bag… Besides that, I don't even like cats.

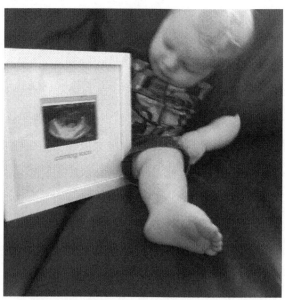

As I look into my daughter's Instagram I am struck by the picture of my grandson Sammy looking upon the ultra-sound image of his little sister or brother. What his nearly two-year old mind cannot yet grasp will soon become a way of living inside the wonder of new life. By experience Samuel's touch, taste, smell, hearing and sight will now expand to incorporate a being different than his mommy, daddy, grandpas, grandmas, uncles and aunts—a brother or sister who will shape him as much as he shapes the little one.

The truth is we are more like Sammy than we know. We are surrounded by the mysteries of life—ours and our neighbors, strangers, fellow workers, family, national and ethnic communities—and are barely cognizant of life's real meaning.

In today's two texts the very meaning of what it is to awaken to the wonderment of the God Story—to salvation, if you will—take giant leaps forward. The Jewish and Christian fishing nets of both Peter and Paul widen in joyful discovery.

Who is saved in the Cornelius story; Cornelius or Peter? Peter confesses that *"I really am learning that God doesn't show partiality to one group of people over another. Rather, in every nation, whoever worships him and does what is right is acceptable to him"* (Acts 10: 34, 35). Apparently, God had already saved in every meaningful sense, Cornelius, who is declared righteous at the beginning of the story and as reaffirmed in Peter's own confession.

In Paul and Silas, we picture the living sign of Jesus in their singing within the confines of a Roman jail and the wounds that attend. Their gift of worship penetrates the jailors heart and evidently their fellow prisoners as the integrity of their refusal to escape jail when given opportunity saves the jailor from possible suicide or death. Had they escaped the penalty of death could have been exacted by Rome.

We are moved by the jailors question, *"Honorable masters, what must I do to be rescued?"* (Acts 16: 30). Rescued? From whom? From what?

Whatever this Roman who certainly believed in the gods— gods to whom he had spent a life giving proper respect in his fear-based religions, especially the new gods; the Roman Emperors—meant, Paul understood the existential mystery in the question and told him of the only Name by which all of us are saved, found, made real; Jesus of Nazareth.

And the net is stretched further. Stretched precisely because there is no human truly beyond the reach of the Story in which God is alive!

Dr. Ray Dunning, an American and Nazarene theologian suggests that the single greatest contribution of John and Charles Wesley to our understanding of this 'way of salvation' is in his doctrine of Prevenient Grace—the ever reaching, active and close Presence of God who lives with, around and in each/all of us to draw us deeply and really (by God's Spirit) into the God—Story, into a living relation with the Trinity of God. This Prevenient Grace is the presence of God that precedes a saving awareness of the life, death and resurrection of Jesus Christ.

The Wesley's were clear that all spiritual formation begins and ends with Christ's work in and through us. However, they understood, Christ's work to be underneath and before and above the specific moment when we first heard The Story of God's saving acts in time.

Whatever our culture, context or religion God finds a way to bring us to an awareness of God's love in Jesus Christ.

Prevenient then, is the whole movement of God from before time and made real in time in the Christ event (life, death, resurrection, ascension, intercession). Prevenient includes the active searching and cultivating mission of the Holy Spirit in every culture, among every people group and in every person, as we are drawn into Christ's Story.

And just like my grandson looking upon his sibling, we tend to see one another in tortured and caricatured ways until God somehow makes real in and between us the mysteries of our universal human experience.

Reflections on "Casting the Net Wide"

> *"Honorable masters,*
> *what must I do to be rescued?"*
> *(Acts 16: 30)*

Q: Does the jailor's response strike you as odd? …What do you think he was asking? …Rescued from whom? …Rescued from what?

Q: What initiated in the jailor, his response? …What effect might it have had on him, his household and the other jailors? …or on Paul and Silas?

> *"Whatever our culture, context or religion*
> *God finds a way to bring us to an awareness*
> *of God's love in Jesus Christ."*
> Terry (Above)

Q: What are the implications of Terry's statement above?

Q: What do you think of Wesley's doctrine of Prevenient Grace?

Q: What does it mean 'to be saved'?

Consider how you were made aware or brought inside the Jesus Story—if you have as yet.

Q: If not, why not now?

Reflect and turn it to prayer.

Week-6: SUNDAY—LUKE 5: 12-16, LUKE 16: 19-31, REV 21: 9-14

STORY 24—ON FISHING: STUCK IN THE NET

A Personal Story about being caught in the net with My Native American friend, who fell off the wagon… Artie, sadly, is now deceased.

It was 12:45 AM when I finally got home. My wife asked me. "Was he on something?" "No," I answered, "He was just sober enough to be depressed."

Today was Christmas Sunday, one year from the day my 'not so recovering alcoholic friend' had fallen off his two-year wagon. The mornings service was magical; a near perfect blend of sight and sound, of sign and testimony, of song and feeling. The hearts of believers and pre-Christians had been touched, a number of whom came from our neighborhood. The evening's Friends and Family Communion services were intimate and deep. About 10:00 pm I was finally getting around to a belated hospital visit when the emergency call came. My 'not so recovering alcoholic friend' had let my wife know he needed to talk. "Honey," she said, her voice echoing the sound of conflicted feelings, "I'm not sure, but he says his mind is slipping." So at 10:45 pm I drove up to his house not knowing if I was walking into:

1) Depression, or;

2) An overdose, or;

3)   Hallucinogenic reaction, or;

4)   Simple (not) manipulation.

His home was completely dark and stayed that way throughout our hour's conversation. Empathy and arguments ensued. He altered between curses directed at me and the church for our failures, as he perceived them and pleas for help and expressions of being tired of the last year's journey.

Sometimes he was lucid and at other moments he was tortured by the demonic lies that held him captive. An hour in I had concluded that he had invited me into #1 (depression) and # 4 (manipulation), depending on the moment. I stayed with him because the volatility of his mood swings created the remote, but real potential of suicide.

As I left and stood in darkness with one hand on his door, he asked me for bus tickets so that he could (presumably) make his way downtown to a social worker to begin the process of treatment. "Artie", I responded gently. "No, I'm not helping you in that way anymore. You know that. If you want to get to that appointment, you'll have to find a way."

As I drove away and made my way to the park where I often pray, I thought to myself, 'He is responding to the heart of my prayers for him over the last two months. I've been asking God to awaken him to the one-year anniversary of his fall. He is awakening.' I prayed: "God help him. Only You can save him now."

Reflections on "On Fishing: Stuck in the Net"

"No man can redeem the life of another or give to God a ransom for him—the ransom for a life is costly, no payment is ever enough—that he should live forever and not see decay." Psalm 49: 7-9

Q: Why do any of us, me included, refuse the reach of God's salvation?

Q: If we are to really be inside the Story of our neighbors, offering the 'saving Presence of Jesus inside the God Story' what might be the cost? ...Is the cost part of our salvation? ...How so?

Q: What is hell? ...Define it: Is it punishment or loss? ...Is salvation escape from Divine punishment or hellish addiction—wounds; the result of a God excluded life?

Reflect, confess, give thanks for where you see Jesus in your own life and then give Jesus Story and your own away.

Next:
Healing

7 HEALING

... The Dung Gate

INVOCATION:

FATHER, YOU HAVE INVITED US TO COME TO YOU AND REASON TOGETHER. YOU HAVE PROMISED THAT IF WE ENTER THE CONFESSIONAL WITH YOU THAT EVEN *"THOUGH OUR SINS ARE LIKE SCARLET, THEY SHALL BE AS WHITE AS SNOW; THOUGH THEY ARE RED AS CRIMSON, THEY SHALL BE LIKE WOOL"* (ISAIAH 1:18). BUT WE ARE AFRAID AND LIKE JOB OF OLD NEEDING *"SOMEONE TO ARBITRATE BETWEEN US, ...SOMEONE TO REMOVE GOD'S ROD FROM US"* (JOB 9: 33-34). AND SO YOU HAVE TAUGHT US TO PRAY IN JESUS HOLY NAME.

FATHER, WHEN YOUR SON WAS ON THE EARTH THE SICK WERE BROUGHT TO HIM AND THEY WERE HEALED. AS I LIVE IN THE CITY I SEE THE BLIND EVERYWHERE. EVEN WE, WHO ARE IN CHRIST LIVE MOSTLY IN THE SHADOWS. FATHER—SPIRIT— SON, SHINE ON US.

AS I LIVE IN THE CITY I HEAR VOICES LOUD AND CONFLICTED, YET FEW LISTEN. EVEN WE, WHO ARE IN CHRIST ARE TOO BUSY PROCLAIMING OUR RIGHTFUL PLACE TO HEAR. COME

FATHER—SPIRIT—SON AND GIVE US EARS TO HEAR AND HEARTS THAT LISTEN.

AS I LIVE IN THE CITY I STUMBLE AMONG WOUNDED PEOPLE. EVEN WE WHO ARE IN CHRIST WALK CARELESSLY AND ARROGANTLY AMONG THOSE WHO ARE MOST VULNERABLE. COME, FATHER—SPIRIT—SON AND HELP EVERYONE AS WE WOULD YOU.

HELP US TO REASON TOGETHER, FATHER, WITH YOU AND YOUR SON IN THE SPIRIT. MAKE US THE CHURCH. AMEN.

PSALM OF THE WEEK: PSALM 32

COMMANDMENT OF THE WEEK: "YOU SHALL NOT MURDER."
DEUTERONOMY 5: 17

DAILY SCRIPTURES:

MONDAY—GENESIS 12: 1-7 & 13: 1-13

TUESDAY—II CORINTHIANS 4: 1-18

WEDNESDAY—ROMANS 11: 32-36 & 12: 1-2, II CORINTHIANS 5: 11-21

THURSDAY—MATTHEW 8: 5-13

FRIDAY—NEHEMIAH 2: 1-4, 7-13, 19-20 & JOHN 4: 1-9

SATURDAY—MARK 11: 15-18

SUNDAY—GENESIS 14: 17-20, II SAMUEL 5:6-10, ISAIAH 58: 5-12, JEREMIAH 29: 4-7, DANIEL 9: 1-19, LUKE 19: 41-48, REVELATION 21: 2

FROM
GALATIANS 4: 26

BUT THE JERUSALEM THAT IS ABOVE IS FREE, AND SHE IS OUR MOTHER.

Week-7: MONDAY—GENESIS 12: 1-7 & 13: 1-13

The Dung Gate - 1968

The Dung gate, near the Temple Mount, leads down into the modern Arab center of Silwan. Once encompassed within a much larger walled city it was just a door in the wall. With Jerusalem's walls now shrunken it has been widened to accommodate buses and cars moving from the Temple mount into the historic city of David.

The Gate is aptly named for through the centuries as Jerusalem felt the violent embrace of Europeans, Romans, Turks, Arabs, Muslims, Christians, Jews and people of the gods, it was this gate that allowed the heaps of rubbage to pass to the valley of Tophet below.

Dung is what we call 'throw-a-ways'. Jerusalem's throw-a-ways have ever changed according to who is on top of the heap. What remains is the need of some on top to call all the rest, 'Dung'.

STORY 25—URBAN DUNG

An Imaginative Biblical Story based up Genesis 13 when Abram & Lot separate with Lot choosing the southern Jordan Valley, near Sodom...

Abrams eyes moistened as Lot feeling self-assured as young men do, turned and set out for his encampment to instruct his servants to prepare to leave for the southern Jordan Valley and make camp near Sodom and Gomorrah.

Abram, standing high above the Salt Sea (Dead Sea) on the plains of Zoar stood frozen as if a pillar on the sea's eastern shore, made of salt. Abram knew the place for he had briefly encamped near the suffocating dry and heavy heat of this lake that looked like a goat's bath of milk, so laden with salt. The air surrounding stifled breath, the moisture sucked out pushing the salt deeper into the ground and over time leaving vast salty deposits against the mountains that rose just east of her shores. Once Abram had climbed the mountain and entering a cave was shocked to discover columns of what he first thought was white rock. But as he drew closer and noticed the brittle texture of its face he broke off a bit and placed it in his mouth, curious, having never seen such a formation. To his shock it was sheer salt, hardened, brittle, fragile—yet strong; obviously the result of the timeless rhythms of the sea below carried by waves of waterless winds.

A tear formed on Abram's cheek as he remembered the experience and his first encounter of Sodom, in the lush green plain to the south of the sea. He remembered how taken Lot was with the city, its youth and vigor, alluring him late into many evening hours. Abram was surprised at the number of Sodom's children who slept on the streets too poor for shelter, even in such a rich city. 'How?' Abram had wondered, 'could a king and his people allow their kindred to live as peasants amidst such wealth.' And Abram had noticed another thing; the numerous slaves, especially women, dressed—if he could call it such—but blatantly attired to stir the passions of any man who could never venture to touch what he did not own.

Before leaving the city and making a covenant to never return Abram had discovered the sad truth. These slaves were used for the entertainment of the wealthy to pursue whatever passion aroused them and in plain sight of all their ivited guests.

'And now', Abram's dark thoughts continued to pour out of him as he turned to go to his own encampment and prepare his own for the movement to the northern lands above the great and salty sea; 'Now his own flesh and blood, Lot whom he had taken from the city of Ur'—away from the pleasures and gods and temptations of urban life— 'had chosen to leave off this exploration of the promised land for a city far worse than he had left'. And his inner thoughts formed a cry… 'May God Most High forgive me for what I have done to my nephew this day!'

MY THOUGHTS 28—URBAN DUNG

I grew up in rural America and within what is still a largely rural evangelical faith community—Nazarene. I used to sit by the hours creating on paper pictures of cities—ancient and future—and then play out imaginary stories to go with them. For days I would draw out the infrastructure—streets, shopping centers, theatres, stadiums, government buildings or military bases—and then pretend I was the King or

President until I tired of it and moved on to another adventure. Sometimes it would be ancient cities in Israel or futuristic cities under the ocean or in space. Looking back, it is clear that I've always loved the city, from child hood. What I did not yet understand is that I also had internalized a prejudice—a Dung view—of urban life.

When I went to college, where did I go? To what was then a small rural community, Nampa Idaho, as far away from the sinful and distracting urban centers of Portland and Seattle as the Church could take me.

What began to re-shape my world view was four influences, including;

> My family moving to Boise, Idaho—a small city—at a time when I had my first 10 speed bike and the freedom to explore, and;
> An inward desire that I initially thought was all about ego (and in part, it was) to never pastor in a rural community, but only in a city, and;
> Pastoring in Seattle, Washington and the sense by God of being called as much to the whole city as I was to my church (and feeling a bit guilty at that), and;
> The influence of Ray Bakke and many others who changed my 'salvational' views from personal (only) too communal and from people to include land and places, including the renewal of the universe and all who live within it.

In the first fifteen years of my mission in Seattle my heart was taken to every part of the city, to every faith and cultural community to simply pray. Today, it is the Duwamish Tribal community and their lodge, not three miles away. But the transformation in theology and heart and mind in my own life is 'salvific' just as Peter's first visit to Cornelius.

To live in the city is to face the prejudice of 'Urban Dung'. In "Theology as Big as the City" Ray Bakke puts it this way:

"The evangelicalism I grew up with had a theology of persons and programs, but it lacked a conscious theology of place. Protestants generally had cut themselves off from 'parish' thinking—an ongoing commitment to their place of ministry—so that when a church's location became 'inconvenient' it simply relocated to a new place, often near a freeway (reflecting our society's shift from a walking to an automobile culture). Along the way, we abandoned real estate that had been prayed for, fervently by Christians before us—and along with it abandoned any commitment to the neighborhoods we left behind. ...It is a theological bias toward Greek individualism and away from a biblical holistic theology, which for me includes not only the physical aspects of persons but also the geography in which we have identity and security.

Does God care only about people, or does he also care about places, including cities?"

From "A Theology as Big As the City" by Ray Bakke, pages 60-61"

Reflections on "Urban Dung"

If we truly believe God cares for places and communities as well as individuals, how would that change the way we see:

- ➢ Where we work?
- ➢ Our neighborhood?
- ➢ Our own Church within a neighborhood or city?
- ➢ Another people group?
- ➢ Other nations?

Experiment: Go to your favorite place to reflect on these questions and pray there.

Q: Why is this your favorite place?

Reflect, confess, give thanks for where you see Jesus and turn it all to prayer.

Week-7: TUESDAY—II CORINTHIANS 4: 1-18

MY THOUGHTS 29—RECONCILING URBAN & RURAL CULTURE WARS

Reflections on the Church within the Urban/Rural Cultural Wars

Reconciliation is the very center of the Church's mission; Reconciliation with God, the environment, within humans, communities, nations and between humans, cultures and nations.

Reconciliation never happens between strangers. A person is reconciled to her/his own past only as we re-know it or to another only as we know each other. The greatest enemy of reconciliation is not hatred, but ignorance and prejudice; the inability or unwillingness to see ourselves and each other as human. Until we choose to live beyond name calling, bullying or stereotyping dialogue reconciliation is impossible.

Our small, multi-cultural, multi-economic and urban faith community loves to make fun (all in good spirit) with our friend from the south. No, not south America—just the southern United States. Brian is an out-going people lover willing to say just about anything that comes to mind. He is constantly walking into urban myths and PC leanings with his southern morays. And we, on many Sundays and Wednesdays laugh with him—sometimes at him—from both the pulpit and pew.

The truth is it would not matter if Brian was from North Carolina or Idaho. What matters is that he is on the rural side of the urban/rural divide.

It has been noted that **the gap between those who live in cities and those who live in the open spaces of America or the world for that matter may be the 21st Century's real challenge for nations and faith communities.** The United States is divided between blue states and red, Republican and Democrat, liberal and conservative, independent or communal. Yet, what makes these divisions powerful is the differences in values, tastes and world views of urban verses rural peoples. Britain's recent vote for independence from Europe through BREXIT was attributed largely to rural votes within the country.

Why this cultural and geographically centered war?

Although an oversimplification, rural communities retain attachments to familial relations, lands and faith traditions as a-priori. The myths or world view assumptions of rural communities or tribes tend to be accepted as universal; hence an emphasis upon conserving and independence.

Cities, by nature are culturally, socially and spiritually inter-active. Myths or world view is seen as part of a narrative unique to each cultural, tribal or religious heritage; each story taking its place alongside others. Emphasis is upon diversity and the inter-connectedness of the human family and the environment.

Strikingly it appears to be a manifestation of the modern/post-modern divide.

Too often, in the American Experience, liberal Protestant communities reflect the urban experience while the Evangelical—conserving traditions the rural. So the church is itself caught up in the rural/urban narratives (myths) defending and enlarging them rather than listening, engaging and transforming each into a narrative of the Kingdom of God; of suffering love.

The evangelical community is often identified with a restoration theology of taking America back to a supposed earlier and largely Christian culture—without a transformational social presence that identifies social and cultural sin as evidenced in racism. Do we really want to go back to segregated schools and lunch counters? Sadly, the current Republican America 1st political culture seems the faith mission for many evangelicals.

The Liberal Protestant traditions identify with marginalized urban people groups and the Presence is often co-opted by and servant to social justice causes but isolated from the very reconciliation which makes social justice possible. And so, while appropriately proclaiming 'Black Lives Matter' the reality of a child in the womb being lost, especially in impoverished and mostly African American Communities is missed.

America's political theatre (and the church with it) is clearly split along urban/rural lines leaving many in our pews who despise either Hillary Clinton or Donald Trump based upon political and cultural association. The Biblical call to pray for and engage our leaders (conservative or progressive) with a servant model of public service is lost inside partisan political activism; and that motivated (on both sides) by faith.

Please do not hear me suggesting that activism socially, culturally or politically is antithetical to the mission of the Church or her parishioners'. If anything we have precious little of it. What is missing is the pre-eminence of a gospel of hope and reconciliation based upon Jesus, who revealed the power of sacrificial love. The Church of Christ must find a way to live in and between the modern/post-modern world views. Each contribute to our human experience. Each bring to the table world views in which the gospel of our Lord can live, affirm, challenge and transform. What then is needed is a Church that can live in and between this political—social—cultural urban and rural experience helping those on either side to hear the other and Jesus.

The very power of the Southern Christian Leadership Conference of Dr. Martin Luther King was the very suffering love for White America that either passively or assertively facilitated Jim Crow. Dr. King saw his mission, in part, to save white America from itself.

What America, indeed the world needs, is a Church committed, as was Jesus to identifying with the marginalized while retaining connection with the empowered and so introduce one to the other, not as caricatures, but as fellow humans.

Interestingly, it seems to me, that it is the Catholic Church that has come closer to living out this gospel than either Protesting Liberal or Conserving traditions, notwithstanding its own grievous sin against culture in the sexual scandals of the church. I would suggest the reason is simply that the Roman tradition retains a world and local connection, a rural and urban historic presence, tribal and Western that keeps its priests, sisters and lay persons committed to broad social justice with reconciliation at heart.

Reflections on "Reconciling Urban and Rural Culture Wars"

"Go up and down the streets of Jerusalem, look around and consider; search through her squares. If you can find but one person who deals honestly and seeks the truth, I will forgive this city." Jeremiah 5: 1

"And I sought for a man among them, that should make up the hedge, and stand in the gap before me for the land, that I should not destroy it; but I found none." Ezekiel 22:30

"What if only ten (righteous people) can be found there?' He answered, 'For the sake of ten, I will not destroy it.'" Genesis 18: 32

One person could have saved Jerusalem, the city of God's love. Just one. That person was not found. Ten righteous people could have saved Sodom? They could not be found.

Q: Have you ever seen one person make a real difference in a community?

> *"We always carry Jesus' death around in our bodies so that Jesus' life can also be seen in our bodies. We who are alive are always being handed over to death for Jesus' sake so that Jesus' life can also be seen in our bodies that are dying. So death is at work in us, but life is at work in you."* II Corinthians 4: 10-12
>
> *"So then, from this point on we won't recognize people by human standards."* II Corinthians 5: 16

Q: What would it look like if a conserving Protestant Church took these verses to heart? ...How would it change the way we pray for or relate to those who do not share our political or cultural views?

Q: What would it look like if a progressive Protestant Church took these verses to heart? ...How would it change the way we pray for or relate to those who do not share our political or cultural views?

Q: What might happen to the Church in America if we really took these verses, indeed just this chapter, to heart?

Q: What might happen to our country?

Experiment: Go to a conservative Protestant Church this week and just sit and pray for its pastor and people. Then go to a progressive Protestant Church and do the same. Blessings!

Week-7: WEDNESDAY—Romans 11: 32-36 & 12: 1-2, II
CORINTHIANS 5: 11-21

STORY 26—DUNG OR FERTILIZER?

Personal Memories living inside a gifted and clueless Church

George came to me, respectfully as Africans do when speaking with a minister. He was from Ghana, Africa and had for several months made our church his home, literally. All I knew was that he was a righteous man with a tender and loving heart who spoke in a gentle and almost cadenced British accent; surrounding each word with a kind of spiritual mystery. Theologically, George was a Word-Faith, Pentecostal and fundamentalist street preacher who stowed away in the bowels of an ocean going Liner to make his way to America, his missional calling, and with the purpose of preaching on its streets.

Now, Word-Faith simply means that if one prays for it, believing and with good heart you will receive it. And did George pray. He cleaned out an old closet about 5' square and would pray for 3-8 hours a day. I didn't have to ask him why a closet? I knew. Jesus had instructed us to go to our 'closet' and pray. When he prayed in public he'd go through three emotive and verbal changes. He would start in English and as his passion increased would change to his native tongue and again when nearing the high point and end of his prayer he would slip into a prayer language and then end in English. As a pastor of a non-charismatic church I was always grateful that our people didn't really know the difference between his native tongue and his divine language.

George was loved by all, incredibly humble, a very hard worker. About a year after being with us he came and asked me if I knew what brought him to our church? I was curious because my sermons were definitely not Word-Faith, so I stopped what I was doing and listened. He said, "Pastor," and then he'd pause for emphasis and repeat. "Pastor, when I was in Africa God gave me a vision of this Church and so when I saw it, I knew I was called to Seattle and to here." Who was I to argue with God? And then with a gentle smile and not an ounce of judgment he added. "Pastor..." that pause thing again. "You see pastor, this little church is doing more good works among the homeless and tribal communities than churches who are a lot bigger." Now, had he stopped there, I would have only smiled in pride. "But," (why do people have to add the but...), "no one here is praying. You will succeed only by prayer. So I'll do your praying for you." Now it was my turn to get quiet and meet his insightful and challenging compliment. "George," I said, pausing... "George, you are right and I am so thankful for you." And I was, deeply.

George has moved on to other cities in his mission. On occasion he will stop by the church to encourage, offer a word of prophecy (which is incredibly timely) and say hi. The last time he came I was especially depressed and ready to give up. That was about six years ago. I had just returned from a pastoral retreat wherein God said, 'Not yet...' And with very specific verbiage, then God framed it in a scripture, which at this writing I do not remember.

The 'not yet' was significant because by every sign it was time. I was in the early stages of deepened depression and was no longer giving the church energetic leadership. In any event that next Sunday George showed up, hugged, smiled and waited to briefly talk with me after the service. I was about to go into a board meeting which was now going to be re-shaped simply on the basis of my intuiting of the Spirit's assurance. I invited George to join the board in a meal and leave after the meal. He told me he could not, but he had a message for me from God. Then in everyday English George told me to not give up, using the very specific phrase I had intuited as God on the prayer retreat. George then re-affirmed that all the promised financial blessing that he had always assured me would come upon our faith community was still going to happen. I always dismissed that part of his prophecy with a smile. Then he concluded by paraphrasing the very same scripture God had given me on retreat.

What has happened in the five years of waiting? From the very timely and creative planning of a neighbor down the street we are in a multi-year plan with a developer who managed the multi-year renovation for Seattle's famous Pike Place Market. In what is typically almost politically impossible our land has been unanimously approved by the Seattle City Council for a new comprehensive neighborhood plan. (Only 2 of the 41 private plans were approved this last year—ours being one). When completed we should realize sufficient income to restore our historic building, complete with a community park. Beyond that, my son is now pastor and leading with exceptional wisdom and heart.

Reflections on "Dung or Fertilizer"

George was right. At that point in our mission in Seattle neither I, nor our people were praying. When George left I began a city wide journey in prayer and significantly, in no small part, due to his example.

For those who might worry, so far God has spoken to me only in English—no angelic prayer language.

At heart, though, what I've come to experience and not simply believe theologically is how central prayer is to seeing the city and everyone in it—through God's eyes. Our ability to live in between the dividing lines and with those who are marginalized by culture or the church (homeless, immigrants, tribal communities, homosexual community) is only because of prayer. The Kingdom of God will simply not come without it. Only God can make fertilizer from what we perceive as dung.

> *So then, from this point on we won't recognize people*
> *by human standards.*
> II Corinthians 5: 16

The power in prayer is not Word-Faith, but Faith in the Living Word. Prayer aligns us into God's way of seeing ourselves and each other. All healing starts with renewed relations with ourselves, our neighbor and enemy and God. We cannot do anything meaningfully with or for anyone unless we are literally God's heart and hands engaged, walking along side and in great mercy.

Q: Your thoughts?

Q: Have you ever thought of prayer as changing our heart instead of God's?

Q: For whom do you need new eyes?

Listen, confess, repent and act.

Week-7: THURSDAY—MATTHEW 8: 5-13

Story 27—Dung Smells

Personal Memories living inside a gifted and clueless Church

The service had been good; the music, laughter, stations for the offering of our heart and lives and sermon all meaningful—especially Holy Communion.

Two men had entered the service partially inebriated. Both are good men when they are not drunk; each knowing Jesus, but lost in the helplessness that addiction is. They sang with heart, their amens just a little too loud and one occasionally repeated some of the phrases of our pastor when preaching—which in our church happens a lot. We have an incredibly loving and intuitive 39-year-old man with a mental age of, maybe six... the result of cerebral palsy. He sings or at least raises his hands and makes a joyful noise. His amens are often timely and he is forever speaking out during the sermon, sometimes with incredible insight. About 40% of our congregation is from the streets or tent city or the projects. They're all family and so, like family, our pastor has to be good at dialogue sermons, whether she or he wants to or not. He is.

After the message one of my street friends who was inebriated wanted to talk and pray. For the better part of a month he has been moving towards detox and treatment. He knows the system and how to make it work for him. He will, I believe, make it one day. But today he was sad in that because of a two-week binge (typical last hurrah) he missed a critical appointment that would have resulted in guaranteed access to treatment. So, he faced starting the process all over, jumping through hoops and hopefully learning that staying as far away from his addiction as he possibly can would be better than embracing it as one last attempt at a new high.

Now, he hasn't been here in two Sundays. I hope it's good news. It might be.

After praying and while watching him leave, I thought, 'what an incredible church. No one, not one person, felt even slightly uncomfortable in their presence… or if they did; they wouldn't make a big deal of it.'

MY THOUGHTS 30—DUNG SMELLS

Children learn early to use words as a weapon. Who is **'in'** and who is **'out'** is the stuff of name calling. In this game we use words to isolate others who become sacrificial lambs. They will be 'cast out' so that we and those who laugh with us are 'in'.

This encounter between a Roman Centurion and Jesus is in three of the four gospel accounts of Jesus life. Why? Is it because of the centurion's faith? A faith that did not need to see in order to believe? That is surely part of it. However, what is extraordinary—even scandalous—is the interaction of Jesus and this Roman soldier. Each pushed past a dozen 'adult-names' just to speak with one another, including:

pagan,

   Jew,

enemy,

   self-righteous,

pig,

   rebellious,

oppressor,

   terrorist,

dung, and;

   dung!

These names and more kept them apart, strangers, unable to cooperate without becoming a traitor to their compatriots.

So the deeper miracle was simply the conversation, initiated by the Roman (pagan-enemy-pig-oppressor-dung).

"'Lord,' he said, 'my servant lies at home paralyzed and in terrible suffering.' Jesus said to him, 'I will go and heal him'" (Matthew 8: 6,7). The centurion saw in Jesus a benevolent person with authority. Jesus saw in the in the centurion a son of man whose faith made him a son of God. This is the real miracle and the probable reason for its inclusion in the gospels. It is also one of the reasons Jesus was crucified. His compatriots thought him a traitor—dung.

Reflections on "Dung Smells"

Our homeless are no longer out of sight. Men, women and children gather every day for food. Food can usually be found. Housing cannot...

Q: When you bypass a homeless person, what are your thoughts and feelings?

Take some time and honestly reflect on your initial responses to homeless persons. Write them out.

In Jesus response to the Roman soldier's faith he notes that *"many people will come from everywhere to enjoy the feast I the kingdom of heaven with Abraham, Isaac, and Jacob. But the ones who should have been in the kingdom will be thrown out in the dark"* (Matthew 5: 11-12).

Q: So how does Jesus description of who is 'in' and who is 'out' strike you?

Q: How should it affect the way we see our cities, our rural communities?

Think, confess, feel, pray.

Week-7: FRIDAY—NEHEMIAH 2: 1-4, 7-13, 19-20 & JOHN 4: 1-9

MY THOUGHTS 31—A TASTE OF YOUR OWN DUNG

The return of Israel from exile is an extraordinary tale similar in many respects to the 'Exodus Story' of the 19th and 20th centuries as modern Jews from the world over returned to what they perceived as their ancient homeland preceding and following the holocaust of Nazi Germany. This modern exodus from Europe is a story of Israel, once again the immigrant community returning in the emotional call of 'their homeland' and those in Palestine feeling increasingly threatened and displaced by this new wave of 'immigrants;' perceived strangers taking their land and jobs, destroying their own cultural heritage. To this day the world, especially Israel and the Palestinians, are living out the hostilities inherent.

It is the story of America and Europe who in very different circumstances are wrestling with immigrant populations seeking economic opportunity or political and religious refuge but who run into a wall (imagined and literal) of distrust, prejudice and hostility.

Nehemiah's return is no different. He seeks repatriation of his people to their homeland. They come in waves. Nehemiah was not the first and he will not be the last.

The tragedy inside this story is the mutual distrust and rejection of the Arabs and mixed races who now lived in what had once been Judea and Nehemiah's people in returning. In facing their hostility, Nehemiah makes it very clear that he does not fear the present inhabitants. He declares in their leaders hearing; *"The God of heaven will give us success!... As God's servants, we will start building"*. And then he makes abundantly clear that *"you will have no share, right, or claim in Jerusalem"* (Nehemiah 2: 20).

And so begins a 400 hundred year religious and cultural hostility between what Israel would call these half-breed Samaritans—as they saw them—and the entitled people of God now returning as legal immigrants to what they believe is their native land.

STORY 28—JACOB'S WELL

Introduction: A moment of rest when Mary and Joseph are making their way from Aunt Elizabeth and Uncle Zechariah's home back to Nazareth to face the perceived shame of Mary's immanent birth.

An Imagined Story from within a Biblical Context—A Prequel to John chapter 4...

Joseph helped Mary to find a place of rest near the well. He left her, the donkey and their belongings carefully nestled together and began his walk into Sychar to purchase food for the rest of their journey. Mary lay her head back to rest a little, thankful that the journey to Nazareth was almost done. She longed to see her mama and papa, knowing that Joseph's acceptance of her and her mission and Elizabeth's story would allow them to welcome her, unrestrained by social conventions.

'Yes,' Mary's thoughts rambled on, 'the wedding would have to be moved up so that God's son would be seen as the legitimate son of Joseph.' While it was considered a sign of weakness and an opportunity for gossip among the women of Nazareth, Mary took comfort in knowing that it would not be considered a sin, given their public betrothal. Mary smiled at her next thought. 'The irony of it all, Joseph was now in a Samaritan village buying food, and that, if their neighbors knew, would be considered the greater indiscretion!'

Samaritans and Jews were like cousins fighting for the same land and ownership of the spiritual heritage of the fathers. It was an old dispute now filled with prejudice, producing walls of distance. Good Jews would never pass through Samaria, but would instead take a much longer route to the east of the Jordan. 'But then,' Mary's thoughts continued on their sarcastic journey, 'we are not good Jews—only the ones chosen by God to raise the Messiah!' She giggled at the thought.

"May I help you?" Mary looked up and into the face of a very young and beautiful woman, whose eyes already looked tired and old. "Would you like a drink from Jacob's well?" Studying her face and seeing no sign of evil intent, Mary simply nodded, adding, "That would be nice, thank you." Mary was a little shocked that a Samaritan woman, this Samaritan woman, would speak to her, a conservative Jew, made obvious by the prayer tassels she was holding. She had taken them out to pray while Joseph went into the village.

Looking at this young girl, not any older than she, Mary noticed that she was dressed somewhat provocatively. 'I wonder why she is here at this hour?' Mary thought to herself, for she knew that women all over Palestine would come early in the morning, and together, to gather the day's water, not in the middle of the day when the sun is out, and never alone. "Here, take this." Mary received the gift and lifted it to her lips eagerly. The water was cold, freshly drawn, tasting pure and satisfying. Mary motioned for the woman to take a seat, asking for her name.

Hesitantly, Rebecca sat down, surprised at the kindness of this pregnant Jewess. However, it was not long before what each held in common overcame what divided them. They laughed over the chores that each was expected to do and the idiosyncrasies of their husbands. Mary had discovered that Rebecca had already been divorced and remarried. 'That,' Mary thought, 'probably explained the midday trips to the well, to avoid the judgments of the other women of the village.' Mary felt compelled to acknowledge that she and Joseph were only betrothed, knowing that her indiscretion, as Rebecca would have perceived it and Mary's willingness to confess it, only seemed to melt their instant friendship. Mary told Rebecca of Zechariah and Elizabeth and the mysteries surrounding John's birth. Only her own mystery did she keep from her, not wanting to shatter the trust between them.

"To blessed children, then!" Rebecca exclaimed, raising her cup as in a toast. Mary responded in kind, but added… "And may Yahweh give you this blessing. May you live to see the Messiah of God." Tears welled up in Rebecca's eyes, for never had she known such acceptance, even among her own, certainly not from a Jew who spoke to her as a daughter of Abraham.

Mary looked over Rebecca's shoulder and saw Joseph in the distance, climbing the hill. "There he is!" she declared with pride. With that, Rebecca quickly gathered her belongings and stood to leave. The wall between Jew and Samaritan once more asserted itself. Mary did not object, for she now knew Rebecca and understood her desire to avoid rejection by a Jewish man shocked by his betrothed's indiscretion. "Thank you, again," Mary said as Rebecca started to walk away. Rebecca stopped briefly, looking back and gave a responsive nod, her eyes moist with water. Then, she turned and made her way down the hill, head down, careful not too illicit a response from Joseph as they passed.

From: "The Advent of God through Mary—A Devotional Journey in the Christmas Season as Seen through Mary's Eyes," Week 3: Friday, by Terry Mattson

Reflections on "A Taste of Your Own Dung"

In Terry's Thoughts about Nehemiah's story he infers that Nehemiah's own perceptions, even prejudices, may have helped to shape the relations between the returning Jewish immigrants and those who had lived in the area surrounding old Jerusalem for generations.

Q: So what do you think? ...Are there always two sides in a dispute?

It should be noted that many of the people groups that made up what later became Samaria—Galilee were also displaced 'people groups' by the ancient power of Nineveh. Unlike Persia who tended to repatriate people groups back to their homelands, help them prosper and begin trade relations, Assyria purposely took peoples from their homelands and resettled them in other areas they had previously conquered and devastated by removing the original inhabitants en masse. Their purpose was to conquer and subjugate by delinking the land from the peoples they conquered.

Q: What is particularly difficult in this Biblical Story for the Jewish immigrants? ...for those who had lived there for a relatively brief time?

Finally, consider the imagined narrative between Mary and the Woman at the well.

Q: Of course this story probably didn't happen, but might it have? ...How might Mary and Joseph, themselves immigrants to Egypt, shaped Jesus own relation with those on the outside?

Q: What is the church's place today in the modern and epic political, social, cultural battles over immigrant populations in our own country?

Pray for your country and your own Church's mission within it.

.

Week-7: SATURDAY—MARK 11: 15-18

STORY 29—STEPPING IN DUNG?

A Personal Story—An early experience in cross-cultural and cross-racial mission

The clouds hung low over the whole city making real the threat that weather was playing with our Bible School mission at High Point Park.

There we were, thirty white people, kids mostly, at the center of old High Point—in those days typical of government projects throwing all the poor and racially mixed communities together in sub-standard housing, stacked on each other like timber being prepped for a fire.

Now, I was not entirely unaware of the tensions and realities of this place not six blocks from my own home, next door to our comfortable middle class and white neighborhood. The ominous clouds hanging quite literally over the whole of Seattle darkened the mood already present in a cultural and racial black and white tension that was evident by the presence of young would be gang bangers hanging around on the outside of the park, seated on their bikes, watching— as we were joyously unloading the backdrops, basketballs, theatre equipment, food and drink deeper into their hood. I wasn't feeling joy, but worry, as I watched those who were eyeing us, restrained only by the presence of their older brothers who were huddled just to the left of us, between the school and park.

I remember offering a prayer up to the heavens hoping it would rise above the clouds that were threatening. "God, help us—soften all our spirits!"

Slowly, cautiously the first kids came out from the shadows making their way past their own brothers on bikes, testing the green space. These few were quickly surrounded by the thirty teens of Kalispell Montana Nazarene church in laughter and Frisbee and tag just as the first rays of sunlight began to open the sky just above the park. Soon, more kids gathered changing the atmosphere or at least lowering the threat as we—Black, Samoan, Filipino and white kids were intermixed—hostages together. Even some of the would be gang bangers put down their bikes and walked over hanging out toward the back. My friend, Peni, who grew up in this project and had known the power of drugs and gangs and violence stood to greet all the kids and open in prayer.

As we walked off the field two hours later I felt the rush of witnessing a miracle, evidenced by two observations.

High Point is called that precisely because it is the highest point in Seattle. Driving away that evening and after clearing the housing area and park I looked up and noticed that all of Seattle remained covered by heavy dark clouds, except for the space immediately above High Point Park—it was bright with the remnant of sun.

It would be a week or two later that the second miracle emerged in the telling. About six months before I had visited a young man in Harborview Hospital who had been shot in the stomach, the result of gang violence. We talked and laughed and he let me pray for him. I was told that indeed there were older gang members present that evening two weeks before, but that they had been warned off by one of their own who simply said. "Leave this pastor alone. He's good. He came and visited me when I was in the hospital."

MY THOUGHTS 32—CROSSING THE RACIAL DIVIDE

Black lives matter—Blue lives matter—All lives matter…Which is it?

If you had asked me that question before spending 20 years of urban ministry I could have answered it easily. "All lives matter!" I would have said, adding… "duh, of course Black lives matter and cops matter—precisely because all lives matter."

That was long before I could feel and reflect in an urban environment my own prejudicial feelings when driving past African Americans wearing hoodies or feel what was for me, a new awareness of 'white privilege'.

Our church is made up of immigrant communities, primarily Samoan and Filipino. In each community pastors are esteemed and white pastors more so. When I'm seated next to my Samoan friend and pastor—Rev. Taulima Onge—who has dedicated his whole life to ministry and who holds a Seminary degree…I am quickly reminded that this white dude who never even completed his under-graduate work is always given first place at any table, white or Samoan. In conversations my brother will always wait till each white pastor has said their piece before he will speak and then only if asked. If we are waiting in line and I open the door to encourage him to go first he will pause and wait for me. If we walk into a restaurant the host or hostess will inevitably look to me and ask the question, "How many tonight?"

If I am seated on a bus no one lifts their head to observe another until three or four Samoans or African Americans happen to get on. Quietly, subtly the atmosphere changes. All eyes are up.

If I am shopping alone in any store I am unaware of eyes looking, but when I go in with my Samoan brothers I become keenly aware that security is ever observant.

So, you see, when my African American or Native American sisters and brothers hear me say... "All lives matter!" ...they want to cry out; "Don't you get it? That world doesn't exist. In your white privileged world all lives don't matter!" And when I retort that I'm merely saying that "all lives should matter" they are quick to point out that what I really mean is that "all lives should be valued just as ours obviously is."

Upon reflection, I think the Black Lives Matter movement gets it and clearly. Very often, even in our evangelical mission, we are leaving a subtle underlying message... "Come know our God who can love you as much as God loves us." **It is an arrogant 'I'm on top of this God thing' reaching down kinda message to those 'without God's kind of love' that fails to grasp the love of the One who on the cross felt the full sting of the Empire's rejection and asked "Why, God, have you rejected me?"**

The real problem with my High Point story is that God was forced to create a protective miracle to protect the hood from this white invasion of ignorant, but well-meaning do-gooders. Had we done it right, we would have simply and quietly moved in, making our home in High Point or partnered with a ministry from the hood and silently come alongside week by week instead of trying to do the 'big splash' thing whites love to do so much.

Reflection on the Text:

So what does this have to do with Jesus cleansing of the Temple? Everything!

Jesus frustration as remembered by Mark, focuses on the question of access to a quiet and holy place, especially for the Gentiles in the outer court yard and surrounded by the noise of business—even holy business. *"'Is it not written,'"* Mark is told that Jesus continued, *"'My house will be called a house of prayer for all nations'? But you have made it 'a den of robbers'"* (Mark 11:17).

One of the beautiful things about this ancient Temple of God is the nature of access for two groups lacking political or social power: Jewish women and lepers. Each had a space in the inner court, a point of access reserved for them—a kind of 'black lives matter' space that acknowledges simply being included in the 'all' doesn't quite get there—because the all is exclusive or privileged and not equal.

Reflections on "Stepping in dung?"

Black lives matter—Blue lives matter—All lives matter...Which is it?

Q: Which is it? ...Why?

Q: What do you think of Terry's point that the Black Lives Matter movement really gets it; That 'All Lives Matter' is another way of saying 'we like our white privileged place?'

Terry suggests that much of our love is really arrogant. We perceive ourselves on the 'inside' of God's love inviting others to our place of privilege instead of fully identifying with those who feel no privilege at all. Of the High Point mission:

> *"Had we done it right, we would have simply and quietly moved in, making our home in High Point or partnered with a ministry from the hood and silently come alongside week by week instead trying to do the 'big splash' thing whites love to do so much."* Terry

Q: Your thoughts?

Q: How might congregations that work through these issues be a 'living sign of Christ'?

Reflect and turn it all to prayer.

Week-7: SUNDAY— GENESIS 14: 17-20, II SAMUEL 5:6-10, ISAIAH 58: 5-12, JEREMIAH 29: 4-7, DANIEL 9: 1-19, LUKE 19: 41-48, REVELATION 21: 1-7

MY THOUGHTS 33— JERUSALEM'S MAGIC: HOPE FOR THE CITIES OF THE WORLD

We began this journey through the gates of Jerusalem by asking, "Are we there yet?" Having walked through the Dung gate and witnessed with Israel even a small portion of the continuous struggle, promise, successes, wealth, arrogance, sin, failure, wounds and destruction that have come through or within this gate we are inclined to ask a different question: "Will we ever get there?"

In moments of human history such as ours; when the cultures of the earth run straight into tyrants seeking to impose the final and eternal Caliphate and when weapons of mass destruction are within the reach of these whose apocalyptic (Iran, Isis) or irrational (North Korea) visions make their use seem probable, we are tempted to despair; to close our eyes and await our final destination. But we cannot hide, for each new day awakens us to yet another reminder that terror is exceedingly powerful even as relatively small pin pricks, a life here—ten there—for they carry in their womb the potential of a later Armageddon upon one of the cities of the earth. And so despair forms the question: "Does it all matter?" "Do our prayers and work for cities filled with peace, justice and abundance, with dance and joy make a difference?" Will the cities of Humankind become the places of Shalom imagined from the first pages of The Book in its first Creation narrative: "It is very good!" ...or will we always

267

live in the despair of a garden turned hostile, full of weeds and bugs and death as revealed in the third chapter of the book.

Perhaps that is why Jerusalem, as the City of God remains the eternal hope of three world religions. Each ask the same eternal question. "God, when, will You come and save us from ourselves?"

The last time God acted within the powerful forces of nature, all hell broke loose—save for Noah and his family and the animals that survived the deluge of angry water—and seemed the only response God could imagine; cleansing as it may have been. Then, according to this ancient story of Israel, God repented—changed directions—and began living into a new story of God's love filling the earth, of Jerusalem coming down to earth. And so God placed His bow and arrow in the sky, forever refusing violence as an answer and turned the water deluge into the promise of baptism— entering the deluge as the Son of the Living God in the waters of the Jordan.

And it is Jerusalem that keeps the promise of Shalom a living memory—a living hope. It is the Dung Gate and all of history's violence breaking into the hellish (Hinnom or Gehenna) valley below Jerusalem that becomes the very place of promise; of God's eventual return by way of the Eastern Gate.

From the pages of Hebrew Scriptures, we are introduced to this city's first Priest/King, Melchizedek and to its name, Salem (City of Peace). The Jebusites rename Salem, calling it Jerusalem. David captures it as part of a political attempt to unify the twelve tribes with neutral ground. But what transforms this terra forma into a heavenly city is one King who becomes a priest, David. He does it by three interweaving gifts; integrity, mystery and humility.

David is a war-lord, to be sure, but unlike most of the Kings of the Earth, he rises to be the ideal of most Kings; to be a shepherd to his people, Israel. The image of the Shepherd

King predates Israel at least as early as Sumer. But it is David who actually rises from within the trade craft to Shepherd his people. The mystery is revealed in the Psalms. *"God brought him from shepherding nursing ewes to shepherd his people Jacob, to shepherd his inheritance, Israel"* (Psalm 78: 71).

From his early shepherding David experiences the stars of the universe and is prompted to begin writing and playing the Psalms which form the heart and soul of Eternal Israel. Finally, it is his 11-year battle with the 1st King of Israel, Saul, and his refusal to by force take the kingdom that becomes the covenant of peace that allows all the tribes to make Jerusalem, the City of David, their capital, their Shalom.

With integrity, humility and worshiping mystery David's Israel makes one other extraordinary leap of faith. This city is to become the place of the Holy Temple and within the reach of God's Presence a city of Peace and reconciliation for all Israel's enemies. The beginnings of Eternal Jerusalem are captured in the peaceful rule of David's son, Solomon and celebrated by the Sons of the Korahites in Psalm 87. *"Glorious things are said about you, the city of God! I count Rahab and Babel among those who know me; also Philistia and Tyre, along with Cush—each of these were born there. And of Zion it is said: 'Each person was born in it, but the one who will establish is the Most High' "* (Ps 87: 3-5). And so King David's cry that these same enemies are destroyed evolves into a promise of blessed peace (Shalom) precisely because Israel's experience of God in David transcends the human David. God's bow and arrow (rainbow) in the sky gets a bit closer.

Centuries later the Christian church captures these promises for the whole world in the son of David, Jesus and by means of Jerusalem, the Eternal City. John envisions a city without walls as falling out of the heavens to a renewed earth free of pain and tears, full of justice. And we, especially in these troubled times, are invited to walk through Jerusalem's gates and back into the story of humankind as it is taken up into the Story of God!

In the centuries that have since passed Jerusalem has been subject to every political, moral, legal and violent intrigue; nearly destroyed twice. At one point it had no more than 200 people living among the fallen stones. Today, Jerusalem remains at the center of three religions, torn by their inter-weaving interests and vulnerable to terrorist threat, both state and state sponsored.

Even so, this weekend a Jewish Rabbi, a Muslim Inman and a Christian priest will repeat a ritual passing a key from one to another allowing access to holy places that are shared, as their fathers have going back centuries—to share a piece of land; in the hope of God's promise that every city in the world matters. Therein lies my own hope!

Reflections on "Jerusalem's Magic: Hope for the Cities of the World."

This week you have walked anew in the city or village. You have followed the passion of God who desires to renew everything and everyone... who sees no one as dung. Still you have been reminded of just how very far we are from John's vision of Jerusalem breaking into the cities and villages of this world.

Q: In what is your hope placed?

Q: Have you ever thought of God loving places as well as persons?

Q: How will this journey through the Dung Gate of Jerusalem affect your own experience in your city or village?

Reflect and turn it all to prayer.

Next:
It's a War!

8 IT'S A WAR!

... The Horse Gate

INVOCATION:

"FATHER, IF YOU ARE WILLING, TAKE THIS CUP FROM ME; YET NOT MY WILL, BUT YOURS BE DONE." AMEN.   LUKE 22:42.

PSALM OF THE WEEK: PSALM 3

COMMANDMENT OF THE WEEK: "YOU SHALL NOT COMMIT ADULTERY."

DEUTERONOMY 5: 18

DAILY SCRIPTURES:

MONDAY—REVELATION 12: 1-12

TUESDAY—JUDGES 4: 1-16 & 5: 1-3

WEDNESDAY—II CHRONICLES 22: 10-12 & 23: 1-19

THURSDAY—MATTHEW 4: 1-11

FRIDAY—LUKE 22: 31-34, 39-46

SATURDAY—LUKE 22: 47-62

SUNDAY—JEREMIAH 17: 19-27, ZECHARIAH 9: 9-10 & 12: 1-5, EPHESIANS 6: 10-17, II CORINTHIANS 6:1-10 & 12: 7-9, JOHN 13: 1-17, HEBREWS 4: 14-16, REVELATION 12: 13-17

FROM
MARK 3: 22

THE LEGAL EXPERTS CAME DOWN FROM JERUSALEM. OVER AND OVER THEY CHARGED, "HE'S POSSESSED BY BEELZEBUL. HE THROWS OUT DEMONS WITH THE AUTHORITY OF THE RULER OF DEMONS.

Week-8: MONDAY—REVELATION 12: 1-12

The Horse Gate

Nehemiah's Jerusalem

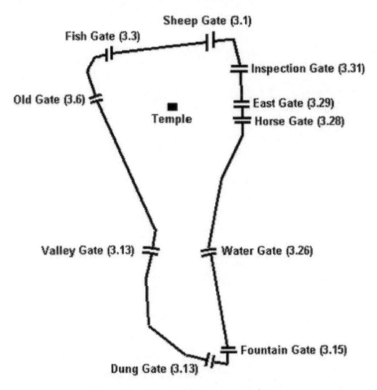

According to Nehemiah 3: 28 the Horse Gate was located between the Water Gate and the Sheep Gate and gave access to the King's stables, which are thought to be near or within the Temple compound.

MY THOUGHTS 34—WAR! WHAT IS IT GOOD FOR?

"This gate represents military strength or spiritual warfare. The actual Horse Gate was at the end of the bridge which led to the Temple of Zion. …The Horse Gate reminds us that a real battle exists for the souls of mankind. Gatekeepers are, above all else, warriors involved in spiritual warfare…

God is raising up churches to emphasize this spiritual warfare in the earth. They are good at training intercessors and many times host conferences or seminars to help newer believers through the 'boot camp' of Godly warfare."
From "Can You Feel the Mountains Tremble?", by Dr. Suuqiina, page #84

Many refer to our time as modernity; the age following the enlightenment in which reason and the scientific method replace mysticism. We moderns (and post-moderns) abhor the brutality of the ancients, but easily forget our own. We outlaw 'capital punishment' while turning a blind eye to the annihilation of ethnic and religious communities in our own world. We abhor the ancient sacrifice of children for economic reasons before the gods while perfecting the abortion of our own for many of the same reasons. And how easily we forget World War I and II, Pol Pot, Hitler, Sadam Hussein and Isis.

The Holy book is not blind to human brutality and intrigue. The Book lumps us all together as sons and daughters of our first parents, Adam and Eve. Their child, Cain, was a murderer. Near the beginning God chose not to take Cain's life as the penalty for killing his brother, choosing instead to isolate him and so protect our infant civilization from additional violence. Only later, after the flood and following a time of great violence, did God allow human societies to remove by death the 'guilty'.

The Bible, reflecting the cultural contexts in which it was written, makes war a central motif. In it, God and His universe is pictured as having fallen victim to the violence of one, Satan, an angelic being whose arrogance and deceit corrupted God's universe. The 'fall' into chaos lies at the heart of The Story, as God seeks to redeem Adam's race and through us, the universe from certain destruction (Eph 3: 10, 11).

Jesus indicated that living his life, with its commitment to 'radical peace', is possible only for those who are willing to approach the journey in peace as a 'war'. *"Do not suppose that I have come to bring peace to the earth. I did not come to bring peace, but a sword"* (Matt 10: 34). He further indicated that the Kingdom would come only to those who took it by force. Even so, Jesus was clear that ours is a different kind of war, waged not with weapons of destruction, but of right-relationship and good heart.

St. Paul picks up this same theme when he writes, *"By the meekness and gentleness of Christ, I appeal to you... For though we live in the world, we do not wage war as the world does. The weapons we fight with are not the weapons of the world. On the contrary, they have divine power to demolish strong- holds"* (II Cor 10: 1, 3-4).

Yes, we are in a war and are at war! But it is a war upside down, like no other. We win it by surrender and suffering, by good cheer in the face of seeming defeat. We win this war only by losing.

Pope Benedict captures the essence of our war in reflecting upon the sixth petition of the Lord's Prayer, "Lead us not into temptation." It is a strange request when we realize with James that no one should say *"when he is tempted, 'I am tempted by God'; for God cannot be tempted with evil and he himself tempts no one'"* (Jas 1: 13). Benedict goes on to remind that Jesus was 'led by the Spirit' into the wilderness to be tempted of the devil because:

> *"Jesus must suffer through these temptations to the point of dying on the Cross, which is how he opens the way of redemption for us. Thus, it is not only after his death, but already by his death and during his whole life, that Jesus 'descends into hell,' as it were, into the domain of our temptations and defeats, in order to take us by the hand and carry us upward."*
> From "Jesus of Nazareth", by Pope Benedict XVI, pages #160-164

So, in Jesus we too are led by the Spirit into a wilderness of trial or testing; possibilities designed by God to secure in us 'the Kingdom of God'. As Paul writes: *"The whole creation waits breathless with anticipation for the revelation of God's sons and daughters. Creation was subjected to frustration, not by its own choice—it was the choice of the one who subjected it—but in the hope that the creation itself will be set free from slavery to decay and brought into the glorious freedom of God's children"* (Romans 8: 19-21).

Reflections on "War! What is it Good For?"

Edwin Star wrote the lyrics and song that frames the question of this writing… "War! What is it good for?" His answer: "Absolutely nothing, except'n for the undertaker."

Like it or not, we are at war—within. God, of course, never intended war, but in creating beings capable of love most certainly foresaw the possibility that creation itself could enter war with one another and ultimately God. It is a cosmic war with eternal consequence.

Q: How does this strike you?

The Bible makes war a central motif. In it, God and the universe is pictured as having fallen victim to the violence of one, Satan, an angelic being whose arrogance and deceit corrupted God's universe. The 'fall' into chaos lies at the heart of The Story, as God seeks to redeem Adam's race and through us, the universe itself from decay—restoring the Shalom described in the first account of creation.

> "God's purpose is now to show the rulers and powers in the heavens the many different varieties of his wisdom through the church. This was consistent with the plan he had from the beginning of time that he accomplished through Christ Jesus our Lord"
>
> (Ephesians 3: 10-11).

Q: Have you ever thought about your spiritual struggles having cosmic impact? …What do you think?

Q: So what kind of war have you ever know, if any? …Whom does it affect and how?

Reflect and turn it all to prayer.

Week-8: TUESDAY—JUDGES 4: 1-16 & 5: 1-3

MY THOUGHTS 35—ON WOMEN & SALVATION HISTORY

The 'first lady' of the human race, Eve, fell prey to the 'war of worlds'. Satan deceived her and she Adam. In Adam all the sons of men and daughters of women taste death— separation from God.

In Catholic theology Mary, the mother of our Lord, becomes the queen of heaven and earth. She is the woman in John's vision who battles with the dragon. From her womb the Savior of the universe and His Church was born. Through her obedience God, the Son, reclaims all of Eve's daughters and Adam's sons.

Deborah, in the time of the Judges, is a type of Mary; one of the daughters of Eve from whom destruction is reversed and salvation flows. With humility she offers to Barak, her military champion, the honor of battle. But he refuses the honor, willing to risk his all only under the banner of Deborah's initiative.

Deborah and Mary give us a living picture of the Holy Spirit, the third Person of the Trinity of God. Like these women, the Holy Spirit is humble and self-effacing, always receiving and nurturing, never initiating.

From the Father—Son, the Holy Spirit pours out holy—love and becomes the nurturing womb from which God's Story is born. In the opening verse of The Book the Spirit forms from chaos the universe. The Holy Spirit is present in each unfolding revelation. The Spirit is uniquely present in the birth of Jesus, by Mary (Luke 1: 35). In the world the Spirit walks along side of each/all of us, forming in us the place of God's dwelling. In the Holy Spirit we are nurtured and fed.

Our relation to God is intended to be that of a woman before her lover. We are the bride of Christ. The Father—Son initiate and by the Holy Spirit in us, Jesus life, death, passion and resurrection are formed. Like these women of old we become vessels through whom God's Story takes form.

Reflections "On Women & Salvation History"

"Our relation to God is intended to be that of a woman before her lover. We are the bride of Christ."
Terry (above)

Terry is suggesting that the feminine-masculine in nature expresses something about the relation of the Father—Son—Spirit, with the Spirit taking on the more historically feminine quality of responding, not initiating—of nurturing, not commanding.

Q: Your thoughts and feelings?

Q: Have you ever thought of your relationship with God as that of a woman before her lover? ...How would that change the way you engage God before engaging the world?

Q: If true, how does this idea effect or affect the way we see women in 'salvation history'?

Q: Which women have played a significant role in nurturing your own faith? How so?

Offer a prayer of thanks to God for the women in your own life who have formed you. Then offer the same prayer for some of the women of The Book who have shaped The Story of God.

Week-8: WEDNESDAY—JOSHUA 3: 1-17

MY THOUGHTS 36—WAR TURNED INSIDE OUT

The Horse Gate's Memory:

"When Ahaziah's mother Athaliah saw that her son was dead, she took over. She began by massacring the entire royal family."
(II Chronicle 22: 10a The Msg)

This is an exciting Story of intrigue, corruption and treason all centered around the right of ascension of a child King—in waiting. It is worthy of the best in fanciful novels. In a time of Judah's struggle between two competing political families— one devoted to the ways of the Temple and one passionate about embracing a new and culturally diverse future—a corrupt Queen had taken over the throne by killing her grand-children. It was Jehosheba, daughter of a wicked King, Jehoram and sister to the Queen (Athaliah) and wife of Jehoiada, the priest (talk about mixed influences) who protected Joash from the murderous Queen Athaliah. Joash was a grand-child of a righteous King who had devoted himself to the Lord. So Joash was kept safely hidden away for six years in The Temple of God. Athaliah oblivious to his existence, ruled the country.

Athaliah is the living picture of a wicked queen who is willing to sacrifice her family, even her grandsons and potential future Kings, in order to capture and keep power. She overcomes all her enemies, save one, the child. (It is a pre-story of Herod and Jesus.) She is bested, however, by her sister in law, Jehosheba, who has chosen the way of the priestly office through her husband. (Again, sound familiar?)

Jehosheba responds to the treachery by hiding the child (the rightful King) until the day of God's choosing. Jehosheba acts, courageously and prayerfully and saves the Kingdom in the process.

Only now can we begin to see the true nature of our battle. The usual weapons of this 'heavenly war of worlds' are born of independence and arrogance. Like Queen Athaliah, we each/all take up our swords to do battle and so define ourselves as separate, indeed better than one another.

Even the Church falls prey to this temptation, as witnessed in the Crusades or in modernity; usually by way of using political means for spiritual ends. This is not the way of our Lord, however. Huckabee had it right when he suggested that Jesus was just too smart to run for political office.

Instead, Jesus invites the church to surrender and become weak. In the center of our ego starved identity he wants to make himself a 'servant king' and us with him (John 13: 1-17).

As the Holy Spirit awakens us to our real need and mission, we are invited (never pushed) to lay down arms and surrender our rights. We are invited to love our enemies and befriend those who would misuse us.

As we obey, we are quickened to respond like a lover to the wonderment of a God who walks among us in the clothes of the:

o poor, or;
o homosexual, or;

- single mother, or;
- mentally slow, or;
- unborn child, or;
- the aged.

As we respond to God with us we are transformed inwardly and taken up into the Jesus Story.

- ➤ Through weakness, power.
- ➤ Through surrender, self-control.
- ➤ Through service, we govern.
- ➤ Through grace, we are saved.

This is the genius of the Biblical Story!

An epilogue: And so, how did the story of Joash turn out? By intrigue the High Priest gathered on one day Levites and the heads of the clans into Jerusalem and in the Holy Temple declared Joash, son of David, King over Judah.

The queen ran into the temple, tore her clothes and cried out "Treason!" The soldiers who were in league with the High Priest pursued her out of Temple and once she had entered under the Horse Gate, killed her.

The reason is simple. The political murder could not take place in the Holy Place of God. Even in ancient Israel there are hints of the nature of the victory to come; not by sword but in the laying down of the very Son of God, Son of David to the cruelty of the Empire.

Reflections on "War Turned Inside Out"

As we obey, we are quickened to respond like a lover to the wonderment of a God who walks among us in the clothes of the:

- *poor, or;*
- *homosexual, or;*
- *single mother, or;*
- *mentally slow, or;*
- *unborn child, or;*
- *the aged.*

  As we respond to God with us we are transformed inwardly and taken up into the Jesus Story.

  Terry (above)

Q: Has God ever come to you dressed up as one of these?

Q: How did you respond?

Consider how God continues to walk among us in the most vulnerable surrounding. Listen for God.

Week-8: THURSDAY— MATTHEW 4: 1-11

STORY 30—THE DRAMA OF THE AGES

An Imaginative and playful (if not quite Biblical) Story— When Good & Evil Finally Meet...

based upon Matthew 4: 1-11

He sat across from him unseen. The now familiar music filled the auditorium of the ages with drama; light'ning flashed! The evil one stepped into the arena and took his seat. The Game show of eternity,' Who Wants to Be A god?', had begun.

With deep, dark eyes the evil one turned his attention to this Jesus of Nazareth. Jeshua looked exhausted and hungry. 'Not a very impressive sight', the host of the universe's most famous game show thought.

Then he spoke. "You alone have been selected by the," he hesitated, for he knew he could not pronounce His Name, holy and righteous, stumbling ever so slightly he continued, "By the One who calls Himself, ...well, shall we say, you have been selected to play. Now you know the game. You have three life lines. Prayer and self-denial, which I would remind you've already used in these last forty days. You have one life line left. The Word of the..."

Again, the evil one, host of the ages, hesitated and thought, 'He must find a way to properly pronounce 'The Name,' a name that eons earlier had fallen so easily from his lips.

Choking, he continued. "The Word, which you have not used…Now, tell me, Jeshua, how are you feeling?"

For the first time, the young man sitting across from this angel of darkness looked up. He did not speak. He did not need to. His body cried out for him. "I am hungry."

The host continued. "Are you?," followed by a brief cough and resetting; "Question number one. Are you truly the son of God? If you are prove it."

Behind this young Galilean the most beautiful music emerged, filling this vast arena. Light, soft and silhouetted, moved across the floor. The sand stone rocks in front of him looked real and inviting, like the freshly baked bread his Mary would make. Selection A came upon the screen. "Is it A: Command these rocks to become bread?", the evil one asked, a subtle sneer could be detected in his voice.

From in front of and just underneath, Jesus heard the sounds of city life awakening to a new day. Another light, brilliant and white flooded the scene below him. He found himself seated on a high wall. He recognized it as the holy temple. Below him, on the outside of the wall was a vendor baking bread. The fragrance now reached his aching body, luring him to take the bread and eat.

How he longed to do just that.

With some difficulty, Jesus stood up, his body barely able to keep balance from exhaustion and hunger; and walking over to the edge lingered, dizzy, longing for just one taste of the bread below, 'almost,' he thought, 'within reach.' Selection B now emerged on the screen behind him. The host read the words. "If you are the son of God, jump off! …and." The host now stood and moved alongside his contestant and through a low guttural laughter continued; "I'll tell you what. I'll give you a hint from your third life line. "Do not scriptures say… 'He will command his angels concerning you, and they will lift you up in their hands, so that you will not strike your foot against a stone?'"

Jesus could not hear the audience, though he knew they were there. Dark eyes by the millions awaited his response. More than a few souls' eternal destiny hung in the balance. The stakes of this game were indeed high.

The host continued. "So you have it, only two responses, A and B. We have eliminated the other two as an expression of our joy at witnessing this most auspicious moment." His eyes, glazed with hatred, glared into Jesus.

Again, the aroma of baked bread surrounded Jesus. For the first time he looked directly at his host and spoke.

"It is written. Man does not live by bread alone, but on every word that comes from the mouth of YHWH."

The evil one shuddered within. How he hated that Name, the one he could no longer pronounce.

Turning from his host and looking again over the high wall, Jesus continued. "It is also written: 'Do not put the LORD your God to the test."

Suddenly darkness filled the theater. An eerie silence enveloped the space that moments earlier had smelled of bread and the sounds of Jerusalem.

Slowly a new light filled the vast darkness and in front of them, Jesus could see all the kingdoms of the world. The evil one had withdrawn back to the chair. Jesus stood alone, high atop what seemed a mountain.

The host spoke. "Okay, so you are the son. I have one more opportunity. All that you see, I will give you, if you will bow down and worship me. You will not have to wait until your Father allows. You will not have to suffer. The world will be at peace and this war of the ages at an end. Think of the opportunity I am giving—Shalom!"

The thought of bowing to this darkness repelled Jesus. How he longed to escape this charade and return to the cavern in which had been praying. Lifting his hand and pointing to the evil, Jesus spoke as though commanding him. "Away from me, Satan! For it is written: 'Worship the LORD your God, and serve him only.'"

Then the devil slid away; The sounds and smells and sights of the desert returning. Angels of light came to him. Real light, not like the images of light against the blank screen he had just witnessed. And the warmth of their light comforted him.

Reflections on "The Drama of the Ages"

Q: What reoccurring temptation, if any, troubles you? ...Why that one?

Q: Are you more vulnerable to the hungers of the flesh or temptations to power or questions of identity?

On the night Jesus confronted Peter with his immanent betrayal by denying he knew Jesus, he comforted him by assuring Peter of his eventual restoration and then added that he had prayed for him.

Jesus is—right now—at the right hand of the Power of God praying for you and me.

Write out what you think that prayer might be in this season of your life. Then give thanks.

Week-8: FRIDAY—LUKE 22: 31-34, 39-46

MY THOUGHTS 37—JESUS WAR—THE HELL OF LOVE

> *"Christ's prayer in the garden of Gethsemane is the noblest of all prayers by its virtue and power to atone for the sins of the world… Victorious in eternity, Christ's love on the earthly plane spells extreme suffering. No one has ever known such suffering as Christ endured. He descended into hell, into the most painful hell of all, the hell of love."*
> From Archimandrite Sophrony in "His Life is Mine", page #91

It is in the garden that we see most clearly the high priestly ministry of Christ, as He who is from glory, anticipates the cost of His full descent into the human story; what Sophrony calls the 'Hell of Love'.

At the center of 'salvation history' is the reality that we—the sons of Adam and daughters of Eve—are all connected. We are really one tribe, yes, but it is more. It is like we are the individual cells that make up one body—the human family.

In Jesus, then, God is both the Creator of each individual cell and enters God's own Creation as a healthy cell—made healthy not by righteousness but by our sin and chaos. Jesus becomes the anti-body by 'becoming sin' in order that we might become the 'righteousness of God.' As Paul put it: *"God caused the one who didn't know sin to be sin for our sake so that through him we could become the righteousness of God"* (II Corinthians 5: 22).

Five moments in the life of Jesus form the cross from which our salvation flows. Not only our salvation, but that of the whole universe.

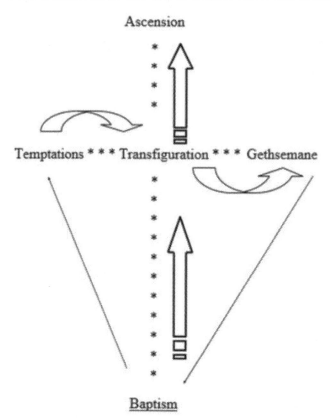

Ascension

Temptations * * * Transfiguration * * * Gethsemane

Baptism

Into the abyss of human need Jesus descended by means of the baptism. His call affirmed in the likeness of a dove, the Spirit delivers him into the evil one's hand

for forty days. We, with him, emerge into his life and mission. On the mountain of God's choosing, Jesus is transfigured. This is the center of the story and where Israel's past, baptized in Moses and tested in Elijah, meet with her Creator, Jeshua (JAWEH).

From this moment of transfiguration Jesus again descends and sets his face toward Jerusalem and to a garden just beyond her gates. For this very night Jesus came into the world. All of the enemies of God gather at Gethsemane, crushing down this Son of God, now Son of man. From the weight of this human drama the wine of salvation flows.

Having drunk the cup, Jesus once again ascends another mount, the Mount of Olives, where his glorified presence is taken back into the heavens. Only now we are with him and in him. He, the Son of Man and the cross may now be fully formed in us. As the Son of Man he rises to the heavens, one who is able to sympathize with us in all our temptations (Hebrews 4:15).

Reflections on "Jesus War—the Hell of Love"

"Up to the time of the Transfiguration, our Lord had exhibited the normal, perfect life of a Man; after the Transfiguration everything is unfamiliar to us. From the Transfiguration onwards, we are dealing not so much with the life our Lord lived as with the way in which he made it possible for us to enter into His life. On the Mount of Ascension the Transfiguration was completed, and our Lord went back to His primal glory; but He did not go back simply as Son of God: He went back as Son of Man as well as Son of God. That means there is freedom of access now for anyone straight to the very throne of God through the ascension of the Son of Man. At His ascension our Lord entered Heaven, and He keeps the door open for humanity to enter."

From "The complete Works of Oswald Chambers", page #681

In all of his descriptions of salvation history Terry seems to suggest that it is the actual life of Jesus that is to be formed in us—between us; that Jesus life becomes the 'stuff of our individual and communal lives'.

Q: Have you ever thought of the Christian life in this way? ...If true, what are the implications?

Q: How might the idea of 'salvation history' effect and affect the way you see your own spiritual struggle?

Q: How might the idea of 'salvation history' effect and affect the way you see your life within the salvation of 'all things'?

Consider where you are, in this moments, within the five movements of Jesus life?

- ➢ **Baptism** as Identity in Christ
- ➢ **Temptation** as Spiritual War
- ➢ **Transfiguration** as Transformation
- ➢ **Gethsemane** as Full Surrender
- ➢ **Ascension** as Holiness

Q: Where are you in this moment?

Q: If you were Jesus, where would you lead you next? ...Why?

Turn it all to prayer. Listen for God.

Week-8: SATURDAY—LUKE 22: 47-62

STORY 31—RISING FROM THE SHADOWS OF FAILURE

An Imaginative Biblical Story—Peter's failure...

based upon Luke 22: 47-62

Peter woke up his body drenched in sweat, his heart pounding—fear still pushing him like a potent Psilocybin (mushrooms) against his body's need for sleep, for respite from the nights dark shadows. Peter's eyes darted around gathering information from the real world, for just a moment grateful that what he had just experienced was not real. In the nightmarish moments before awakening to the shadows of Jerusalem's pre-dawn morning—it looked to Peter like, maybe the 10th hour (4 a.m.) given the mix of light on the horizon almost ready to break in—his memory from the events of the evening before flooding back in.

The anxiety had first tumbled in upon him during the celebration of Passover when Jesus said—in front of all— that he, The Rock, Simon of Bethesda—would deny ever knowing him. Like waves against the rocky caverns of Galilee's Sea the images poured over him; The sword and rebuke by Jesus, fear, running, staying near but out of sight and then—denying.

Peter gathered his cloak tightly about him, his shame returning in the awakening. 'Perhaps', his thoughts troubled him further, 'the demons within his nightmare were still with him.' Just before awakening Peter saw himself lying, crouched like an infant in his mother's womb when he looked up and over him were six venomous snakes—cobras— striking at him, each in turn.

As if to shake off the images Peter body shuddered and he sat up, now fully awakened to his surroundings, an alley way in the heart of the old city, his back against the inner wall of a courtyard.

Then Peter remembered another thing as he now mentally began to replace the steps leading to this foreboding place. 'How,' he wondered, 'did it come to this? How could he?' But an even deeper fear seized him; 'Run!' And so, Peter made his way out of the alley into the eerie silence of a Palestinian night, his eyes darting about for signs of movement in the cold stillness. 'But where?' his thoughts raced. 'If only he could access water and end it all—water! ...of course, the Holy Temple and pool of Bethesda.' With renewed energy Peter made his way to the Temple and to the pool that carried a double meaning in both Hebrew and Aramaic; shame and mercy, disgrace and grace. 'For me,' Peter's dark thoughts ore whelmed, 'its waters would end his shame as he deserved no mercy.'

Minutes later Peter found himself alone in the Temple courts, now hiding in the shadows. Looking around for any guards, by stealth he made his way over to the Pool of Bethesda, where Jeshua had healed the paralytic man. As Peter leaned over the pool. His mind reflected on the betrayal of the one Jeshua had healed that day. 'Had not the paralytic Jeshua healed also betrayed him there?' It had been Sabbath and in order to save himself from being rejected by the Temple authorities, he had turned on Jeshua, the one who healed him, and pointed the authorities in his direction. 'How he had wanted...,' Peter remembered, ...'had wanted to spit on the paralytic for his ungrateful cowardess—Who's the real coward?' Peter's troubled conscience objected; 'had he not followed Jeshua for the last three years?'

For a very long moment, he simply stared into the water, feeling its invitation to death and reprieve—'indeed, mercy from these haunting memories!'—when suddenly a powerful gust of wind filled the Temple. Peter looked up and around. The light of the moon glistened on the waters of the pool revealing a stirring within them. Peter knew the ancient belief, that healing would come to those who entered its waters while the angel stirred them. But within Peter was an older, darker understanding of water's power; the home of the gods and demons of the underworld. Instinctively, he dove in, totally immersed. At first he ceased all effort, hoping the waters might become a tomb ending his tortured soul.

Then, his body took over and he struggled to straighten himself up, and rise above the waters for breath. He stood, strength filling his limbs; and then collapsed once again into the shallow waters to his knees. Peter cried out, to no one; "I do not have the courage of suicide as I do not have the courage of faith," his hands covering his face as to hide his renewed shame. *"Simon, Simon,"'* Peter remembered and with it the feeling of hurt that always accompanied when Jesus called him by his given name. It was as if Jesus was reminding him that before he was Peter, the rock, he was another. His memory continued; *"'Look! Satan has asserted the right to sift you all like wheat. However, I have prayed for you that your faith won't fail."'* As if by magic, a sense of calm suddenly came over him as remembered anew Jesus prophecy, *"'When you have returned, strengthen your brothers and sisters"* (Italics from Luke 22: 31-32). When I have returned,' Peter's mind recounted again.

As the first ray of morning light had just broken through the high colonnades surrounding the pool, Peter slowly gathered himself and stood preparing to leave the darkness of the water's invitation; leaving the shame, renewed in grace. 'But where?' he asked himself. 'To the place where it began. John Marc's home—but not yet'. He must first go to Gethsemane and think and perhaps, pray.

Reflections on "Rising from the Shadows of Failure"

"Simon, Simon, look! Satan has asserted the right to sift you all like wheat. However, I have prayed for you that your faith won't fail. When you have returned, strengthen your brothers and sisters."
Luke 22: 31-32

On the night Jesus confronted Peter with his immanent betrayal by denying he knew Jesus, he comforted him by assuring Peter of his eventual restoration and then added that he had prayed for him.

Jesus is—right now—at the right hand of the Power of God praying for you and me.

Write out what you think that prayer might be in this season of your life. Then give thanks.

Week-8: SUNDAY—JEREMIAH 17: 19-27, ZECHARIAH 9: 9-10 & 12: 1-5, EPHESIANS 6: 10-17, II CORINTHIANS 6:1-10 & 12: 7-9, JOHN 13: 1-17, HEBREWS 4: 14-16, REVELATION 12: 13-17

MY THOUGHTS 38—THE REAL WAR

I don't think my grandson, Sammy, was much more than a year old when I received the first Instagram showing him seated, alone and snuggled firmly in a child's saddle on top of a huge horse—a beautiful and graceful animal inhabiting God's creation—his dad standing proudly by, ready to protect as needed. Sammy is now two and has been in two horse shows to date. Frankly, I am grateful he will grow up in the rugged heritage and independence that surrounds horses.

The Horse Gate in Jerusalem had little to do with Israel's spiritual and mystical center of worship and more to do with its political world; as it gave access to the Kings of Israel to their stables and to the Temple. Horses were and are signs of wealth and power; of independence—indeed war.

One of the poignant images in Israel's prophetic history is that of the Messiah coming into David's City, his City, riding on a donkey—not a horse—and entering through the Gate Beautiful, or the Eastern gate.

The donkey in ancient times was the symbol of peace. When a ruler came into a city on a donkey it simply meant that he came in good will and with peaceful intent. But when he came to the city riding on a horse it meant war usually—or at least the threat of war. The horse was a sign of a powerful and conquering warrior.

In the Kings of Israel David rides on a horse and Solomon a donkey. David is the warrior king, Solomon the diplomat who rules in wisdom.

We live in a world ruled by horses, not donkeys. Women and men seek power, most often it seems for powers sake. Even the church has historically seemed to come into new geographical and spiritual territories riding on a horse as was the case in the Crusades and in most of the missionary efforts of the 17th-19th centuries. A sword often accompanied the church. The practical Horse Gate in ascendance.

Jesus vision was radically different:

- ➤ Through weakness, power.
- ➤ Through surrender, self-control.
- ➤ Through service, we govern.
- ➤ Through grace, we are saved.

Each of us battle somewhere. We are at war within ourselves to determine if we will ride on a donkey in peaceful surrender to Holy—Love or a horse asserting our own insecure, addicted ego needs.

As we respond to God with us we are transformed inwardly and taken up into the Jesus Story until finally, in the end, God's Kingdom is welcome in the earth as it is in Heaven.

This is our only hope as individuals, cultures and as a human family.

Reflections on "The Real War"

"The personal Holy Spirit builds us up into the body of Christ. All that Jesus came to do is made ours experimentally by the Holy Spirit."

From "The complete Works of Oswald Chambers", page #681

Jesus vision is radically different:

> ➤ Through weakness, power.
> ➤ Through surrender, self-control.
> ➤ Through service, we govern.
> ➤ Through grace, we are saved.

Q: Which of these phrases best reflect what God has been doing in your life?

...How so? ...Describe it.

Q: What is left undone?

In Ephesians 6 Paul lists a number of pieces of armor for us to wear about our lives.

Q: Which of these do you possess in good measure?
...Which need repair or perhaps, to acquire?

> ➤ Confessional Honesty
> ➤ A Heart longing for the good and right
> ➤ Quick to pursue Peace in all relations
> ➤ Identity firmly set in Jesus
> ➤ Faith
> ➤ Word of God
> ➤ Prayer

Listen quietly now to God the Father—Son—Spirit. From this place, go.

Next:

Hope

9 HOPE

... The Eastern Gate

INVOCATION:

FATHER. FROM BEFORE TIME YOU SAW OUR WOUNDED AND REBELLIOUS SPIRIT. FROM BEFORE TIME YOU, TOGETHER WITH THE SON-SPIRIT COMMITTED TO OUR RE-CREATION, BY THE SACRIFICE OF LOVE, THE LAMB OF GOD.

THANK YOU FOR THE LAMB, JESUS, WHO IS WORTHY TO OPEN THE SCROLLS OF TIME AND BRING BACK MEN AND WOMEN *"FOR GOD, FROM EVERY TRIBE AND LANGUAGE AND PEOPLE AND NATION"*. THANK YOU FOR MAKING US A PEOPLE WHOSE LIVES COUNT, PRIESTS WHO SERVE GOD AND THE NATIONS.

"WORTHY IS THE LAMB, WHO WAS SLAIN, TO RECEIVE POWER AND WEALTH AND WISDOM AND STRENGTH AND HONOR AND GLORY AND PRAISE!"

WE, YOUR CHURCH WILL SAY THE AMEN, FALL DOWN AND WORSHIP HIM WHO IS, WHO WAS AND WHO IS TO COME! AMEN.

BASED UPON REVELATION 5
NOTE: ITALICS ABOVE FROM REV 5: 9B, 12B

PSALM OF THE WEEK: PSALM 100

COMMANDMENT OF THE WEEK: "YOU SHALL NOT STEAL".
DEUTERONOMY 5: 19

DAILY SCRIPTURES:

MONDAY—EZEKIEL 1: 1, 25-28 & 2: 1-4, 9-10 & 3: 1-3 & 4: 1-7 & 5: 8 & 6: 8-10

TUESDAY—EZEKIEL 8: 1–18 & 10: 4-5, 18-22 & 11: 1-6, 22-25

WEDNESDAY—LUKE 14: 1-23

THURSDAY—LUKE 19: 28-48

FRIDAY—PHILIPPIANS 2: 1-11

SATURDAY—II CORINTHIANS 5: 1-21

SUNDAY 1—ZECHARIAH 14: 1-9, LUKE 21: 20-28, JOB 19: 23-27, REVELATION 5: 8-14

FROM
LUKE 2: 25

A MAN NAMED SIMEON WAS IN JERUSALEM. HE WAS RIGHTEOUS AND DEVOUT. HE EAGERLY ANTICIPATED THE RESTORATION OF ISRAEL, AND THE HOLY SPIRIT RESTED ON HIM.

Week-9: MONDAY—EZEKIEL 1: 1, 25-28 & 2: 1-4, 9-10 & 3: 1-3 & 4: 1-7 & 5: 8 & 6: 8-10

The Golden Gate, as it is called in Christian literature, is the oldest of the current gates located in Jerusalem's Old City Walls. Jews used to pray for mercy at the gate, hence the name Sha'ar Harachamim, the Gate of Mercy. In Arabic, it is known as the Gate of Eternal Life. In ancient times, the gate was known as the Beautiful Gate.

The modern version of the Gate was probably built in the 520s CE, as part of Justinian I's building program in Jerusalem, on top of the ruins of an earlier gate in the wall. An alternate theory holds that it was built in the later part of the 7th century by Byzantine artisans employed by the Umayyad khalifs.

The gate is located in the middle of the eastern side of the Temple Mount. The portal in this position was believed to have been used for ritual purposes in biblical times.

In Jewish tradition, this is the gate through which the Messiah will enter Jerusalem. Ottoman Sultan Suleiman I sealed off the Golden Gate in 1541 to prevent the Messiah's entrance. The Muslims also built a cemetery in front of the gate, in the belief that the precursor to the Messiah, Elijah, would not be able to pass through, since he is a Kohen. This belief is erroneous because a Kohen is permitted to enter a cemetery in which primarily non-Jews are buried.

The Golden Gate is one of the few sealed gates in Jerusalem's Old City Walls, along with the Huldah Gates, and a small Biblical and Crusader-era postern located several stories above ground on the southern side of the eastern wall.

Note: Information summarized from Wikipedia

STORY 32—RETURNING FROM EXILE

A Personal Story—Hope Returned...

Written in September 1999, lifted from devotional notes reflecting on events years earlier while enjoying a meal

I was sitting in a restaurant in Vancouver, Washington. I had been reading, thinking and meditating.

The waitress was good to me. She had brought me a glass of ice water and a second glass filled with ice. I would transfer the ice water into the glass stuffed with ice, never allowing the water to rise even close to the top of the ice. When finally chilled, I would drink from the water, cold and refreshing.

My days of wandering in a spiritual desert of thirsty lust were forever behind me. Barely, behind me, but forever, I knew. God was again speaking within.

In the year or two previous to my recovery God had removed everything I held precious, save Joetta, my wife. My sin had taken from me the ministry and a place of spiritual leadership in my church and community. God, my heavenly Father had stripped me in His loving anger. Worst of all, The Spirit had stopped speaking within. All was a dark silence.

I had thought I would never again enter the ministry. It was all gone. Still, as I sat reflecting—looking back—a tear of joy began to fall down my cheek.

This morning I had been reading from Romans, chapter eight. The text suddenly captured my attention. *"Who shall separate me from the love of God?"* (Rom 8: 35), Paul had asked.

It was then that I saw the truth of my recent journey. It was clear and pure and felt as fresh in my soul as the perfectly chilled glass of water would in my mouth. 'God had never abandoned me,' I thought. As I continued the meditation I became aware that the Trinity of God's dark silence was like that of a good friend who listens as you pour out your heart. The silence is respectful, quiet, aware that there are no words of comfort. My own complaint, like David's was like a broken record or scratched CD. *"Will the LORD reject forever? Will he never show his favor again? Has God forgotten to be merciful?"* (Psalm 77:7).

Angry with me God had been. "Terry," The Spirit had spoken on one day. "If you do not repent. If you do not stop hurting Joetta, I will destroy you!" Never before, nor since have I felt such anger. There was no animosity, only a sad and powerful determination to protect Joetta from me. I got the message and responded.

But on that day in that restaurant, in a land of spiritual exile and humbled, I realized another thing. My prayer, given at an altar, years earlier had been answered. All my life I had tended towards anxiety, compulsive and crippling. In desperation, I had sought the help of the Lord. And now it dawned on me. I could not imagine a worse series of events than those I had just lived through. I had lost everything and especially the trust of the church in ministry. But now I was past it. Peace as I had never known had reigned in my life in the months following God's gracious restoration of fellowship within. My whole world knew of my sin, but God had not abandoned me.

What I did not then know was that in the near future I would again serve my church, first on the board and then as a worship leader. Before a board of twenty-five my pastor, Galen Olsen, would affirm my life and my friends and peers would all stand and applaud me. For what? For failing God and them?

The meditation of Ann Julian of Norwich—a thirteenth century mystic—had become true in a measure, even in this life.

> *"Also, God showed that sin shall not be a shame to man, but a glory. For just as every sin brings its own suffering, by truth, so every soul that sins earns a blessing by love. ...For the soul that comes to heaven is so precious to God, and the place so holy, that God in his goodness never allows a soul that reaches heaven to sin without also seeing that those sins have their reward. And the soul is known to God forever and joyfully restored with great glory.*
>
> *...And then God brought happily to my mind David and others without number from the Old Law, and in the New Law he brought to my mind first Mary Magdalene, Peter and Paul, and those of India, and St. John Beverley—and also others without number. And he showed how the Church on earth knows of them and their sins, and it is no shame to them, but is all turned to their glory."*
>
> From "The Joy of the Saints", by Robert Llewelyn, page #205

In this single moment of meditation at a restaurant in Vancouver, I did not know, nor could I, the full extent of restoration God had in mind. All I knew then was that God had indeed been gracious to me. Never again would I place my trust in me or my talent or my commitment to Jesus or my calling from Him.

My trust would ever and only be in the One who did not leave me, when I deserved to have been left.

A quiet peace had marked the last months of my life. God, even in and through my sin, had answered my desperate prayer.

Reflections on "Returning From Exile"

Exile is where Israel is as the book of Ezekiel is opened. Glory has been lost and with it all hope. But in the midst of its exile and in a land far away from home, God would speak, through His prophet, one Ezekiel. Ezekiel would speak of 'glory lost' and 'glory restored.'

Terry paints a picture in which God is passionate; silent, angry, personal and always present. He speaks of a 'season' of loss, in which God uses even his sins to answer his hearts cry for 'peace'.

Consider your own life:

Q: Have you seen the 'hand of God' at work in your life? How so?

> *"Also, God showed that sin shall not be a shame to man, but a glory. For just as every sin brings its own suffering, by truth, so every soul that sins earns a blessing by love…*
>
> From "The Joy of the Saints", by Robert Llewelyn, page #205

Q: Could it be that even our sins become part of God's image restored in us?   …that without sin, we should not become all that God intends?

Q: Your thoughts?

Consider just how well you 'see God' and turn it to prayer.

Week-9: TUESDAY—EZEKIEL 8: 1–18 & 10: 4-5, 18-22 & 11: 1-6, 22-25

STORY 33—GLORY LOST

A Biblical Imaginative Story—Glory Lost...

Based upon Chapter 36 of Jeremiah

Introduction:

In the span of my life, I have witnessed our culture move from "Leave it to Beaver" to "Bachelor's house", from "Denise the Menace" to "Criminal Minds".

Now, truth be told, not everyone shared in the innocence of earlier times. Nor would I wish to take us back to segregated lunch counters or a grocery store that was all white and European. Still, though the playing field has leveled some and a healthy tolerance (even acceptance) is clearly emerging, our streets are violent, our schools are centers where power has too often overwhelmed achievement and our sexually charged culture knows little of lasting commitment or worth rooted in character.

It is an ancient story. Human cultures tend to move to ever deepening levels of moral chaos and leave in their wake violent ends. In Judah's experience moral confusion often began in the country side high places as the sensual gods of economic prosperity vied for the people's allegiance. Yahweh, in contrast to them, seemed demanding, narrow and judgmental. From these 'high places' Israel's heart was drawn away. Inevitably, even the Holy Temple in Jerusalem would not escape their lure. With each succeeding generation a new moral low would be discovered.

At the time of Ezekiel's writings, Jerusalem had been surrounded and was being destroyed. Her rich and powerful, her educated and political classes were led into Exile by the Babylonians. Ezekiel, in his vision, describes the final scene in Yahweh's Temple as the passionate love and holiness of Yahweh is squeezed out of his own house.

The promise inside the vision is that Yahweh would one-day return by means of the same gate He had left, the Eastern Gate.

The following is an imaginative story based upon chapter 36 of the book of Jeremiah, prophet of God Most—High, one considered a traitor by the ruling elite. Jeremiah prophesied just before and during the fall of Jerusalem by the Babylonians.

The Story:

A shadow hung over the land. Babylon the great was on the march once again. Her armies had conquered Assyria, defeated Egypt at Charchemish and now were preparing for their final conquest of Jerusalem, the fortress city of David, Solomon's glory. The dwelling place of Yahweh.

King Jehoiakim was restless in spirit. The desert cold penetrated the rock walls of his winter palace, filling it with a crisp silence, broken only by the occasional crackling from the open fire pot located in the center of the chamber.

Jehoiakim moved from his window overlooking the temple. His people were gathered, as he should have been, in a great religious observance; a fast to Yahweh, asking for his deliverance from the growing threat to the north of Jerusalem.

'The fools!', Jehoiakim thought to himself, 'holding onto dreams, when political skill was what was really needed.' He had learned his lesson as a young man of twenty-five, watching his older brother Jehoahaz as he was taken captive by the Egyptians. Jehoiakim laughed as another thought intruded. 'I wonder how my brother fares. Now he was a fool. He simply did not know when to compromise. But not me." Jehoiakim had remained faithful to Egypt until Nebuchadnezzar's army had swept over Egypt. He then paid tribute to Babylon's rule and taxed Judah heavily for it. But fortunes had seemed to turn. Babylon's army had been beaten badly just months before. Jehoiakim had stopped his payments of tribute and reached out again to Egypt. He had thought to himself, 'had not Egypt been Israel's birth mother. The power of Egypt would save him. Not myths long forgotten, except by a few zealots like his father Josiah.

As the King turned toward the fire his body took comfort from its warmth. But his soul was icy cold, frozen by an inner rage, tempered only by cunning and anxiety. The chilling news from the front hung over him. Babylon's King would want more than tribute now, if Egypt failed him. That much he knew.

Piercing through the darkness was the sounds and smells of the worshipers at Temple. Turning from the fire, he wondered, 'Why had he allowed the fasts to even be conducted?' And yet he knew why.

Babylon's army would one day come. He would need all of his people united. Followers of the God of Abraham and of Egyptian gods as well.

Now Jehoiakim smiled at his own brilliance. He had again set up idols to the gods of Egypt in the same Temple where prayers were now rising to Yahweh. Jehoiakim, King over Judah, would be ruler of all the people's gods. His was a diverse nation, rich in culture. 'And for now I will tolerate men like Gemeriah and Elnathan,' he reminded himself. These were powerful men whose fathers had served King Josiah and his religious reforms. 'For now...but the day will come when I can do more than restrict Jeremiah, the prophet. I will kill him as I did Uriah.' A smile formed on the King's face. The glow of the fire began to lift his spirit. 'But not today,' his thoughts continued to rush in on him. 'Besides, who knows. Today, I might even have Jeremiah released.' Laughing at the notion, he began to speak aloud to no one. "Yes, I might go and listen to the traitor myself. A kind of political favor to the followers of my father's God."

Stepping away from the fire and into the courtyard, the King saw Gemariah approach. 'Some days are just full of irony,' he thought as he lifted his hands in welcome, his face all smiles.

"Your majesty." Geramioah bowed low in honor. "Your majesty, we, that is your humble officials, are all assembled near the fire pot in your Secretary's office. It is warm. We invite your presence among us." 'His presence, yes, it really was his presence that mattered', his thoughts betrayed by the arrogance in his eyes. "You honor me Gemariah, as your father honored King Josiah before me."

Actually Jehoiakim had not looked forward to this meeting. These men, officers in his court, had asked to report to him the words of Jeremiah, read at Temple by Jeremiah's scribe. Why they held this traitor in such honor the King did not understand.

Jehoiakim entered the office of his Secretary for the Affairs of State. He took a seat near the fire pot and spoke. "Thank you gentlemen. I had wanted so much to join in the festivities to my father's, to our God, but you know recent events have forced me to retreat to this winter palace where I can think more clearly. I understand that you hold Jeremiah's words in some honor, as do I." With that the King ordered his scribe to open the scroll and begin reading. "Hear what the LORD says to you, O house of Israel. This is what the LORD says; 'Do not learn the ways of the nations...For the customs of the peoples are worthless." As the scribe continued to read Jehoiakim's thoughts wondered, though his body communicated rapt attention. It was a skill a good politician must perfect. Still, some of the words caught his attention. "Tell them this." The scribe had raised his voice for the clarity of Jeremiah's words demanded emotional response. "These gods, who did not make the heavens and the earth, will perish from the earth and from under the heavens. But God made the earth by His power; he founded the world by His wisdom and stretched out the heavens by his understanding."

Jehoiakim looked around him, the cold icy anger again shuddered through his being. Suddenly, Jehudi the scribe, noticing the King's discomfort stopped reading, to which the King merely forced a smile and rolled his hand. "Continue please."

Jehoiakim's thoughts moved away from the reading once again and the empty chill in his soul penetrated his spirit. Again the scribes voice became more urgent capturing the King's attention. Jehoiakim felt like the prophet's words were leaping from the scroll and burning into his heart. "The people of Judah," the scribe continued, "have done evil in my eyes, declares the LORD. The have set up their detestable idols in the house that bears my Name and have defiled it. They have built the high places of Topheth in the Valley of Ben Hinnom to burn their sons and daughters in the fire— something I did not command, nor did it enter my mind. So beware. The days are coming, declares the LORD, when people will no longer call it Topheth or the Valley of Ben Hinnom, but the Valley of Slaughter, for they will bury the dead in Topheth until there is no more room."

Jehoiakim knew that valley. He had often gone there to escape the pressures of the palace, to drink, to offer sacrifices to the gods and to find the warm comforts of the priestesses.

Again the words of God took hold. "I will bring an end to the sounds of joy and gladness and to the voices of bride and bridegroom in the towns of Judah and the streets of Jerusalem, for the land will become desolate."

Jehoiakim's icy heart now boiled in hot rage. He forgot himself and who he was with. He rose from his seat and grabbed the scroll from Jehudi's hand. On a table near him was knife, which he grabbed and used to rip through the words of Jeremiah. Then he stopped, remembering where he was. He looked around the room. Everyone was silent. No objection was heard, except for the astonished responses of their faces.

Gemariah, Elnathan and Delaiah also stood in stunned silence as the watched their King rip through the holy Word of Yahweh's prophet.

The King took control of himself and let his action seem that of a dramatic gesture, instead of a lunatic's rage. Forcing himself to relax, he let out a cold laugh and took what was left of the scroll and tossed it in the open fire pot. At last he spoke, slowly and in quiet but determined tones. "Jeremiah is a traitor. He may mean well. But our people are nervous and his words increase fear. Well, the days of fear driven religion died with my father. Have him killed!" His voice was getting louder with each word, but always in control. Then looking directly at his Secretary for the Affairs of State, declared. "We cannot forever tolerate treason, even in an open and tolerant society!" With that he left the room.

Reflections on "Glory Lost"

Ezekiel, chapters 8-10 paint a picture of God's glory literally being pushed out of the Holy Temple. In the space below list the types of sin which God accuses the people of:

Q: Of these sins, which have you entertained in your (temple) life?

Q: In your life is glory fading or being reborn?

Q: In your church is glory fading or being reborn?

Turn your reflections to prayer.

Week-9: WEDNESDAY— LUKE 14: 1-23

STORY 34—GLORY RIGHT IN FRONT OF US

A Biblical Imaginative Story—The Messianic banquet…

Based upon LUKE 14: 1-23

Introduction:

As Jeshua entered through the outer portico of Simon Bar Joseph's house he immediately noticed the man. He was standing just inside the courtyard with a small crowd of neighbors and other poor village dwellers who had come into Simon's outer court to catch a glimpse of the prophet.

Jeshua always attracted attention, but most especially when the Pharisees were involved. The invitation to this banquet was given, according to custom, a month of Sabbaths before. The hour of the dinner was not revealed, of course, until the day of the event, also according to custom. Some in the crowd had been there when Simon's servant had first invited Jeshua. Jeshua immediately accepted. Now the day had come. Simon, ever the graceful host, had sent out his servants to all of his wealthy invited guests and to the prophet and told them to come to his house at 6:00 o'clock, today.

It was 5:00 p.m. and several of the invited guests were already comfortably gathered in Simon's outer court together with neighbors curious about the coming event. All were aware that Jesus of Nazareth would be coming. About five minutes later Jesus arrived and entered apparently oblivious to the gathered, except one invalid seated near the outer gate. Jeshua stopped and looked into the eyes of longing in front of him. The man blocking his path was desperately ill. Glancing around, Jeshua observed the question on each person's face. Would Jeshua, here and on this day, insult the leader of the Pharisees in his own home? Would he break the law and heal this poor man who would never, healed or not, see beyond the outer court of Simon's luxurious home? It was Sabbath, for at least another hour. He had been invited to arrive a little before all the other guests for private conversation with Simon.

Looking up and past the man to Simon whom Jesus saw approaching, Jeshua spoke. "Tell me, Simon, is it lawful to heal on the Sabbath or not?" Simon did not respond. Although he privately agreed with Jeshua on this matter of the law he knew many of his guests did not. "Very well," Jeshua said, and looking again at the suffering one, he reached out and touched him. Quietly Jeshua leaned forward and whispered something. The man's eyes lit up with joy, but took from Jeshua his queue and left at once.

One could feel the tension in the air as the news spread among Simon's guests, most of whom had now made their way into the inner court. Moving toward his host, Jeshua again spoke. "Tell me Simon, if your son or even your ox would fall into a ravine on the Sabbath, would you not immediately pull him out?" Simon nodded, acknowledging the obvious and lifting his hand artfully directed his guest to the inner court and away from the public's eye. Nothing more was said by anyone of this awkward moment as they entered into the inner court where a number of Simon's guests had already gathered.

Jeshua looked around, a sparkle in his eye. He liked these events. He should, for he went to more banquets, parties and feasts than any prophet of God before him. And for that reason he was accused of being given to drinking too much wine and eating too much food. Banquets, in ancient Israel, were a sign of God breaking in on human history.

Someday God would come. His coming would bring joy and plenty to the nation of Israel. All of the guests at this dinner knew of this belief. When Messiah came it would be called the Messianic Banquet.

As Jeshua made his way further into the inner court he noticed how most of the guests were up near the front of the table, all politely maneuvering to take the more honored place near Simon. Jeshua took a seat at the very end and entered into a quiet conversation with one of the village's elders, a humble man who was no longer concerned with his place.

Simon quietly, but quickly moved over to Jeshua and asked him if he would not join him at his left, the place reserved for the honored guest. As they moved together to the front the other guests greeted Jeshua and Simon politely. There were no smiles. Jeshua took the place of honor at Simon's bidding, the guest who had occupied the seat moved to make room, noting the host's invitation to Jesus. Every eye was on Jesus. There was an eerie and jealous silence.

Hearing the feelings living inside this polite, yet silent welcome, Jeshua's thoughts turned to His Father's house in the heavens and the celebrations hosted in the inner courtyards of Yahweh's heavenly palace. The contrast was revealing. Jeshua looked around and mused. 'They didn't have a clue. They did not understand that the Messianic banquet had already begun in their presence. They were not celebrating. There was no joy here.'

An inner compulsion swelled up within the master. Lifting his voice and taking a cup of wine in hand, he pleaded. "Do you not see what is happening?" They did not, of course. He continued. "When someone invites you to a wedding feast, do not take the place of honor, for a person more distinguished than you may have been invited. If so the host who invited both of you will come and say to you, 'Give this

man your seat.'" Jeshua quickly glanced over to the
Pharisee who had to make room when Simon ushered
Jeshua to the front. Jeshua continued. "Then humiliated, you
will have to take the least important place. If, however, you
take the least important place then you will be honored in the
presence of everyone when the host asks you to please
come and take the seat near him." Turning now to Simon, he
continued. "Simon, you are an elder in this village, known by
everyone in the holy city as a gracious host." Simon smiled,
knowing it was true. The High Priest himself had more than
once sought an invitation to his home.

Jeshua continued, speaking quietly. Everyone strained to
hear. "You have honored me. I thank you." Simon smiled
gently and nodded. Jeshua continued. "But Simon, what if I
were only a man and not a rabbi. Would you still honor me?"
Looking away from Simon and to his guests, he continued.

"When you give a luncheon or dinner do you not invite only
your friends, your family or your wealthy neighbors? Of
course, and it is because you know they will invite you back
and so repay you. I tell you, invite instead the poor, the
crippled, the lame, the blind. Then you will be truly blessed.
Though they cannot repay you, you will be repaid at the
resurrection of the righteous in my Father's house."

Jeshua's remarks cut through to Simon's heart. His guests
were shocked at the brashness of this young prophet.
Embarrassed for Simon, they looked around for something
to do or someone to talk with. An older guest, wanting to
break the awkward moment, spoke up, lifting his cup as
Jeshua had done earlier. "Blessed is the man who will eat at
the feast in the kingdom of God". "Shalom," was the
response of every man around the table.

Jeshua's heart was stirred at the contradiction in all of this.
Standing and walking toward the Pharisee, he began a story.
"A certain man was preparing a great banquet. Invitations
had been sent out well in advance to his guests. Thirty days,
I think it was. On the day of the banquet he sent his servants
to announce the time, just as Simon did. 'Come,' they said,

'for everything is ready.' To the servant's surprise, each invited guest began to make excuses. The first said, 'I have just begun a new business. Profits are low. Please excuse me.' Another said, "I have just bought five new oxen and you've caught me at the worst possible time of the day. I must drive them before I finalize the deal. Please, excuse me.' Still another said, 'I just got married. The law makes allowance in the first year for us to delight only in each other. We need our time alone.'

Jeshua was now at the end of the table. Every person was fully engaged. "The servant came back and reported all of these excuses to his master.

Then the owner of the house became angry and ordered his servant to 'go out and invite those who could never pay him back. Those in need. The poor, the crippled, the blind and the lame.' The servant, knowing his master's heart had already done that. 'Sir,' he said, 'we've done as you requested already. Still there is room.' Then the master told his servant. 'Go out then, into the streets and into the country lanes if you must!'

Jeshua was now moving back on the other side of the room and towards the front where Simon remained seated. Jeshua now spoke as though he were the voice of the master, pleading. 'With passion, request everyone to come to my banquet. The feast will begin. We will not delay for one moment longer! I tell you, not one of those who received their invitations by formal means will get a taste of the joy at my table.'"

Jeshua stopped and turned looking directly at Simon. Jeshua's eyes did not look away from Simon. The silence between guest and host was deafening. In the stillness of the next seconds, each of Simon's guests began to take the story in. They knew that they, the Jews, were the ones who had received the formal invitations. Simon Bar Joseph was the first to turn away from Jeshua's gaze and began to casually speak to his guest seated to the right of him. Others did the same.

Jeshua slowly made his way back to his seat of honor. Only he knew the real truth. The Messianic banquet had begun, in their presence, on this very Sabbath day and the only man eating at the Lord's table was absent, home, rejoicing that he had been healed on this very day!

Reflections on "Glory Right in Front of Us"

Q: Why do you suppose that YHWH, whose glory was forced to leave His own Temple, chose to come back into Israel's life in this very quiet and human and vulnerable way?

God moments are all around us. Jesus is still coming to us, today. The writer to the Hebrews warns us not to *"forget to entertain strangers, for by so doing some people have entertained angels without knowing it"* (Hebrews 13: 2). Then he goes on to say: *"Remember those in prison as if you were their fellow prisoners, and those who are mistreated as if you yourselves were suffering"* (Hebrews 13: 3).

Q: When have you seen Jesus, up close and personal?

Q: Has he come to a community you live in dressed up in some else's feet or hands or eyes?

Consider and pray.

Week-9: THURSDAY—LUKE 19: 28-48

STORY 35—THE RETURN

A Biblical Imaginative Story—Pushed Out & Looking for His Return…

Based upon LUKE 19: 28-48

Introduction:

In Ezekiel, chapters 8-10 we are given a vision revealed to the Exiles in Babylon through their prophet Ezekiel. In this vision Ezekiel witnesses the eschatological moment when YHWH is pushed out of God's own Temple due to the multitude of private and public idolatry practiced by the priests of Judah—within the very confines of this sacred space. God's glory is seen as being progressively removed, first to the portico of the Temple, then to the Eastern Gate and finally to the Mount of Olives across from the Temple Mount where God's glory is finally lifted and removed from the face of Judea.

The promise inside Ezekiel's revelation is that God would eventually return by way of this same route, beginning with the Mount of Olives and through the Eastern Gate and into the very Temple Mount from which God is banished. This is the story of God's return in Jesus of Nazareth.

The Story:

Jeshua entered under the portico of the east gate as the crowd rushed around him. Even the disciples, now comfortable with his daily teaching in this holy place, continued on into the court where they assumed Jeshua would be teaching. It was Passover day.

Standing alone, Jesus looked up at the high columns supporting Solomon's porch, just outside the inner Sanctuary.

The morning mist had settled in giving the impression that the mighty columns continued to rise into the heavens. The sun was breaking through the clouds, it's rays forming the silhouette of a crown; Jesus knew what it meant. His father in heaven was watching.

Leaning against the wall just inside the East Gate, Jeshua whispered to his Father. *"Father, the hour has come. Glorify Your Son, that Your son may glorify You. For You granted him authority over all people that he might give eternal life to all those You have given him...*LORD, the very life of eternity is..." For a moment his prayer was interrupted as the crowd now gathering before him caught his attention. *"This is eternal life,* Father, that these you have given may *know You, the only true God,* and Your Son, *whom You have sent. I have brought You glory on earth, Father, by finishing the work you gave me to do. And now, Father, glorify me in Your presence with the glory I had with You before the world began"* (Italic selections from John 17: 1b-5).

Closing his eyes and leaning his head against the wall, Jeshua felt as though his head were cupped by the Father's hand. In the next instant, he heard the sound of rushing wind. A glowing fire fell down through the cloudy mist and in his imagination he saw the promise of Ezekiel being fulfilled. Starting from the Holy of Holies, the fire spread throughout the city and rested on the heads of a few gathered in a room; the very room in which he would celebrate the Passover later this evening.

The ground, in Jesus mind, began to shake and he was transported to the middle of a valley full of dead bones. He recognized it as Ezekiel's vision; the same vision that He, the Word, had given Ezekiel centuries before. Jeshua was now watching the Holy Presence of the Trinity. The Father spoke and Jeshua reached out into the valley across the bones attaching tendons and covering with flesh. Suddenly by the millions, the Breath of God filled each one, creating a vast army.

The Father again spoke to His Son in the quiet of intuited thoughts that Jesus had come to trust as the very Breath of God. "My beloved Son, when You become the offering of sin and I, for a dark and seemingly eternal moment turn my back upon You, know that I will fulfill the words of the prophet Ezekiel, by Your offering. All of human pain, her wounds and sin will be poured into You and by way of The Holy One the taste inside death shall be shared in Us. But we shall overcome. Jesus remembered the promise. *"When I open your graves and bring you up from them...I will put my Spirit in you and you will live"* (Ezekiel 37: 12, 14).

Jeshua breathed deeply, as though his human spirit was taking comfort from God, His Father. He opened his eyes. Once again he was surrounded by the sights and sounds of His Father's Temple. The disciples were gathered across the court  yard mingling with the people, full of the joy of the moment. They had no idea what was about to befall them. The sun had now dispersed the clouds above Solomon's porch.

The noise of the money changers and their greed filled this holy place. It certainly was subdued from earlier in the week, but present still. Anger swelled up within him. 'Would no one understand?', he thought to himself. 'This is my Father's house. It is to be a house of prayer. It must be so.' And so he moved out into the open court yard and toward the steps where he would take his place and begin to teach. On this day, he would make it, His Father's house.

Reflections on "The Return"

"Jeshua breathed deeply, as though his human spirit was taking comfort from God, His Father. He opened his eyes. Once again he was surrounded by the sights and sounds of His Father's Temple. The disciples were gathered across the court yard mingling with the people, full of the joy of the moment. They had no idea what was about to befall them.
From Terry (above)

The disciples were clueless as to the real significance of this moment. Ezekiel's prophecy was being fulfilled before their very eyes. They thought they had a clear vision of what the moment of God's return would look like. They thought wrong. They were unaware, caught by surprise in a tornado of events. Jesus arrest and trial were hours away; not months, not even days and they were each/all blind to it when unfolding before their very eyes.

Q Are we still clueless today?

Q: What is the 'hope' of Jesus soon return? …Is it pretty much the same as the disciples hoped for? …How so?

Q: Are we, like them, simply looking for a Messianic savior who will deliver us from our present hour? …from the earth?

Consider whether your own vision of God's Kingdom coming, of God's will being done on earth as it is in heaven is too little; and pray.

Week-9: FRIDAY—PHILIPPIANS 2: 1-11

MY THOUGHTS 39—WHAT KIND OF HOPE—POWER OR PERSUASION? PART I

We humans seem to be at the center of a truly cosmic war. What is at stake is the willing allegiance of beings and communities who, like the Creator, can choose. From the writings of Israel, it is clear we are not alone in this war and may even play a decisive role. Angelic beings, who have been engaged in this war far longer are apparently divided with roughly one third choosing a god other than the Living God. Job, perhaps the most ancient source in Jewish writings opens with the Creator still responding to the devil in the hope of persuading him to *"consider* (His) *servant Job,"* whom Yahweh declares *"blameless and upright, a man who fears God and shuns evil"* (Job 1:8). In this story/drama, likely lived and/or written before Abraham, the central issue is faith. In this trial Job declares, *"I know that my Redeemer lives, and that in the end he will stand upon the earth. And after my skin has been destroyed, yet in my flesh I will see God. I myself will see him with my own eyes—I, and not anther. How my heart years within me!"* (Job 19: 25-27).

Paul, centuries later and writing a circular letter to the Churches of Asia Minor hints at the import of the people of God in this cosmic war. *"His* (God's) *intent was that now, through the church, the manifold wisdom of God should be made know to the rulers and authorities in the heavenly realms, according to his eternal purpose which he accomplished in Christ Jesus our Lord"* (Eph 3: 10-11).

While in Jail, Paul declares the central hope of the gospel. *"God exalted him* (Jesus*) to the highest place and gave him the name that is above every name, that at the name of Jesus every knee should bow, in heaven and on earth and under the earth, and every tongue confess that Jesus Christ is Lord, to the glory of God the Father"* (Philippians 2: 9-11).

As a child of twelve I was conversant with Rapture theology. Even then evangelical preaching made me aware of Israel's rebirth in 1948 and of her later unification of Jerusalem. I understood these events as historic, from God's perspective and as signs of promises kept and of Christ's soon return. I remember meditating upon Daniel 8-10 and Ezekiel 38 and seeing the Soviet Union (Russia) in the story as the conquering nation of the north. As a young and older adult, I have been impressed with the emergence of the European Union as real and a possible re-configuration of Rome's glory as some believe. The pace at which she has unified and begun to engage world events is staggering. When President Bush formed the quartet of geo-political powers (America, European Union, Russia, United Nations) for the political, economic and military search for the peace of Jerusalem prophetic bells went off in this child's (adult's) mind. I continue to watch the global political evolution of our world through a child's curiosity.

As an adult, a Wesleyan and one who serves Jesus Christ I am even more impressed with the more historic understanding of Christ's body effectively and successfully transforming human culture by persuasion instead of power. Over and again Paul uses the **'universal all'** when speaking of the mystery of Christ poured out into the world, in Jesus life and death and through the Church. Yes, often the 'all' is provisional, but not always. At least he does not seem to condition it always. *"For God has bound all men over to disobedience so that he may have mercy on them all"* (Rm 11: 32).

The hope inside his vision is fulfilled in language, not of conquest, but of weakness. *"And being found in appearance as a man, he humbled himself and became obedient to death—even death on a cross!"* (Phil 2: 8). The very next word is therefore. *"Therefore God exalted him... That at the name of Jesus every knee should bow"* (Phil2:9a,9c). Up until the last decade I assumed it was true because God would make it true. He would, by power, coerce men and women, children and teens to bow, weather they wanted to or not.

The problem inside such an interpretation is two-fold.

The immediate Biblical context is humility and suffering, Christ's and Paul's. He is writing from prison. He sees in his chains the kingdom of Christ advancing, having effect among the Emperors Praetorian guard and in the Church (Phil 1: 12-14). As the church struggles in her weakness, Paul sees her faith perfected as she shares in Christ's own suffering. Power and suffering are vitally connected in Paul's Philippian letter (Phil 3:10). The 'every knee' referred to is the result, not of power, but of sacrificial love doing its more perfect work.

The power motifs in end times Biblical references (rapture, conquest following tribulation and millennia reign) are often interpreted by evangelicals as finding their fulfillment in the absolute failure of the Church to be transformational. Like Israel of old, the Church is simply biding time, extending the offer of escape from the terrible day of the Lord's wrath, poured out in judgments upon the earth. The Church in these scenarios becomes a blip in the story of man until the final dispensation comes. God, in most of these gospels is patiently waiting for every child who will, to come home and will then close the door, leaving outside His kingdom the fallen angels and the hopeless dupes he controls. Only in a powerful act of war is God able to set things right and cast into jail (a living and continuous hell) those who reject him. The anti-Christ of Revelation is simply the last and greatest human to defy God's will.

I don't know about you, but I find these visions of human destiny horrific. They are horrible not because they are painful, but because God is viewed as a complacent participant in their horror. The God inside these stories too often comes off as an angry and distant Being, willing to allow 'the many' to live in continual agony and torture for the sake of the few who choose Him. It is a costly grace indeed!

In these pictures human history is moving nowhere. It is simply an unwilling participant in a war of worlds, older than time. History is the context of the current battle, awaiting the unveiling of the real victory. If true, then the incarnation of God is reduced to drama, a powerful visual, nothing more.

Christ did not come to transform history but to make way for an alternative history to develop in some other place. Indeed, there is little hope in a universe where a few win and feast while most are 'left behind!'

Reflections on "What Kind of Hope— Power or Persuasion? Part I"

Q Have you ever considered Paul's statement about 'every knee bowing' as voluntary instead of compulsory?

Q: What are the implications if that is correct?

Reflect and turn it all to prayer.

Week-9: SATURDAY—II CORINTHIANS 5: 1-21

MY THOUGHTS 40—WHAT KIND OF HOPE—POWER OR PERSUASION? PART II

At this writing (August 2016) the Middle East and Europe are experiencing significant, reality altering changes.

In Europe an emerging Russia captures Crimea and further threatens Hungarian independence, halting at the very least its European tilt. The Baltic states face a re-emergent Russian bear within a European Union torn by increased ethnic and cultural tensions, threatened by radical Islam with Great Britain adrift and Turkey in its own political turmoil, apparently considering rapprochement with the Bear.

In the middle east the Islamic Caliphate is now in competition with a resurgent Iran for political domination of events, Iraq slowly disintegrating, Syria at war with itself while Egypt escapes the clutches of the Muslim Brotherhood but at the expense of democratic institutions. Once again Russia has re-emerged as a significant player as the United States signals its retreat.

European Christianity is in full retreat while its American cousin is increasingly seen as irrelevant; concerned primarily with its own deteriorating place in the larger culture. Inside the vacuum left by a shapeless Christian witness is the possibility of spiritual renewal through cultural exile as in the Biblical and reoccurring experience of Israel or extinction.

The Coming Great Tribulation:

As a result of our deepening Euro-American drift toward materialism, sensuality and secular based models of humanism our world is opening ever wider space for the emergence of a power centered future. The current political environ in which Hillary and Trump compete is all about power—left or right. The vacuum of empty souls, uncommitted relationships and a lack of transcendent values may indeed lead us into a great and world felt Tribulation echoing the prophetic witness. Environmental, economic, health and hunger crises may yet converge to bring about John's apocalyptic vision of a world where 1/4 of the planets inhabitants are killed, a future where only the powerful survive.

From within salvation and secular history, it would appear that Yahweh allows us humans great freedom, even if a holocaust is the result. Real evil seems to lurk in the shadows. With each passing decade it seems the heavenly 'war of worlds' has greater, not lesser, impact upon this world. So then, the real questions, eschatologically are:

1) **To what end is history moving?** and;

2) **What is the meaning of history, if any?**

Evolutionary thinking (secular and theistic) is hopeful that ever more sophisticated social, economic and spiritual answers will emerge from the tensions of people—cultures—governments—scientists wrestling with a world in chaos, resulting in ever increasing social—political—spiritual skill sets. In this emergent view of world history, throwing off the social constraints and paradigms of our ancestors will allow humans to explore new kinds of social and political gatherings, leading to a more practical and peaceful co-existence, based on tolerance. The post-modern sees in this maze of competing world views (cultures and sub-cultures) the kind of diversity from which a new age is born.

Many in the evangelical and reformation Church, looking through a lens of 6,000 years of salvation history and within

2000 years of experience in Christ see another probable outcome; deeper chaos leading to cataclysmic events, as we devolve into fractured communities, without purpose or meaning. Power will emerge, brutal and controlling in such a world.

Millennial Reign of Christ:

For the 19th/20th century dispensationalists, chaos is necessary. These evangelicals see history as a stage upon which each Act in the play is radically different—even unconnected—to the Act that precedes or follows.

The new age of Christ (Act IV) will come only by power, not evolution or transformation. This power, however, will be benevolent. God enters human history to end it and begin Divine history, on God's terms. Jesus saves each of us who call upon Him, in time, but allows those on the planet who have rejected His offer of salvation to fall into a still darker night; one reserved for God's enemies. God wins. Satan loses. God's people win big. Satan's people lose big. End of story! Correction. End of the short story. This is the hope to which a large part of evangelicalism is committed.

Let us enlarge our questions and reflect from within this evangelical—reformed tradition.

1) **To what end is history moving?**
   Toward a new heaven and a new earth.

2) **What is the meaning of history, if any?**
   The purpose is to populate this new heaven and earth with the 'real' believers.

3) **What is the destiny of those who never believed?**
   Hell.

Such a world view is deeply unsatisfying when set alongside the historic view of the Church for it does not carry in its wings the larger Story of God among humans. It reduces the heavenly 'war of the worlds' to one of power, resolved ultimately by means of power. As a result:

- ➤ Power trumps love, and;
- ➤ Power trumps sin, and;
- ➤ Most humans are born and lost so that a few can be saved, and;
- ➤ The incarnation of God is unnecessary, and;
- ➤ God being wounded for our sin is unnecessary beyond individual soul salvation, and;
- ➤ The Church of Christ is unnecessary in historic terms, and;
- ➤ Secular evolutionary theory is more hopeful, in terms of this planet's future than is this 'end times' scenario.

At the heart of this theological vision is the failure to see in Christ and His Church the manifest commitment of Yahweh to the weakness of love, as transformative and healing—to see God as better than ourselves!

STORY 36—GUILTY LOVE

A Personal Story—on what drives our love?

Last evening, while visiting my not so recovering alcoholic friend, we went out into the freezing cold of night to find his friend. He wanted to invite his friend out the cold and into his home. Initially I left my friend off at a makeshift homeless encampment, located on the back porch of an Assembly of God Church and facing into an isolated alley way. As I drove away I noticed a young man among the four who seemed a teenager.

'Dear Lord,' I thought, 'how can this be?' About a block down the road, I pulled over and walked back into their encampment to offer food and blankets. In the course of buying McDonald's meals and securing blankets for the new friends I met I found myself questioning what motivated me. Was I concerned for these homeless, especially the young teen? Was I instead just trying to salve my own guilty sense of obligation—knowing that the night before I had not given the homeless so much as a thought and tomorrow night it would again be—out of sight, out of mind?

More Questions:

Matthew reminds us, that if we, though evil, *"know how to give good gifts... how much more will your Father in heaven give good gifts to those who ask him!"* (Matt 6: 11).

Now admittedly, the gifts I gave to the homeless men may have been more for myself than them. In fact, that awareness drives this folk theology.

How can a 'good Being' who rules ultimately by power allow in God's universe evil that goes unnoticed?

I wouldn't. I wouldn't subject billions to a hell, even of their own choice, simply to create and encourage others who would choose me. So how can God?

Reflections on "What Kind of Hope— Power or Persuasion? Part II"

Q: Have you ever considered the popular 'end times' teachings popularized in books like "The Late Great Planet Earth" or the "Left Behind Series" as essentially un-hopeful?

Q: How do you feel about popularized 'end times' teachings?

Q: What do you think of Terry's analysis?

Consider what a hopeful outcome to God's Story among humans would look like. Write it out. Talk with someone about it. Pray about it.

Week-9: SUNDAY 1—ZECHARIAH 14: 1-9, LUKE 21: 20-28, JOB 19: 23-27, REVELATION 5: 8-14

MY THOUGHTS 41—THE HOPE INSIDE WEAKNESS—PART III

> *"The power motifs in end times Biblical references (rapture, conquest following tribulation and millennial reign) are often interpreted by evangelicals as finding their fulfillment in the absolute failure of the Church to be a transformational presence... I don't know about you, but I find these visions of human destiny horrific".*
> From "Jerusalem's Gates—A Devotional Journey", Chapter 9, "What Kind of Hope?", Part I

The Hope Inside Weakness:

A few years ago one of my professors, Cathy Cox, asked a question that has forced me to re-think hope by asking:

"In terms of the human race: Do we really believe the cross of Jesus is stronger than Adam's wound?"

I had to admit, I did not. You see, if the dispensationalists are right, the clear answer is 'no'. Satan, though placed in the limits of confined space, nevertheless lives in his hellish Kingdom with the vast majority of humans. And if, the eternal nature of his place is torment, I do not see how such an outcome is victory, even for those who escape? How is such an outcome a victory for the Creator who longs to restore all persons and material to fellowship with the Trinity of God?

As a Wesleyan I have been given two powerful lenses through which to interpret prophecy and all of scripture.

> ➤ One is the belief that Jesus death on the cross has real impact on all humanity, not just some, and;
> ➤ Secondly, that God is everywhere in the Trinity of God's universe seeking to restore everyone.

In the first centuries of the church the debate raged around the 'reality' of Christ's humanity. If God becoming man meant anything, it means that God has entered into human history in a vital way; a transformational way. Therefore, Jesus life, death and resurrection have real impact upon our life, death and resurrection. In fact, all of history is valued, if God entered it in more than a visual way.

Wesley taught that Christ's death offers atonement for all of Adam's children, including Adam, in terms of our 'original unrighteousness' and the wounds that attend. This is true, without human response. Further, he believed that our own personal sin/sins are provisionally cleansed and healed in Christ's passion and death, provided we become willing participants by faith.

Further, Wesley describes humanity's ability to respond to God's gracious offer of Divine Presence, in Christ, as a 'gift of God', a prevenient grace. God is everywhere, in all times and places, present to all persons acting to bring God's children home to Divine relationship and to themselves. God's Story and ours intersect in the life of Christ, in the Holy Spirit and through the Church. Our story (His-Story—History) become intertwined in Jesus of Nazareth and His gospel.

If these two concepts are accurate as they are Biblical, then one conclusion follows: **The cross of Christ is more powerful than Adam's wound. It is the very weakness of Christ and his life that is the transforming relationship in which all of Adam's children participate, both really and provisionally.**

Finally, the cross becomes God's participation inside the human story of pain and isolation. *"God* (The Father) *made him* (Jesus) *to be sin for us, so that in him we might become the righteousness of God* (II Cor 5: 21). This entering into the Story as a co-participant places the 'glory of God' alongside our own lost glory. Where Ezekiel's vision of 'glory lost' was an occasion of God being powerless before human willfulness in that our human decisions are respected, John's vision of 'glory returned' is a powerful image of the weakness of God being more persuasive than the strong holds of Satan. *"The Word became flesh and made his dwelling among us. We have seen his glory, the glory of the One and Only, who came from the Father, full of grace and truth"* (John 1: 14). This is the same glory that Ezekiel saw returning to Christ's temple.

Finally, then, if all this be true, salvation is inclusive and must be worked out in human history. Salvation, must touch 'all' of God's children, at least provisionally and in 'all' seasons of history.

To this end, I have come to several conclusions about 'end times' prophecy. They are as follows.

1) With one of my teachers at college, Dr. Weigelt, **I am a 'pan-millennialist.'** With respect to all the particulars of 'end times' I simply affirm it will all pan out and to a good end. As Ann of Norwich wrote from one of her visions. *"At one time our good Lord said: 'All things shall be well…You shall see for yourself that all manner of thing shall be well.'*

2) **Human suffering is extreme and God's suffering with us equals the need.** No one is 'left behind' in God's history, except as a person refuses. God's gift is 'eternal' and intended for all of his beings, Satan included, if only. I have no doubt that if it is in God's power to redeem everyone, even against their will, He would. Unfortunately, redemption is not a matter of power, but of love (persuasion). Power, a rock can make, but only love can call a human being or angel into fellowship with the Trinity of God. In a parable Jesus described this joy of the Father in Heaven seeking His

children back. *"If anyone owns a hundred sheep, and one of them wanders away, will he not leave the ninety-nine on the hills and go to look for the one that wandered off?... In the same way your Father in heaven is not willing that any of these little ones should be lost"* (Matt 18: 14).

3) **The assurance that in the cross of Christ, 'all' of Adam's sins and the wounds which attend are forgiven, healed and cleansed clearly infers that every son and daughter of our first parents will be able to make a free choice about the Trinity of God, without the pull of Adam's sin (and his children's multiplied wounds) affecting the choice.** In other words, God has a mystical solution wherein 'all' are clearly invited. Who, under such a circumstance would say no. Perhaps many.

I am not suggesting in this that our own personal sins/sin and experiential history is removed from the choice we ultimately make. The church and Jesus agree that what we do in these seventy years has real and lasting impact on who we are in eternity. I am merely suggesting that God is just and merciful and will assure clear-headed and clear-hearted freedom in that choice. It is a prevenient gift, that goes before our salvation.

4) **The Church is Christ, present in human history, by the Holy Spirit.** History is moving to a redemptive and restorative place. As such the primary function of the church is redemptive. We are called to 'live Christ' in his suffering and so somehow to attain the resurrection. God's purpose is to redeem by suffering love 'all' of his children who are lost. *"Not that I have already obtained all this, or have already been made perfect, but I press on to take hold of that for which Christ Jesus took hold of me...I want to know Christ and the power of his resurrection and the fellowship of sharing in his sufferings, become like him in his death, and so, somehow, to attain to the resurrection from the dead"* (Phil 3: 12, 10-11). In this sense, 'the end times' began with the birth of Christ and the Church.

5) If there is no 'magical' (power centered) way to redeem 'all' in history, then the possibility of redemption (even in hell) must be continual or the final judgment must be about non-existence rather than 'continual prison.' **I cannot imagine heaven being 'real' if 'eternal punishment' is in store for the vast majority of God's children.** I certainly see 'hell' as real. I see its beginnings in many I know, even now; including my own personal experience. It is not hard to imagine 'hell', only a place of 'eternal prison' without the possibility of parole (redemption). C.S. Lewis describes hell as God's last act of mercy, in Mere Christianity. It is God's way of confining both the power, influence, effect and affect of hellish choice in his universe.

The secular humanist sees in evolution a hopeful future based upon 'freedom' from God's rule and law. While hopeful, it is also wishful thinking. Only the 'faith of the Church of Christ addresses significantly the human tendency to 'devolve' morally and in social and political relations. The Church rightly is viewing human evolution through a much longer lens of revelation than is available in most of our culture.

However, the hope offered in so much of the late nineteenth and twentieth century, in Protestant and fundamentalist thinking is equally blind. It is a short sighted version of 'redemption' centered in power.

Perhaps, in the context of two world wars and a multitude of others, such theology looks hopeful. But it is a hope that few will enjoy. Most will be lost to God. God's opening question to Satan in the account of Job, *"consider my servant Job,"* (Job 1: 8) rings hallow indeed. Satan wins. God loses. In fact, the evolutionary model, though not based upon truth (accepting as it is theistic and Christ-centric), is preferable.

Every week I pay my tithe. Why? Not because it is commanded, but because it is the historic 'witness' of those who believe in God's Story. For me as a Christian, it is both my wave offering in light of my personal experience of

Pentecostal hope and my down payment or tithe in my belief in the resurrection of Jesus and his bride.

I do not know what tribulations lie ahead as a result of human arrogance. I do know that *"my Redeemer lives, and that in the end he will stand upon the earth. And after my skin has been destroyed, yet in my flesh I will see God. I myself will see him with my own eyes—I, and not another. How my heart years within me!"* (Job 19: 25-27).

Reflections on "The Hope Inside Weakness—Part III"

The cross of Christ is more powerful than Adam's wound.

Q: Do you really believe this? ...If so, how would that effect the way you see salvation history?

Consider Terry's conclusions—as follows:

1) With respect to all the particulars of 'end times' I simply affirm it will all pan out and to a good end.

2) Human suffering is extreme and God's suffering with us equals the need. No one is 'left behind' in God's history.

3) The assurance that in the cross of Christ, 'all' of Adam's sins and the wounds which attend are forgiven, healed and cleansed clearly infers that every son and daughter of our first parents will be able to make a free choice about the Trinity of God, without the pull of Adam's sin (and his children's multiplied wounds) affecting the choice.

4) The Church is Christ, present in human history, by the Holy Spirit. History is moving to a redemptive and restorative place.

5) If there is no 'magical' (power centered) way to redeem 'all' in history, then the possibility of redemption (even in hell) must be continual or the final judgment must be about non-existence rather than 'continual prison.'

Q: Your thoughts?

"Our culture is characterized by the absence of transcendence, a culture in which Christianity is not seen as a force determining the shape of things… But I am quite sure that the Church will not lack creative energies even in the future… Saint Benedict probably wasn't noticed at all. He was also a dropout who came from noble Roman society and did something bizarre, something that later turned out to be the 'ark on which the West survived.'

…(Today) "Christianity is suffering an enormous loss of meaning, and the form in which the Church is present is also changing. The Christian society that has existed until now is very obviously crumbling. In this respect the relationship between society and the Church will also continue to change, and it will presumably continue in the direction of a de-Christianized form of society…

On the other side, however, Christianity will offer models of life in new ways and will once again present itself in the waste- land of technological existence as the place of true humanity. That is already happening now".

From "Salt of the Earth" by Pope Benedict XVI, pages 126-128

In this writing Terry is reflecting Pope Benedicts optimism that a church 'in exile'—identifying with a larger and deeper existential threat created by a lack of transcendence and faith will lead to a renewed Church and culture.

Q: What do you think?

Q: Is there reason to hope within this troubled season in history?

Consider what needs to emerge from your own faith in these times and turn it all to prayer.

Next:

Divine Appointment

10 DIVINE APPOINTMENT

... The Master Gate

INVOCATION:

WE GIVE THANKS TO YOU, LORD GOD ALMIGHTY, THE ONE WHO IS AND WHO WAS, BECAUSE THROUGH YOUR GREAT POWER DEMONSTRATED IN JESUS DEATH AND RESURRECTION, YOU HAVE BEGUN TO REIGN. THE NATIONS ARE ANGRY, LORD. THE TIME APPOINTED FOR YOUR WRATH HAS YET TO COME, THE TIME FOR JUDGING THE DEAD AND REWARDING YOUR SERVANTS AND PROPHETS AND YOUR SAINTS TOGETHER WITH THOSE WHO REVERENCE YOUR NAME, BOTH GREAT AND SMALL.

FATHER, ALL WHO DESTROY THE EARTH WILL THEMSELVES BE DESTROYED. BUT WE PRAY AND HOPE THEY ARE FEW, PERHAPS NONE. WE LOOK FORWARD TO THE DAY WHEN THE KINGDOMS OF THIS WORLD HAVE BECOME THE KINGDOM OF OUR LORD AND OF HIS CHRIST! AND HE WILL REIGN FOR EVER AND EVER. AMEN.

ADAPTED FROM REVELATION 11: 15-18

PSALM OF THE WEEK: PSALM 118

COMMANDMENT OF THE WEEK: "YOU SHALL NOT GIVE FALSE TESTIMONY AGAINST YOUR NEIGHBOR." DEUTERONOMY 5: 20

DAILY SCRIPTURES:

MONDAY—LUKE 2: 21-24

TUESDAY—LUKE 3: 1-23

WEDNESDAY—ROMANS 6: 1-11

THURSDAY—JOHN 17: 17-18

FRIDAY—LUKE 4: 1-13

SATURDAY—LUKE 7: 18-23

SUNDAY 1—JOHN 12: 37-50 & 17: 20-26

FROM
MATTHEW 16: 21

FROM THAT TIME JESUS BEGAN TO SHOW HIS DISCIPLES THAT HE HAD TO GO TO JERUSALEM AND SUFFER MANY THINGS FROM THE ELDERS, CHIEF PRIESTS, AND LEGAL EXPERTS, AND THAT HE HAD TO BE KILLED AND RAISED ON THE THIRD DAY.

Week-10: MONDAY—LUKE 2: 21-24

THE MASTER GATE

(In Jesus of Nazareth) *"glory and the Passion are inextricable intertwined.*

We encounter this connection in a uniquely concentrated form in the parable about the Last Judgment… in which the Son of Man, in the role of judge, identifies himself with those who hunger and thirst, with the strangers, the naked, the sick, the imprisoned—with all those who suffer in this world— and he describes behavior toward them as behavior toward himself…

The Son of Man is one person alone, and that person is Jesus. This identity shows us the way, shows us the criterion according to which our lives will one day be judged.".

From "Jesus of Nazareth", by Pope Benedict XVI, page #327, 328".

They say only two things are certain, death and taxes.

The story of the Christmas child finds it's beginning as a young Jewish couple make their way to Bethlehem to pay taxes. As an adult Jesus, nor his followers would escape the clutches of either death or taxes. *"Give to Caesar what is Caesar's,"* (Matt 22:21b) was Jesus own response to a Pharisee who tried to trap this young Rabbi into suggesting that good Jews could avoid taxes.

Of all Jerusalem's gates the Jewish pilgrims going up to Jerusalem would know of the Master Gate. On feast days they would make their way from the far reaches of

Judea/Samaria and come through or at least to this gate. Why? To pay the temple tax.

If you wished to do business with the High Priest's office you came to this gate. It was also known as the 'Inspection Gate'. It was here that the poor of Israel would present their offerings for approval or rejection. All too often a blemish would be found, forcing the believers to pay the temple or its vendors a high and exorbitant fee for a dove or lamb without blemish.

Jesus, the Son of God, knew this and it was likely through this gate that his anger poured out and into the temple's center of human power; the Master Gate!

MY THOUGHTS 42—BEGINNINGS—AN APPOINTMENT WITH THE STORY

CHILD BAPTISM—APPOINTMENT 1

He meant it as a way of 'identifying with my professional calling'. He is an honest business person in my community and we were talking by phone about our insurance policy. In the course our conversation, I noted that an additional bit of insurance would provide my wife some comfort. His response was, "well, now the very best insurance you already have and give away daily." I got it. I understood that he was talking about Christ's death, passion and resurrection. I agreed. It was his next statement and the casualness, even humor, with which he said it that troubled me as he continued, "...not everyone in Seattle, in fact most don't buy into that insurance."

I responded. "Well, we'll see." I think he thought I misread his metaphor and began to explain that he was referring to those who do not accept Christ. I responded by suggesting that maybe God had it all worked out so that everyone, or nearly everyone would have a policy. Our conversation ended. This good business man did not want to argue theology with his customer. As we hung up, I'm sure he wondered if I was a Methodist or worse, a Unitarian, instead of a Nazarene.

In our tradition and most evangelical ones, the issue of an adult 'confession of faith' or 'conversion' is central to the gospel as communicated. It is a transactional understanding of salvation. God is 'saving' from his judgment (wrath) those who will run to His Son's shed blood.

The strength inside this tradition is the urgency and personal immediacy of the 'confession'. In the end, if faith is not personal and the result of God the Spirit living inside the believer, then we cannot really live the "Jesus way". For the life of Jesus can only be formed in us by God living in us.

The weakness inside this transactional understanding of salvation is the narrow view of 'salvation' as a bargain with God. Transactional salvation fails to capture the 'communal and relational' nature of salvation.

The narrative of God's Story begins/ends with our testimony (our story) rather than God's Story coming to us, lived before us, all around us and ultimately in us. We are the center of the Story, rather than God's redemptive purposes in history. The emphasis is upon the experience itself, rather than in the relationship the Holy Spirit initiates in us and previous to the moment, around us. Finally, in its fundamentalist expression, transactional salvation is based upon an unbiblical and sad view of God's purposes in the universe and with and in us. God's wrath is deeply misunderstood and the communal nature of salvation ushering in the healing/cleansing and restorative purpose of God in history—society is simply lost.

STORY 37—AN APPOINTMENT WITH A STORY TELLER

A Personal & Imaginative Story—from before me

I sat at a stone table, small and round. Three trees rose from the garden surrounding as a testimony to the God who is Father—Son—Spirit. The air was humid, heavy but with the rays of sun filtering through the clouds and into my heart. This was a memorial sanctuary just outside the old and traditional building rising like a sanctuary before me. As I listened and waited, I almost felt her. A mysterious, feminine presence, of an older and scholarly woman whom I never met, but by whom and through her writings my heart was formed. Mildred Bangs Wynkoop, author of "A Theology of Love". She was not the first woman who had deeply impacted my interior sense of God's presence. Fairy Chism, was a charismatic revivalist in whose ministry I came into my own personal experience of Christ, at seven years of age. My mother also had spent hours listening with patience to my constant need to confess sin.

As I sat in the Wynkoop Memorial Garden feeling connected to her presence I became a little frightened and so brushed the feeling away. But the reality of what I was being taught in that moment remains with me and vividly at this writing, on July 30th, 2008, while on the campus of Nazarene Theological Seminary.

My own journey to, with and in Christ is both human and Divine. Mildred Wynkoop played a pivotal role, when as a young adult, I wrestled to make sense of my own hunger to be holy and the tension of being aware, even at an early age, that I am not holy. Her writings set me free to widen just a little the parameter of 'meaning' and 'mystery' that fills my own participation in God's saving restoration of all life. She pointed me beyond the 'transaction' to the relationship and beyond the relationship to the Lover who moves in all life.

At this writing, years later, I am now keenly aware that my own participation in the saving work of God has as much to do with my own mother and father who presented me to Christ and his Church, as with Wynkoop. Their presentation of me took. The Trinity of God was active with the Church who received and affirmed the continuing and deepening transaction (covenant) with my family. Unseen, the Father was celebrating before time and in time my own journey to and in the Spirit, in and to Christ Jesus.

None of us are saved because of a decision we made, alone. It is the decision of God, before time and Jesus in time, of the church in history and of the Spirit active in all and in me that results in my own participation in the Story of God.

I had an appointment one day with the Church of Christ. And so began my own journey in—too—with Christ by means of His Church.

Reflections on "Beginnings—An Appointment with The Story"

None of us are saved because of a decision we made, alone. It is the decision of God, before time and Jesus in time, of the church in history and of the Spirit active in all and in me that results in my own participation in the Story of God.
Terry, Above

Q: Have you ever thought of your to, with and in Christ as being as much a human journey as it is Divine? ...How does that strike you?

Q: What Divine and human moments have formed or informed your relationship with Jesus?

Reflect on the significant of Terry's thesis and write out a short spiritual biography of your own journey to, with and in Christ. Especially think about those that took place even before you were old enough to envision knowing God.

Then: Give Thanks to God and perhaps, others.

Week-10: TUESDAY—LUKE 3: 1-23

My Thoughts 43—The New Birth—An Appointment with the Church

Adult Baptism or Affirmation of our Child Baptism—Appointment 2

Becoming Real

I have a very poor memory. Feelings I remember, but not events or persons in time. I feel embarrassed in many social situations with old friends, for I am lost to their memory and have to fake it.

One moment I do not need to fake. It is my first recalled awakening to the Holy Spirit in the new birth. Whether the same service or not I cannot say. But I remember singing incorrectly and with passion "and with a concrete (instead of conquering) tread we will push ahead and roll the sea away." Concrete tread made perfect sense to this young boy of eight or nine, already familiar with freeways and bridges crossing the Snake River. It was my original contextualization of the gospel in music.

Even so, it was the feeling of triumphant optimism that captured me in that small revivalist church in Burley, Idaho. Our guest was Fairy Chism, a passionate and old preacher of the gospel. I remember only her kind eyes and the heart inside her stories. I went forward to the altar in response to the invitation to follow Christ. I wept. Somehow, even as a child who probably knew little of sin as experience, my heart was captured with a real sense of sorrow. It was a sorrow not rooted in guilt, but in revelation. I would not know it again, deeply and purely as I did that evening until three decades later. I can still hear my words combining with a child's faith. "Jesus, please come into my heart." Such peace entered and seemed to permeate and stay with me. I was a different little boy. I was now Jesus' boy. I was born again.

While I now clearly understand the need for continuing conversion and the developmental aspect of our deeply personal involvement in this great salvation, I know from experience that children can be significantly engaged with the Holy Spirit. Child evangelism makes perfect sense to me.

Whether as a child, teenager or adult one thing remains biblically clear. The 'reality of Christ' can only be personally and communally experienced in relation to the Third Person of the Trinity of God.

Catholic's confirm by the laying on of hands. Evangelicals have altar calls or their equivalent. Mystics wait in silence for renewal in relation to God. **However, one gets there, the knowing which makes 'real' is the Holy Spirit forming the life of Jesus in us.**

By 'real', I do not mean to suggest that all that comes before/after by 'sign' or in 'relation' to the Story of the Church or the Eucharist is unreal. I know too many authentic followers of Christ, who (if I may be so arrogant) do not yet seem to know if *"there is a Holy Spirit"* (Acts 19: 2b). I simply mean that the Kingdom of God is actualized only in relation to the Trinity of God. That relation is made affective and effectual in the Holy Spirit's Presence in us! The new birth is necessary to that end. It is not the 'end' itself.

Reflections on "The New Birth—An Appointment with the Church"

By 'real', I do not mean to suggest that all that comes before/after by 'sign' or in 'relation' to the Story of the Church or the Eucharist is unreal. I know too many authentic followers of Christ, who (if I may be so arrogant) do not yet seem to know if "there is a Holy Spirit" (Acts 19: 2b). I simply mean that the Kingdom of God is actualized only in relation to the Trinity of God. That relation is made affective and effectual in the Holy Spirit's Presence in us!
Terry (Above)

Terry seems to want to equate 'knowing' and the Holy Spirit's Presence in us.

Q: How does that strike you?

Terry is also wanting to locate the 'new birth' in a larger human experience of our faith journey and of the journey of the Church. He suggests that the new birth is really an appointment with the Church, with 'living' inside The Story of the Church.

Q: How does that strike you?

Q: Have you ever thought of the natural rhythms of the Church's life as the context in which the Person of the Holy Spirit can actualize or make real what is already true—that you are a follower of Jesus?

Q: Have you, as yet, been 'born of God'?

Turn your story and life to prayer.

Week-10: WEDNESDAY—ROMANS 6: 1-11

STORY 38—GODLY SORROW

GODLY SORROW—APPOINTMENT 3

A Personal Story—Dissonance

I was making my way from the West Seattle Highlands descending through the green space toward the Port of Seattle, the rising orange dinosaurs (cargo cranes) that dot the landscape only added to the breath-taking scenery of the deep blue sea splashing in the bright morning sun light of the Seattle skyline. This morning my eyes were not captured by the beauty before me. Tears were gently flowing down the side of my face, my spirit in another place of deep conversation with the Trinity of God. "Father, will I ever be saved?" I heard myself speaking out loud my inmost thoughts. "I mean really saved?" It was not a plea of desperation whose urgency echoed against the lonely caverns of my heart. This cry was a gentle, broken awareness of need. "Lord," I continued aloud. "I know I am saved. I am Yours, but I remain so unholy. Will I never be more than I am, earthy and sensual, filled with longing?"

There was a comfort, even a hopefulness in the echo of my heart. All I heard—felt—intuited was, "Yes." The voice had the signature of the Spirit, who was also listening.

MY THOUGHTS 44—GODLY SORROW— AN APPOINTMENT WITH OURSELVES

Transformational Dissonance—Sanctification Deepening

Jesus was born from the broken waters of his mother's womb. It was earthy, fleshy. Blood and water mingled and the Eternal Son of the Eternal Father was born as a son of Adam, the result of a painful struggle inside the rhythms of Mary's womb. The first event in the life of the One from before time was also a violent gasping for air, pushing through that water liquid that had filled his lungs for his first nine months. It is the moment of his first cry and ours; not his last, nor ours.

Dr. Luke tells us of the cave and straw, the shepherds and of Joseph's humble origins. What we do not see, but surely know, is the truth that even God's only Son was not spared the sign of Eve's curse. (Genesis 3: 15) In fact the rhythms of delivery are the sorrow from which birth is given. As Jonah was in the belly of a whale, so Jeshua made his journey from the very Presence of Glory (Father—Son—Spirit) to our planet inside the darkness of Eve's womb.

Now thirty-three years have passed. Jesus lived his life in relative obscurity until this moment, the beginning of his mission. And what is the sign of eternity's hope? Armies? Purple robes? Dancing? Angels singing? No, it is a further humility, as Jesus kneels into the dirty waters of the Jordan.

Lakes and oceans to the ancients represented the mysteries of darkness. To the Hebrew it was the place of sheol, the home of the dead. To the pagan the waters of the deep were the birth place of the gods and the source of their angry thundering's. And so Jesus came to John and entered in by baptism. He entered into our fears and darkness. He identified fully with our weakness, enveloped in water.

This was neither the beginning or end of Jesus watery story, but it is the sign of His, and through Him, our salvation by and from water. It is no wonder that John's gospel is filled with a watery motif. Of all the disciples John was the closest to Mary. He would have known the intimate details of his birth. He was also the only male disciple to have witnessed crucifixion and the spear that pierced his heart and seen the water and blood which flowed from within him.

Reflections on "Godly Sorrow—An Appointment with Ourselves"

Reflect on the significance of Terry's observations of Jesus watery life.

Q: Have you seriously considered baptism as an awakening to the depth of human sin and wounds? ...as sanctification (being made holy) begun?

Q: Have you ever known a season of Godly sorrow?

Turn your story and life to prayer.

Week-10: THURSDAY— JOHN 17: 17-18

MY THOUGHTS 45—ENTIRE SANCTIFICATION—AN APPOINTMENT WITH LOVE

ENTIRELY AVAILABLE—APPOINTMENT 4

Transformational Congruence—The 'Entire' inside Sanctification

Sanctification—now that's a big word that I've never heard in my walk around life. I mean, no one has ever come up to me and said, "Hey, Terry, how's the sanctification going?" True enough—but no one on the street has ever asked me about the Trinity of God either and how I see and experience God goes to the very center of being human; as does sanctification.

So let's start with some simple definitions.

Definitions:

Sanctifying Grace: Getting inside the Jesus Story so that we become like him and by God's Holy Presence are being restored to God's original vision of who we are to become.

Progressive Sanctification: The moment by moment development of Jesus likeness and story in us.

Initial Sanctification: That moment(s) when Christ is real in us, by the Holy Spirit and are in relation and accepted (justified) by God.

Entire Sanctification: The quality of relation with Christ wherein we love God first as no other and our neighbor as ourselves. The human center of identity being formed in critical moments so we are entirely given over to the Sanctifying Presence of the Holy Spirit.

Well, now that we got a bit of word image on sanctification, including 'entire' let's talk briefly about one other huge impact on the way we humans experience reality; our world view. We are living in one of those 500 year moments when the way we see reality itself is shifting and with it our ideas about Biblical salvation. We are in the beginnings of a shift from **modern** to **post-modern** thinking, feeling, seeing, living.

Now, in terms of what it means to be human and fully alive to God, 'Moderns' focus on character formation. "Give me a truly honest and compassionate man and I will make him a skilled worker, whatever his lack of knowledge," is the paradigm of my grandpa. Life is built around the timeless, eternal character of God and those, who like God, are trustworthy—certain—still; in whatever winds that may blow.

'Post-moderns' define being human as living into God; as making loving choices in whatever circumstance one lives. "Show me a gifted artist who can love through her art or music or writings and I will show you God"—and so leans the direction of my millennial friends. Like water flowing, life is an endless rush of ever changing emotions, circumstances, environs and it is a loving human who can traverse the age with skill, openness and acceptance.

To the modern holiness is about heart—what is the central focus or motive in every interaction or experience? And so sanctification is simply 'centering' one's heart in love and devotion upon God.

For the post-modern the center of human God-likeness is loving relation, whatever may be the interior state of the soul.

Entire Sanctification has all too often been preached and taught in mathematical terms—being entirely holy and loving as God is. While holy—love is a descriptive of sanctification, entire is about us (each and all of us together), not sanctification. The question in 'entire' sanctification is simply this: Am I entirely given over to the Sanctifying presence of the Holy Spirit.

For the millennial, it is a question of the quality of my/our love—are we, am I, accepting and authentic? If my life is congruent—whole—moving in accepting, healthy and loving direction then I or we may describe the quality of our holiness or love as 'entire,' real, gifting.

For the greatest generation, it is a question of heart and passion. Do I love Jesus first, as no other? Whatever my actions, they are worthless unless they express a heart the is congruent it its pursuit of holy—love and in all circumstances. 'Entire' is a quality of relation (called sanctified) but only because the center of motivation and affections (the heart) is united in seeking only to please God.

Whether you live in modernity or post-modernity one thing remains. God has an appointment of love with you and desires that you are given over to love, entirely.

Reflections on "Entire Sanctification—An Appointment with Love"

"When we pray ('Your will be done on earth as it is in heaven'), *we are asking that the drama of the Mount of Olives, the struggle of Jesus' entire life and work, be brought to completion in us; that together with him, the Son, we may unite our wills with the Father's will, thus becoming sons in our turn...*

The Sermon on the Mount provides the key that discloses the inner basis of this remarkable experience and also the path of conversion that opens us up to being drawn into the Son's filial knowledge [of the Father]: 'Blessed are the pure in heart, for they shall see God' (Mt 5:8). Purity of heart is what enables us to see. Therein consists the ultimate simplicity that opens up our life to Jesus...
From "Jesus of Nazareth", page #341-343, Pope Benedict XVI

Pope Benedict XVI is connecting Jesus own full identification with God's will (sanctification) with our own need/ability to be 'entirely' given over to the will of God... It is purity of heart—to will one thing alone; God's will—whatever the struggle in getting there.

Q: Have you ever seen the necessity of responding to God's call to inner sanctity as a necessary part of our salvation; of being made holy—made whole?

Q: Have you come face to face with this appointment as yet? ...You will.

Turn your story and life to prayer.

Week-10: FRIDAY—LUKE 4: 1-13

MY THOUGHTS 46—DEEPENING INTEGRITY—AN APPOINTMENT WITH HOLINESS

DEEPENING INTEGRITY—APPOINTMENT 5

"We know that when he appears, we shall be like him, for we shall see him as he is. Everyone who has this hope in him purifies himself, just as he is pure."
I John 3: 2-3

Progressive Sanctification: The moment by moment development of Jesus likeness and story in us.

Transformational Congruence: The 'Progressive' inside Sanctification

Integrity is a word whose modern meaning comes very close to the Biblical idea of holiness. Integrity in persons infers a quality of character, whose responses and choices involve 'wholeness (health), purity and hope'. Integrity always acts out of loving intention towards others, even when there is great cost to ourselves. Yet what we might do, even in similar situations may vary widely, according to the needs of those with whom we interact and our growing understanding of what's real and healthy and right.

Would I serve the sacraments to a young couple living together without the benefit of marriage? The law is clear. If holiness is based upon law alone, I would not, ever. Yet, for integrity's (holiness's) sake I have. For on more than one occasion I have walked alongside of couples who I believe are in Christ and walking within the permissive will of Christ and yet, have not faced the sin and contradiction of their sexual intimacy outside of the communal and personal union between God and a male and female. I have freely offered the sacrament to such couples, believing that to withhold the holy—love of Jesus would violate love itself and thus be to act without integrity (holiness).

More personally, at this writing—March of 2008, in the last six months I have wrestled deeply with the inmost longings of my heart with respect to sexual desire. Behaviorally, I have never entered into nor believe I am capable (the heart is deceitfully wicked?) of an adulteress relation. Still, a combination of age, counseling and emotional loss has opened up in my conscious mind the fact that the deepest desires of my heart remain pagan. They are more deeply informed by Hollywood than the Church. What was suppressed and/or emotionally healed, until recent months, has re-emerged as a new and more intense struggle. Much of my prayer time is owned with this confession of the sin (not behavioral sins, but underlying affection) and the awareness of hypocrisy. Up until recent months my thought life has remained free in my relationships with women. I have not felt contradictory feelings of being genuinely present person to person and also feeling strong sexual hunger in women's presence. Now, in this season and on some days it seems like it takes 45 minutes of devotional prayer and confession just to get into the day and function. So the question arises? Should I receive holy communion myself? Should I as an ordained elder even offer the sacrament?

My historical holiness community, formed in the intellectual and cultural environment of the late 1800 revivalist tradition would ask me to resign from active ministry at such a confession and seek earnestly the holiness of heart (transformation of character) that allows unity of holy-affection in all my personal relationships. Love is a matter of inner thoughts—being first, understanding that from a corrupt heart comes corrupted behavior. This tradition would move me away from confession and counseling and instead direct me to prayer, fasting and earnest hunger for purity, until given. Once received they would encourage a positive and public confession of faith of the purifying presence of the Holy Spirit.

The twenty first century expression of my holiness community is much more concerned with behavior and compassion based action (living into faith) and would counsel me to seek wholeness (healing) and behave ethically and with loving intention. If that is the mark of my life (and I believe it is) then my contemporary holiness friends would surround me in prayer and suggest I remain compassionately and vitally engaged in ministry. The only question (and it is appropriate) is one of emotional health. Am I healthy enough to do ministry?

Health (Wholeness) or purity (Holiness)? Being or doing?

To the post-modern the moment is everything. You and I are an evolving personality and presence, arising from the Creator's love and moving back to the Creator. Every event of our life forms our heart. Will we live into love or away from love?

Loving and holy action is 'eternal' as God is and will form in us a holy—loving presence (heart). At the heart of the post-modern perspective is a relational—orientational perspective. Faith is looking to God's loving action, not away from God's loving action in our world. Faith is living into what God is doing in the world. Faith is love responding. Orientation of response is the critical central issue of our faith journey.

To the pre-modern/modern the formative issue is not the moment, but our personal being (character). Are we, like the Creator from whom we derive life, holy and loving or corrupted and lost? Likeness in being is the central issue of salvation. Hence the pursuit is focused on achieving a quality of 'character' or 'substance of being' instead a quality of life as lived.

A Biblical argument can be made for each perspective. Each have their historical ancestors. Each draw from a tree of life, dating back to our first parents. As a son on the edge of both philosophical traditions I seek to find a community of understanding that incorporates both, so that I may live/speak to both generations.

Like my 18th century counterparts, I remain convinced that my personal identity—likeness—presence is actual and real and not simply derivative. I am more than an accumulation of events (moments) with Christ forming the connections between and thus co-creating in me, life. I continue to take seriously from my fathers (European-Western) in the Church the 'character/quality' of my being before God. I further believe that as a result of the influence of past events (Adams and all his sons/daughters) the original likeness of my being is deeply wounded and I am born lost in some real sense to the Father—Spirit—Son's eternal presence—likeness—being. Hence I grow up corrupted.

However, with my contemporaries I share a relational—orientational view of salvation. The truth is my likeness—presence, though actual is also derivative and dependent upon the eternal good will and sustaining presence of God's Holy Spirit in the world. Further, Salvation is communicated in time (relationally) and hence the moments—events of my life carry within them the potential of creation and re-creation of my actual being. Through 'salvation history' (actualized moments in time) God is bringing about both my own personal 'story/presence' but also a larger 'Story/Presence'. The Kingdom of God is emerging. It is actual, real and lives inside the identity—dreams—reality of real persons connected over centuries with God.

God is a person, not an accumulation of experiences. We are made in the image of God and are persons. Sin therefore can be a noun and not simply an adjective or adverb. Sin is always deeply personal and involves both intent and action. That is to say that at heart sin is relational. Sin is always a movement away from love. The Biblical narrative of persons in battle, seeking to influence the outcome of 'history' is appropriate for such a world view. Yet sin cannot live apart from persons. A rock or aunt cannot sin. Only persons can. Still the very center of a person's being can be said to be sin-filled, willful, unable or unwilling to respond to God's loving initiative.

Unlike, God, we as persons cannot live outside of events/moments in time. At least not in the universe as we understand it. We are not independent beings, but very dependent upon the good will and presence of the Trinity of God for our actuality. What we do (get it? ...do) does matter. For it is the doing (living our story in time) that frames salvation.

Salvation is not something God does to us or even in us. Salvation is God, living inside our event experience (through the Son and by the Holy Spirit) and forming in the very center of our being (likeness—presence—identity) Divinity. Salvation is always communicated relationally in moments of time. In this sense, God is really connecting the dots of our lives as the Trinity of God forms a communion with us.

Myself as a living person in communion with God and all creation will not be fully formed until I see God face to face. Hence, St. John rightly says, *"What we will be has not yet been made known. But we know that when he appears, we shall be like him, for we shall see him as he is"* (I John 3:2b). It is in seeing the actual presence of Jesus that our own actuality (being) is fully realized. Even so, John goes on, *"Everyone who has this hope in him purifies himself just as he is pure"* (I John 3: 3). 'Purifies' speaks of allowing the moments of our life as lived, to be transformational. It also speaks to the confessional need to be 'aware' of our hope and to long for and seek in each moment that purity of being/heart that is promised in scripture. The term, however is active, always and refers to the orientation of our life as lived.

The confession 'just as he is pure' is a statement of being and relation. We are pure, relationally by being in 'right relationship' with God. However, inside the word is the very real promise that at the center of our being love already lives [See John 13:10-11].

So, what does all this have to do with me, at this writing? Should I or should I not serve communion?

At this writing, I am 54 years of age and experiencing a deeper awareness of loss and as a result an intuitive and hungry awareness of just how broken is my (mental—physical—soul—spiritual) body.

Still, I live with the very real hope of 'seeing Jesus' face to face one day. *"I know that my Redeemer lives, and that in the end he will stand upon the earth. And after my skin has been destroyed, yet in my flesh I will see God; I myself will see him with my own eyes—I, and not another. How my heart years within me!"* (Job 19:25-27). This very hope increases both my hunger for and awareness of the deep love (grace) in which I stand. This same hope also makes me keenly aware of the depth of Adam's wound in me [Romans 8: 24-25]. I am a real person but also a being in the process of formation.

Like Christ there are seasons of deeper temptation, when the eternal questions break into time with power and expose broken spaces. In these desert seasons I am forced to live 'not by bread alone, but by every word that proceeds from the mouth of God.' I do not like these moments. I do not seek them. But I see in them my redeemer, who in his own life, entered into mine.

Integrity lies at the heart of my moment by moment journey. God's and mine.

Reflections on "Deepening Integrity—An Appointment with Holiness"

Terry seems to suggest that that the Sacrament of Holy Communion can be offered to anyone who is authentically following Jesus, even if their own personal story does not live up to God's revealed will.

Q: Your thoughts? …Where would you draw the line?

Q: Does the word 'integrity' carry all of the New Testament means by holiness? …Can you think of a better word?

Psychologists speak of in-congruency; That state wherein our behavior is really different than our self-image. Hence we don't see our behavior, because it doesn't fit into our view or our-self. Deepening Integrity has to do with 'seeing clearly'. Seeing ourselves as God does.

Q: Is your life congruent? What would God see in you that needs fix'n?

> *"We know that when he appears, we shall be like him, for we shall see him as he is. Everyone who has this hope in him purifies himself, just as he is pure."*
> I John 3: 2-3

Q: What is salvation? Is it:

> ➤ The orientation of our life toward God?, or;
> ➤ Loving God out of a pure heart?, or;
> ➤ Growing up into Christ in all ways?, or;
> ➤ All of the above?, or;
> ➤ Something else all together?

Write out your own thoughts about salvation and then prayerfully meditate on the question: Am I saved? Am I being saved?

Week-10: SATURDAY—LUKE 7: 18-23

Story 39—Living that Matters—An Appointment with d'Judge

THE LAST JUDGMENT—APPOINTMENT 6

Introduction:

I do not fear being alone. I enjoy it, for I know that inside me, in my inner being and imagination lies a kingdom wide and deep, filled with intimate knowledge and conversation. Further, I know that I know that I know this one truth: God is love and God loves me. It is enough, even on my darkest day.

However, what I do fear is that in the end my life will amount to nothing. I fear that nothing I write or feel or think or live will ever have impact beyond or even in time. One would hope that the certainty I feel in God's surrounding love would be sufficient to arrest this fear. It is not. For love cannot make a thing true.

A Personal Story—Why Life Matters

Driving home from my last visit with my father, before his death, I wept and bitterly. It was between Woodland, Washington and Longview. This road at night is dark and often a shadow casts its long grey presence over the road, even on a moonlit night, for you are driving near a mountain on one side of the freeway and an open valley on the other. What drove me to tears was not the fear of losing someone for whom I had deep emotional attachment. I did not and do not now. My father and I shared ministry, but we did not share in life together. What created sorrow was the awareness that what was lost between us could not be captured again. It was an eternal loss. Even heaven could not re-create what never was. Yes, heaven could begin a new journey with my father and I hope will. Love will transform our relationship, going forward and may allow us to share the deep inner longings that I suspect we both felt in isolation from each other and family. But heaven cannot magically replace what these fifty years (for me) had never been. It was an eternal loss that wept under the dark shadow of the evening.

Bringing the Story Home:

Why? Why does the story of my loss even matter? Because time matters. How we live our life or don't has significance. It is the judgment of God which assures the possibilities of life, not love alone.

MY THOUGHTS 47—WHY LIFE MATTERS—AN APPOINTMENT WITH D'JUDGE

We live in a time when we despise the idea of 'judgment'. Part of the reason is that we have confused judgment with condemnation. We have seen judgment as a judicial proceeding. Our memories of God, as judge, have been framed by passionate preachers who warned us of eternal torture, if our sins were not judiciously atoned for. Such a view of judgment, reflecting pagan ideas of hell and captured by the church, contradicts the picture of God as loving—It should.

We are also averse to the idea of judgment because we live in a democracy which tries to level the playing field. We are afraid to honor winners because it inevitably infers that there were some who were losers.

It is a mistaken idea of love which compels us to avoid the idea of judgment. God is all love. Love is defined by God's personage. The Trinity of God is a communal Being who is love and holy awe. In creation the Trinity has opened up the possibility of creatures such as ourselves knowing intimately the holy love that is shared between the Father—Son—Spirit.

Not just any idea of love will do. Not just any idea of love rises to fellowship with the only Persons who really matter. Only that love which is 'true, noble, right, pure, lovely, admirable and praiseworthy' [see Philippians 4:8] will rise to live forever. Only such a holy love will have significance and meaning.

The playing field in which we live is not even. The holy—love of God guarantees equal access, true. But this same holy—love also guarantees that there will be winners and potentially losers.

This is the heart of Jesus teaching as John remembers it. *"When a man believes in me, he does not believe in me only"* (John 12: 44). If life were defined by the mathematical ideas of infinite grace extended to us in Jesus we might have reason to buy into theories of atonement that see Jesus death as a substitute for our unrighteous and careless life choices. However, Jesus grace is given in the context of the Trinity of God's holy dreams. Dreams which originate in the Father's heart and form in both eternity and time the context or condition in which life either thrives or perishes. *"I know that his command leads to eternal life. So whatever I say is just what the Father has told me to say"* (John 12:50).

Jesus came to *"the world as a light, so that no one who believes in [him] should stay in darkness"* (John 12: 47). The possibilities of life are endless as we live within the vision of the Trinity of God. However, it is also true, necessarily, that to stray from the light is to place ourselves in the darkness of a 'living hell'. Jesus primary word for hell was "gehenna", a garbage dump just outside of Jerusalem. Jesus often warned his hearers that this same love which will go to any length to see that we live a life of wholeness is a double edged sword. This love will also condemn us. Condemnation here is not judicial as though we were being condemned to punishment. Rather it is truth and love forming the only basis in which we can live and love and prosper. Jesus identified the risk. *"There is a judge for the one who rejects me and does not accept my words at the last day"* (John 12: 48).

It is this future judgment into which we are all living. This judgment guarantees the awesome potential of our life. We can rise at that last day and be known by the Father, who will see in our life, His only Son. If that is the case, then all our words and feelings and living which have the mark of Christ's holy love will live and prosper. We will have just begun. However, there is a down side and it is great. The Father of all might not recognize in us The Son. In that case our life is empty and wasted. We are left to a garbage dump from which only love can save us.

Reflections on "Living that Matters—An Appointment with d'Judge"

Do not fear God. Fear only yourself, living outside of Christ's holy—love…lost.

The Character and dreams of the Father—Son—Spirit form the universe. Living lost to yourself, your neighbor and God's vision, you should fear. The stakes are high.

Q: Have you ever been before a judge? …What was it like?

Q: What do you think of Terry's suggestion that it is not God, but us we should fear—living outside of Christ's holy—love?

It is the judgment of the Trinity of God that assures the possibilities of life—not love alone.

Terry argues that God has a vision and dream and 'life matters' because of it; our life makes a real difference. Hence we either live into love or live into something very different—and that something other is always a dead end street.

Q: How does such a view make you feel? …Is the idea of judgment contrary to love or necessary to it?

Consider the meaning of your own life and take it to the only judge who really cares.

Week-10: SUNDAY—JOHN 12: 37-50 & 17: 20-26

STORY 40—LOOKING EAST—AN APPOINTMENT WITH THE FULLNESS OF CHRIST'S COMING

THE COMING OF CHRIST—APPOINTMENT 7

Introduction:

What is the mission of the Church?

We are to be a community of priests in the city of humankind. We are to offer living sacrifices; living sacramentally and sacrificially in the city of women and men until all creation is truly reconciled to God and one another.

A Personal Story—From the East Side of Kansas City

My spirit felt a check. 'Don't give him anything.' As I turned from the convenience store clerk, having received quarters for a newspaper, I was thinking instead about the young man just outside who had asked me for a quarter, so he could take the bus ride. Usually, I won't give money to someone on the street. Time, food, gas—yes, but never money. "Will you use it for drugs?" I couldn't believe I was asking the question. It's demeaning to the person I'm asking, creates an immediate wall in relation and does nothing to guarantee the person in need is telling the truth. Besides, a quarter? Seriously, Terry? So, as I hesitated, I shook off the intuition of my own spirit, perhaps The Spirit, and went outside and gave him a dollar and a quarter. The attendant inside had said that's what it takes to ride the bus.

I knew I had not approached the young man with equality of heart, only a 'white' guy's guilty response to apparent hunger. I asked him, "Are you hungry?" He looked at me with the look of someone who knows he's about to catch a big fish. "Sure." I invited him into my car to go get something to eat. Third mistake.

I was on his turf, in a city I'd only visited once before as a child, Kansas City. Once in the car he started giving me directions further into his hood, to a pizza place, he told me. I became quickly aware that he was on some drugs. My driving scarred him. Now my driving scares a lot of people, true, but I was doing only 30 on a wide four lane road with little traffic. When nervous, his English was pretty clear of the hood accent—as he gave orders to avoid the side of the road or a car ahead of us. But when I tried some casual and personal conversation he went slang on me. A lazy kind of slang used by inner city kids. Lazy, that is, to my white way of think'n. It was his way of telling me to butt out. He knew and I knew this was not about a relationship, but a hand out. I was white. He was black. From his perspective, I was rich. "Seattle, huh? Must a cost." It was the closest thing to a conversation we had. He was taking the measure of me. I genuinely think he was sizing me up to shake me down. I was praying.

Several times he had ordered me to turn to his favorite rap-jazz station. He seemed frustrated that I couldn't make the radio work in my Trans-Am rental. When we finally got it figured out, he kept turning up the music with the bass speakers dancing. I get so frustrated when a car comes up next to me bang'n some music no one wants to hear. It must have looked pretty funny to people around us seeing an old white dude and young African American street kid kick'n it. I would turn it down. He would turn the radio right back up. We were now locked into a power trip, as we made our way further into his hood. Finally, I turned it down soft and told him to leave it alone. It was the way I liked it.

I saw a Pizza Hut, turned in and got out of the car taking my keys with me. He seemed cool with it. "Live here," was all he said. I went in, paid for his pizza and left him abruptly, wondering where and how I went wrong. It had not been the transformational moment I have learned to enjoy with person's pan handling in Seattle.

Still the day had been good. It was Sunday and had started in an African American United Methodist church I stumbled onto. I was the only salt in the shaker. But I was warmly received. The music rocked. The sermon was powerful and directed at part of my own interior journey. The afternoon had been a mixture of reflection, sleep, silence, eating and reading. A good day.

And now, at the close of the day, around 10 pm in the evening I was parked down in the heart of the city next to a river, windows down, writing in my journal when a well-dressed middle aged African American approached me. He had a story. It was a good one, designed to elicit concern and money.

This guy was smooth and felt sincere. So, I told him, "Listen, I'm not going to give you money, but I will go with you and get some gas in your car so you can take your lady and new born home." I was disappointed when he started back peddling with reasons why he couldn't follow me to a gas station. I offered to go get some gas in a can and bring it to him. He'd been caught, smiled and just lowered his head. The sense of apparent shame was the first honest moment between us. "Okay, this time listen. I'm a preacher from Seattle who works with the homeless. Why don't you cut the crap and just tell me what you need?" In about a minute I knew I had something of the real story, so I responded: "Bottom line, I ain't giv'n you money. I'll take you and buy you some food. "Now, he was sizing me up. He had already showed me his license to evidence who he was.

Given the Bible in my lap and the writing tablet, not to mention some good jazz gospel sounds he decided to trust. And me? I wasn't getting any checks from either The Sprit or my own. I knew it was a little risky but it all felt good.

We started heading, at his direction, straight towards the same part of town I had been frightened in earlier that afternoon. We stopped at a Gates Barbecue. It was an upscale barbecue with atmosphere and a security guard outside. As we talked we cleared the lies. He told me he was a born again Christian. It didn't feel like a con as much as good American religious experience, an inch deep. I suggested a little honesty might be a good thing then. By the time our trip was done, I had met one of the owners of this chain of restaurants, whom Tommy knew, delivered him to a home in the African American community and prayed with him.

I left, grateful to God that I was alive and had just witnessed a Jesus moment. We had moved past mutual prejudices and distrust to respect and equal risk. It was about relationship, not a hand out. It was about love, not power.

He walked away with a real sense that God had met him, because we had stumbled onto his friend and owner of the restaurant, who did offer him the money he needed. In our conversation and prayer, he knew he had been gently loved and confronted by His God. Plus, I was able to tell him about the cool United Methodist Church just up the street from his mom's house. It was a kingdom moment.

MY THOUGHTS 48—GETTING TO THE FULLNESS OF CHRIST'S COMING

All of creations children; rich, poor, red, white, black and every shade between, the powerful and the weak, Muslim, Native faiths, atheist, pagan and Christian are covered with Jesus. His life, death and resurrection permeate all things and land. Our purpose is to make real the Jesus event in all things.

All of God's creation are forgiven of every wounded space that attends Adam/Eve's children. All of God's children are held by the tender mercies that poured into the city by the One who suffered just outside the city gate.

Land itself drinks of this new spiritual water, flowing from Calvary's mount. Nature is fully renewed in Christ. Environmental healing is restored in that One life whose Word first created in the beginning and now through the Church is re-creating.

Even the unseen world, beings not human, but capable of glory, fallen and filled with darkness are reconciled and await the fullness of Christ's coming. Satan himself, deceiver and robber, may yet be received as the prodigal returned home. Job's opening dialogue between the evil one and God makes no sense unless God remains redemptively engaged with this rebellious angel.

What is the mission of the Church?

The church is the first fruit of all creation both in the heavens and on earth. We live and breathe Christ, in the celebration of His mystery revealed in the Eucharist and made real in the Holy Spirit. We are his body, broken. Our sacrificial love is his blood poured out into history in each cultural setting. As we awaken to holy love the world and the heavens will come to live in the fullness of love made real, earthy, timely.

Salvation is the unfolding Story of creation reconciled to herself and her creator in Christ. All of the daughters and sons of Adam are saved, for no one will be left out of God's Story in the end; unless of course we freely and finally choose to live apart from the one and only Son of the Father. It is from this hopeful picture that salvation draws its meaning. Salvation's provision is made real by means of the cross (Christ event) lived out in history through the Church.

Salvation is never about a few souls being captured out of creation (time and place) in order that the wrath of God may be eternally visited upon the rest of creation who remain separated from the life of God. That would indeed be a costly grace.

Salvation is always:

> ➢ Communal, and;
> ➢ Lives in cultural context, and;
> ➢ Involves history and land, and;
> ➢ Is deeply personal.

Salvation is Communal

God is a community of persons so united in holy love that God remains One in essential being. Hence God lives in and between persons. **Wherever holy—love is, God is!** Some expressions of holy—love are fully Christian. They originate and express the Son's human event (life, death, resurrection). Some are pre-Christian. Whenever a community lives in the wholeness of love, God is present.

The Church is a community and lives in communion with the Father—Son—Spirit on earth. The Church is the ever growing realization of the Trinity of God's purpose in creation. The mystery of the Eucharist, as lived in John's gospel is a vivid scriptural example of the Church's current purpose. The church's life is the salvation of Christ, made real in time.

Salvation lives in a cultural context

God delights in the rainbow of life. All of creation evidences diversity seeking unity. We are made in the image of the Three who are One. All, that is, but personal society (human/angelic) who struggle with the original independence of our first parent/arch-angel.

Human society/history is about diversity seeking power. The Nazi holocaust and ethnic cleansing is perhaps the most vivid example of history moving away from instead of toward God's purpose. The heart of our dilemma is here. The best pre-Christian expression of diversity seeking unity is tolerance and limited acceptance. Drive through any American city (like Kansas City) and you will quickly begin to see that our differences divide instead of unite.

[An aside: It was at this moment, in this writing that Tommy approached me in Kansas City, for money].

The church is to live reconciled, breaking down racial, economic, prejudicial walls and by presence seeding 'diversity seeking unity'. It must be a faith lived in real cultural context.

To that end contextualization is only the beginning of our mission. Our real purpose is to move past context and into a new city where diversity is honored and creation is celebrated, not merely tolerated. It would seem apparent that our current American church experience in which Sunday mornings are largely segregated would need to go.

Salvation involves history and land

The greatest tragedy of the modern rapture theology is the absolute ignorance of 'salvation history'. In this tradition, history is moving nowhere. History is simply the context of our individual salvation. The church and Israel before, become the back drop from which God chooses the few. That kind of theology is neither Biblical or imaginative.

The Christian and Jewish revelation is about a suffering God who enters into and redemptively relates to human and angelic history. The Trinity of God is actively involved in the falleness of our story and of both the heavens and earths' environmental de-evolution. God's acts are restorative.

John's Revelation is honest about the result of human sin creating wars, floods, earthquakes, hunger and disease. John however, looks to a new heaven and earth emerging from the totality of our brokenness.

The early and historic debates of the Church around Christ's physical body were critical for they affirmed the glory of all creation. God became material so that we, His body, may affect a real and material transformation of our story into His Story (history) and of our universe into our place in His universe.

In our own community we regularly pray for the environment and for Native American tribal communities seeking federal recognition (Duwamish in West Seattle).

In real, political, economic and physical ways the Church is to live out salvation history in our land and time.

Salvation is deeply personal

I will never forget the Wednesday evening when my evangelical, older and saintly lady was testifying to her personal experience of salvation. One of our previously homeless men, now living in his own home and at that time ministering in our community as a lay preacher bristled at what he perceived to be a 'self-absorbed' and somewhat arrogant expression of salvation. In his early years, he had studied in the Vatican for the priesthood. I knew her story was neither self-absorbed, nor arrogant.

Following his teaching response to her story, I interjected into the conversation that yes, our pietistic tradition can be both arrogant and self-absorbed. It can also be real. If it is real, it had better get deeply personal.

That is one significant contribution that our branch of Wesleyans brings to the body of Christ. We emphasize the need for the new-birth and a life entirely given over to the Presence of the One who is Three. If ever we devalue our contribution we will miss the soul of salvation.

Interior experience of Christ, by His Spirit is necessary. We cannot live Christ unless Christ is fully alive in us. This is foundational. It is also soulful.

However, it is the beginning of salvation, not its largest expression of God's salvational story among and in us.

07/28/08

Reflections on "Looking East—An Appointment with the Fullness of Christ's Coming"

The idea of 'salvation' as restoration of each individual, community, people group and the environment to God and each other is at the heart of God's mission and is fore-told by the prophets as the coming 'shalom' of God in the world.

Q: Have you ever thought of salvation as more than a personal transaction?

Q: How would such a view of salvation change the way you see the Church and the world around you?

Q: If salvation is restoration/reconciliation of all creation instead of a 'coming out party' in the heavens, how does that effect the way I view 'good works'?

Q: What is the purpose of being missional if our presence (as those who breathe Christ) is salvation begun?

"The church is the first fruit of all creation both in the heavens and on earth. We live and breathe Christ, in the celebration of His mystery revealed in the Eucharist and made real in the Holy Spirit. We are his body, broken. Our sacrificial love is his blood poured out into history in each cultural setting. As we awaken to holy love the world and the heavens will come to live in the fullness of love made real, earthy, timely."
Terry (above)

Q: In what ways does your local body of Christ already reflect this reconciling view of Jesus mission?

Q: Can Jesus really come to the world by means of a rich church? ...Is 'brokeness' necessary to living out Jesus as a 'living sign'?

Terry suggests that, in the end, very few will refuse the loving and holy grace of God, given in the Christ event and lived out in the Church. He even perceives the possibility of the evil one coming home.

Q: How scary or hopeful is that?

Consider the mission of the Church and pray for your own community.

Next:
City of Humans, City of God

11 CITY OF HUMANS, CITY OF GOD

... The New Jerusalem

INVOCATION:

ARISE, O GOD AND SHINE, FOR YOUR LIGHT HAS COME. HE HAS COME IN JESUS OF NAZARETH, HIS LIFE AND SACRIFICE GIVEN ON A HILL NEAR JERUSALEM, ON GOLGOTHA. ARISE, O GOD AND SHINE, FOR YOUR GLORY HAS RISEN. HE ASCENDED AND IN HIM AND WITH HIM, WE ARE INVITED INTO YOUR PRESENCE, TO THE JOY OF YOUR LOVE.

FATHER, STILL WE LONG. DARKNESS COVERS US, A THICK DARKNESS REMAINS OVER ALL PEOPLE, COMMUNITIES, TRIBES AND NATIONS. IN THE DARKNESS WE ASK, 'HAVE YOU FORGOTTEN US?' PLEASE COME, QUICKLY LORD AND BREAK INTO OUR DARKNESS THROUGH THE BIRTH OF YOUR SON, REBORN IN US, YOUR CHURCH. HOW WE LONG FOR YOUR GLORY!

WHEN, LORD, WHEN? WHEN WILL THE NATIONS COME INTO JESUS LIGHT? WHEN WILL THE KINGS OF THE EARTH COME TO YOUR CHURCH AS ONE COMES INTO THE LIGHT OF A NEW DAY? AMEN.

ADAPTED FROM ISAIAH 60: 1-3

PSALM OF THE WEEK: PSALM 128

COMMANDMENT OF THE WEEK: "YOU SHALL NOT COVET YOUR NEIGHBOR'S WIFE. YOU SHALL NOT SET YOUR DESIRE ON YOUR NEIGHBOR'S HOUSE OR LAND, HIS MANSERVANT OR MAIDSERVANT, HIS OX OR DONKEY, OR ANYTHING THAT BELONGS TO YOUR NEIGHBOR.

DEUTERONOMY 5:21.

DAILY SCRIPTURES:

MONDAY—ZECHARIAH 2: 6-13 & 3: 8-10 & 4: 6-10A

TUESDAY—ISAIAH 61: 1-11, MATTHEW 11: 1-6

WEDNESDAY—ISAIAH 60: 4-22

THURSDAY—MATTHEW 22: 23-46

FRIDAY—LUKE 21: 1-4

SATURDAY—LUKE 22: 14-38

SUNDAY 1— EZEKIEL 37: 1-28, HEBREWS 11: 8-10 & 12: 22-29, COLOSSIANS 1: 24-29, ROMANS 11: 25-32, REVELATION 21: 1-8 & 22: 1-7

FROM
REVELATIONS 21: 1-5

THEN I SAW A NEW HEAVEN AND A NEW EARTH, FOR THE FORMER HEAVEN AND THE FORMER EARTH HAD PASSED AWAY, AND THE SEA WAS NO MORE. I SAW THE HOLY CITY, NEW JERUSALEM, COMING DOWN OUT OF HEAVEN FROM GOD, MADE READY AS A BRIDE BEAUTIFULLY DRESSED FOR HER HUSBAND. I HEARD A LOUD VOICE FROM THE THRONE SAY, "LOOK! GOD'S DWELLING IS HERE WITH HUMANKIND. HE WILL DWELL WITH THEM, AND THEY WILL BE HIS PEOPLES. GOD HIMSELF WILL BE WITH THEM AS THEIR GOD. HE WILL WIPE AWAY EVERY TEAR FROM THEIR EYES. DEATH WILL BE NO MORE. THERE WILL BE NO MOURNING, CRYING, OR PAIN ANYMORE, FOR THE FORMER THINGS HAVE PASSED AWAY." THEN THE ONE SEATED ON THE THRONE SAID, "LOOK! I'M MAKING ALL THINGS NEW."

Week-11: MONDAY—ZECHARIAH 2: 6-13 & 3: 8-10 & 4: 6-10a

MY THOUGHTS 49—JERUSALEM—CITY OF GOD?

"But then—after the power of evil has reached it apogee— something totally different happens. The seer perceives… the Ancient of Days, who puts an end to the horror…The beasts from the depths are confronted by the man from above…the 'Son of Man,' who comes 'with the clouds of heaven,' prophesies a totally new kingdom, a kingdom of 'humanity', characterized by the real power that comes from God himself. This kingdom also signals the advent of true universality, the definitive positive shape of history that has all along been the object of silent longing. The 'Son of Man' who comes from above is thus the antithesis of the beasts from the depths of the sea; as such, he stands not for an individual figure, but for the 'kingdom' in which the world attains its goal."
From "Jesus of Nazareth", by Pope Benedict XVI, pages #326, 327".

Never has there been a city like Jerusalem!

On Mount Zion Melchizedek, King of Salem, offered sacrifices that pleased God. Here too, Abram offered up his one and only son. How the Trinity of God grieved with him,

389

anticipating the ultimate sacrifice of God's One and only. Here, King David longed to build a home for God. But his dream was delayed as God waited for a son from David's loins whose heart reflected the peace that God the Father always desired for his city. And Solomon reigned in peace, bringing to Jerusalem and Yahweh's home all the kings of the earth to revel in the glory of Jerusalem.

Solomon's life was filled with the spirit of wisdom and justice, like another Son who would one day come into this city. But Solomon's heart strayed. He did not remain faithful to the humility that occasioned his childhood faith. From Solomon's idolatry and sexual addiction flowed a river of sin and destruction. God's home was subjected to every human longing for magic, power, altered psychic states, sexual freedom and violence. In God's home a wicked Queen was killed. Children were sacrificed to secure from foreign god's economic security. Its gold and treasures were removed to pay the cost of her many sins!

This beautiful city of God had become only a city filled with the worst in humanity. Still, God responded by sending to Jerusalem prophets and priests who called its citizens to remember. Through these servants God threatened and pleaded and dramatized profound longing. *"How long will you wander, O unfaithful daughter?"* (Jeremiah 31: 22) In every generation the Father looked for a faithful remnant, who would live before Jerusalem His loving passion. In the end, God found none (Jeremiah 5:1).

Finally, Yahweh had enough and left the Holy Temple and the city that housed God's home. Yahweh left her forsaken with no stone remaining on another. Like a lover scorned He left her to the strangers and animals that roamed this desolate land. But God left with a promise. His return!

In 538 B.C. Yahweh began the return to Jerusalem, in Israel's exiles—now humbled and having a single heart, as God had in days of old. Each labored stone placed upon another was a 'sign of God's promised return'! (Zechariah 2:7-9). In God's heart was a renewed vision of Jerusalem's future. In the fellowship of the Three, who are One, the Father spoke. *"What shall I do? I will send my son, whom I love; perhaps they will respect him"* (Luke 20: 13b). And so The Son of the Father was sent through the Eastern Gate and into a city loved. **And The Son, like the prophets before, was taken and beaten, spit upon and rejected, until finally, at a hill called Golgotha the 'city of humans' met the 'city of God'.**

Jerusalem is the place where heaven and earth meet. However, it is to become the city where God and humans live together, where the city of humankind becomes the city of God. This is the promise of her creation. It is a promise begun in the life, passion, death and resurrection of Jesus. In Jesus, God fully enters the human story. Our story becomes His-story! Our city is transformed into God's.

The problem is that the city of humankind never seems fully open to the city of God. Even we, who in Christ live out Jesus Story and are forming a renewed community of God, often behave more like a city of humans, armed to 'take over' and rule as yet another tyrant. That has been our history all too often.

But that is not the way of God. These two ways; humanity's and God's, are at 'cross' purposes. These two inter-acting stories form a contradiction lived out on a hill called Golgotha.

The contradiction is fully seen in Jesus triumphal entry into Jerusalem. There was no glory or power, only a humility turned into suffering love. The passion of God was fully demonstrated in that last week as Jesus wept over the city, threw out the money changers, taught in the temple, was arrested, beaten and taken out of the city to face a criminal's death.

Reflections on "Jerusalem—City of God?"

"And the Son, like the prophets before, was taken and beaten, spit upon and rejected, until finally, at a hill called Golgotha the 'city of humans' met the 'city of God.'" Terry (above)

Q: What are the implications of God's return to Jerusalem by way of humility (donkey) and within suffering (the cross)?

Q: What does Terry mean in saying at a hill called Golgotha the 'city of humans' met the 'city of God'?

Q: Is your life a reflection of the 'city of God' or 'city of humans'?

Consider just how well you 'receive God' and turn it to prayer.

Week-11: TUESDAY— ISAIAH 61: 1-11, MATTHEW 11: 1-6

MY THOUGHTS 50—ZION—HOME OF GOD?

I live on the edge, my life informed by two visions. Sometimes I feel like the Baptist, looking up from a dark place, wondering if I am following a fantasy. (Matthew 11:3) And then I find myself with him at the water's edge looking up and into the face of the Lamb of God. (John 1:29) Two Visions; one optimistic and the other afraid.

My spiritual ancestors, thriving in the revivalist spirit of the late 19th century were not afraid. Their gospel, though deeply personal and mystical, poured into the cities of America as a social conscience. Their witness was a tsunami, the tidal waters of social reform forming in it's after shock. The abolitionists, temperance leaders and women suffragettes all found a home in this vision. It was the vision of the city of God entering the city of humankind. These pioneers envisioned the twentieth century as a mighty holiness flood leaving in her wake a Christina Century!

However, not fifty years passed and the look of that movement was transformed. Fear drove the evangelical community to look inward, concentrating on institutional instead of communal presence. The Christian century had collapsed under the weight of two world wars, one Hitler and his holocaust and finally, Vietnam and its aftermath.

Increasingly marginalized, these churches sought cultural influence by political means, as in the past. Only the vision was very different. The hope was in preserving a fading

Christian memory in a secular age. The gospel was communicated as an individual commitment with little social or moral conscience. The promise was 'escape' from a future judgment portending even more horrifying world events. Rapturing out was the goal, not transformation from within.

I was born and came of age in this time of chaos producing fear. In the secular world there were still windows of hope. The free speech movement and the early stages of the peace-loving hippie's offered a kind of alternative salvation. It was short lived, dying a still birth in the empty promises of sex, drugs and rock and roll. The civil rights movement, marked by violent reaction, seemed to offer transformational possibilities. This movement was the birth child of the church, at least the African American church and a few liberal white congregations. I remember well Martin Luther King's march on Washington D.C. and the fear and respect I felt as I watched him speak into that little black and white TV in the corner of our living room. My little world seemed to tremble. I could not tell if it was good or bad. To this white child's lens, it felt like both.

I'm guessing that John the Baptist had grown up in a world not so different. Two conflicting visions had informed his childhood. The traditions of his father and of Israel's God was constantly reinforced. It was a conserving message, in times of difficulty. Institutional presence relying upon individual sacrifice would have been the norm. The goal was to preserve the memory of Israel's Story in a time of Roman occupation. But John's heart had early been drawn to the desert, to the Essenes and to a revivalist and renewing tradition that envisioned nothing short of the coming of a Messiah whose gospel would radically change Israel's heart and life. Communal presence was the goal. Institutional presence was the obstacle to what God wanted to do.

And now John is in Herod's prison facing judgment and possible death. What had he accomplished? Nothing seemed to have changed. Jesus, his cousin, had not ushered in a new reality. He still attended the Synagogue and honored Moses seat. And so he asks through intermediaries a question. *"Are you the one who was to come, or should we expect someone else?"* (Matthew 11: 3). In other words, "Have I blown it? Did I lead our people into a blind alley called hope?"

It is Jesus response that captures my attention. *"Go back and report to John what you hear and see"* (Matthew 11:4). And then he lists all the signs of messianic presence identified by Isaiah in year of the LORD's favor. All but one, that is. What is left out is telling. Jesus did not come to proclaim the *"day of vengeance of our God"* (Isaiah 61: 2b).

At the heart of the prophecy that one phrase was a contradiction to the rest of the text. Jesus excludes this one phrase. And its omission would have communicated something of import to John the Baptist.

Jesus is reminding John of two important themes:

- ➢ First to look and see what God is doing in the city of humankind. It is as if he said, 'God is at work in you and me and others. That is all you need to know, John.'
- ➢ Second, he is reminding John that his coming was from the broken heart of God. He was God's sacrifice. His lamb. Vengeance would not come as a result of Jesus action. Only others would do violence. The Son was coming into His city of peace as a messenger of peace.

John's message had been one of repentance, in preparation for the Messiah. It was a message to clear the heart and land of all that was not like God. The contradiction was that John was being held by violence as Jesus would soon know. That would be Israel's hope, God's suffering love. John's mission was to keep faith in God's work and his messenger.

As I have lived with the dreams of my ancestors and the fears of my contemporaries, I have longed for more. The simple presence and hope of the revivalist tradition was only a memory; witnessing echoes of it around the altar as old and young gathered to confess and weep and pledge to one another. But the transformational power of that early tradition seemed dead from my birth. Instead I have wandered in a wilderness of personal and social disappointment. Individual and isolated salvation has seemed empty. Especially if it is salvation from God's vengeance, instead of repentance and renewal as a welcoming grace to who God is and what The Father is doing in His world.

What has emerged in me over many years is the awareness that God is doing something profound. I get to see only glimpses of it. I see it in both the Church and beyond her walls and culture. God is renewing in people the hope of salvation even as the world seems a more dangerous place.

Ministering among the homeless and in a cross cultural context has forced me to de-emphasize institutional presence and emphasize communal presence. And I do not mean to suggest institutional presence is unimportant. It is very important, but should arise from the relational mission of the church as she lives Christ in the city of humankind. Every person I attempt to help makes me keenly aware of my own poverty of spirit and life. Among the homeless I have seen such living faith. Among Native traditions I have witnessed powerful awe, before the Creator.

I cannot live in a church that is fear driven any longer. It seems absurd that the secular community is more hopeful and interested in salvation of the planet and her history than the church.

So, I live in a place of contradiction. I live and witness the hope of the revivalist tradition, but feel very little of its power. Silence has replaced the excitement of intense worship. Listening has replaced testimonies. But Christ I see. In him I feel naked, though not alone. In him I feel the depth of my own sinful heart and cry out for the promise of the Holy Spirit. But I also see through Jesus eyes the city of humans and am compelled to be fully present. It is a presence born of trust in people and God. It is a message of hope and not destruction. The 'vengeance' remains, but only in the hearts of men and women, not God. I am keenly aware that this journey may lead to a cross. So be it, as long as Jesus is seen hanging on it with me.

Reflections on "Zion—Home of God?"

"My spiritual ancestors, thriving in the revivalist spirit of the late 19th century were not afraid. Their gospel, though deeply personal and mystical, poured into the city of man as a social conscience". Terry (above)

Q: How does Terry's description of 19th century holiness strike you? …How is it different in the ways you experience it?

Q: Is your own world view driven by hope or fear or both? …How so?

Q: What makes life in the body fun? What makes it boring?

"What has emerged in me over many years is the awareness that God is doing something profound. I get to see only glimpses of it. I see it in both the Church and beyond her walls and culture. God is renewing in people the hope of salvation even as the world seems a more dangerous place". Terry (above)

Q: What do you see God doing in the World? …Where is Jesus showing up and in what clothes?

Q: Are you in on the action? …How so? …Why not?

Experiment: This week look for Jesus in the city. When you see Jesus turn it to prayer.

Week-11: WEDNESDAY—ISAIAH 60: 4-22

STORY 41—RESTORATION OF JERUSALEM'S PROMISE

An Imaginative Story—The end of A Long Dark Night...

So much had changed in the last 100 days. The gathering storm of the previous year had taken the world by surprise. Although, we should have seen it coming. Especially we who remained committed to the promise of Jeshua's mission in the earth. Most of us were simply keeping a low profile.

I remember watching in horror the events surrounding Jerusalem. For months the armies of the nations had been gathering. Europe and the United States had increased naval presence in the Mediterranean, Black Sea and the gulf area. Tactical nuclear weapons had been placed in active readiness. China and North Korea, together with a radicalized and nuclear Pakistan had been landing forces and armaments in the former Yemen, now the Islamic Republic of Yemen. China's growing need for oil was not to be left to the designs of the nations of the west. Russia, having closed a friendship treaty with Iran and Turkey and in league with Hamas controlled Lebanon and Damascus, had forces within reach of Israel's northern borders.

In the decade before, pandemic diseases, violent earthquakes, floods and starvation resulting from climate change had taken millions of lives. The international community had lived with constant stress, responding with ever more authoritarian structures to meet the needs. In this context the Church of Christ, her ministers and priests were given the choice of cooperating with these structures to meet the medical and environmental needs or being branded as enemies of the New Order. At first it was a no brainer. Our mission to be Christ present clearly led us into social mission. The difficulty came over time as the governments of the New Order became active in population control and Euthanasia. In the last four years the western powers had begun to challenge our Christocentric theology as hostile to the human needs of the world for a united and culturally diverse spirituality.

In Europe the Vatican was militarily occupied and a politically appointed Pope placed in charge by the European Union. In the United States, still religiously diverse thanks to the world-wide influx of immigrants, all church institutions were required to affirm with the IRS their allegiance to the social and health policies of social justice—especially those surrounding Abortive Embryonic research including what had become termed as DNA Holistic Medicine and the compassionate termination of those whose quality of life was perceived as sub-human. Most individual Catholic parishes and Evangelicals and main stream Christian communities found themselves isolated and afraid, branded as Salvationists and Zionists. To fail to register meant far more than loss of tax free standing. Because the IRS was the enforcer of Health Insurance levies churches unapproved lost access to the Health Alliance.

In the Middle East the ancient city of Jerusalem had become the symbol of International tolerance; as the four great powers (US, Europe, Russia & China) had secured a fragile peace with the four regional powers in the larger Middle East (Iran, Turkey, Pakistan and the Hamas controlled territories of old Syria). Jordan, Egypt and Saudi Arabia acquiesced, each focusing on internal struggles and grateful for a balance of tensions that did not immediately threaten them. These Internationals, as they were commonly called, had come together some seven years ago to declare peace between Israel and her immediate neighbors. Europe,

Russia, China and the United States had all agreed to enforce the new agreements. But that was a short lived hope.

Pakistan had radicalized and looked to China as its best strategic hope for asserting its regional importance. Iran with the full support of Russia had finally defeated Isle in what was now greater Iran—covering the old central provinces of Iraq and Syria with Iran in military control of what was central Iraq and Russia and the Hamas dominating large portions of old Syria. Only Kurdistan located in the north of old Syria and Iraq maintained a fragile and costly independence.

Russia, Turkey, Hamas and Iran had become increasingly uncomfortable with Europe's hierarchical place at the table of four. Pakistan's new government, though Islamic, was a very real threat to everyone in the region though apparently appreciating Russian presence if only to challenge Europe and the U.S. At the epicenter was Jerusalem, as it had often been in the past.

100 days ago the battle popularly referred to as Armageddon had escalated. The world had now witnessed multiple nuclear strikes. Millions of people had died as a result, adding to the already stressed international alignments. The final assault was at the initiative of the Russian—Iranian—Hamas Alliance. Russia was the edged of the spear and had poured its forces into Northern Israel. In response the European and U.S. alliance had prepared for one final tactical nuclear assault on Israeli soil to counter this pan Islamic/Russian threat, when suddenly The Event unfolded.

From somewhere beyond Terran space a bright light imploded blocking electronic transmissions. The armies of the nation's immediately surrounding Jerusalem were killed.

All nuclear and non-nuclear weaponized planes, missiles and vehicles were neutralized with no additional explosive impact. An eerie Silence followed. Every nation had ordered its armies to stand down and wait for...They did not know.

Early the next morning, around sunrise the next Event happened. I was sitting in my condo at High Point in West Seattle. Our church property, including the parsonage had been confiscated in the previous year upon our refusal to accept a non-threatening (to the New Order) universalist position. Now our church consisted of a few who gathered for study and community service. Every news channel was picking up the same event. In Jerusalem there was an earthquake of significant impact. The Mount of Olives, in the heart of Jerusalem's suburbs simply split, leaving a deep cavern stretching from East to West as far as the camera could capture. The Temple mount lay in her path. Where the Eastern gate had been there was now an opening, perhaps a football field in depth. CNN's camera was the first to pick up an airborne anomaly. Descending from the heavens was a bright light, filled with the colors of the rainbow. The reporter speculated about a possible extra-terrestrial source. I knew who it was.

Slowly, as the light softened we were able to make out a group of what seemed millions descending from the heavens. They were surrounded by beings of brilliant light, ever changing in color. Music seemed to live inside the light, emanating from the colors. The music was more felt than heard. The commentators at CCN were silent in awe and fear. At the center of this Event was one whose face shown like diamonds, though he still had very human features. When his feet touched the ground the earth once again trembled. I remembered thinking it an after-shock, until I realized that I too was feeling the gentle shock wave, on the other side of the planet. It must have taken another thirty minutes before all the persons in the air came to rest upon the ground. Now the commentators were beginning to speak, saying nothing of import, only filling air time. From my own Biblical studies, I could see that the camera was facing east from the Temple mount and looking across what was left of the Kidron valley, toward the mount of Olives.

Immediately the millions of new visitors followed the One in the center down and into the valley. As the One whose face was brilliant, yet human, made his way down and through what once was the Eastern gate the camera spanned back across the valley giving a wide angle look at the procession. Upon entering the Temple mount this Human One made his way over to Solomon's wall and placing his hand on it, prayed. While he prayed chairs were brought for his comfort and a makeshift platform was formed from collapsible stands, complete with a red carpet and podium. No one had any idea if he would speak or when.

After an hour of watching him pray with full commentary by the usual cadre of experts, the Human One looked up and made his way to the podium. He smiled, his eyes still sparkling, seemed warm. He was wearing a white robe, it appeared. It was hard to tell for the light surrounding him made everything appear white.

One of the ABC reporters, from Jerusalem, stood and asked the first question. "Sir, your honor or Excellency, what or how shall we refer to You? His voice was deep, though gentle. I remember shuddering at the sound of it, still a deep peace filled me. "I Am who I Am." He hesitated and then looking out over the city, continued. "Daniel of old called me the Son of Man. I always liked that title. You may refer to me by the name my mother gave, Jeshua."

Camera lights went off as some correspondents moved away to immediately communicate with their individual audiences. The CNN camera stayed with Jeshua. Another correspondent, this time a woman. "Were you responsible for the brilliant light of last evening and the subsequent cessation of violence between the global powers?" "Yes, well, that is, my Father and yours was." Again, his eyes smiled. Lifting his hand like a practiced politician he stretched out his arm and pointed towards another questioner. The camera angle zoomed in on his hand and wrist. There it was, the sign of violence, where some bloody instrument had pierced him. Standing slowly was an older man, whom Jeshua had picked. He began, with a broken English. "I am not a television correspondent. Only an old man, a Jewish rabbi, before the recent restrictions. Tell me sir, are you the Messiah?"

Jeshua hesitated. He did not immediately answer. One of my friends, sitting next to me, a Samoan spoke for the first time. "Do you realize he is speaking in perfect Samoan?" Answering, I looked at him in surprise. "I'm hearing everything in English."

We both turned back to the television. From within the crowd of visitors there was a stirring. The beings of light were opening a path as one middle aged man stepped forth, together with a dozen persons of varying ages. As the middle aged man approached I had the distinct feeling of having seen him, but could not remember where. As he approached Jeshua, he did so with great deference. He bowed. Jeshua smiled, acknowledging his bow, but in a gesture of warmth gave him a hug. The others gathered in around the podium, behind both Jeshua and the middle aged man. Jeshua spoke. "Let me allow my friend to speak to that question." The man, whose hands were trembling came to the microphone and begun. "My name," he hesitated. "My name is Adolph Hitler. I am the one who is responsible for the Holocaust of the last century." More cameras flashed. A gasp was apparent throughout those assembled and in me. He continued. "I come to this sacred place, to Jerusalem so that I may now acknowledge to every one of my Master's race how horribly saddened I am at the pain I have visited upon you and the world. But," and now turning to the Rabbi he continued. "I am not worthy to answer your question." Looking back at those who immediately surrounded him, about twenty in all, he continued. "But they are." Stepping forward each person came to the microphone and showing the number upon their hands and arms from the Nazi concentration camps each answered, simply, "Yes." The last and apparently the oldest of them now approached. He answered. "And I am your father whom you lost when you were just a boy at Auschwitz. My son, may I introduce you to Jeshua of Nazareth. He is the Messiah, the Son of the Living God."

As Jeshua stepped forward again, he added. "I know this is so much to take in. We shall speak again, soon. But for now, we have much to do. I have brought with me the saints of my Father, together with some whose deep sin is matched only in the depth of their repentance. Together with my holy angels, these will be sent out to every nation and people and to every Church where my name was once held in honor. They shall appoint for me ministers of state and pastors and priests. In many cases they will be the officials who are currently elected or serving. In others they will be dismissed and replaced."

From within the edge of those who came with Jeshua two men came forward, each appearing wise in their own right. Jeshua pointed to one of them and continued. "Joseph of old, once the Prime Minister of Egypt, shall lead in the establishment of new governments. These governments may continue to build upon their traditions provided they follow the ten laws of Moses and the summation of those laws in the first and second great commandments and derive their consent from the people. No government shall have authority, however, to enforce those commands that are related to the honor and worship of my Father."

Then looking to the other he continued. "This is Peter, my rock. He will be responsible to appoint or reappoint my pastors and priests. All buildings and property taken by the world powers are now returned." Turning to Peter he gave what appeared to be an aside. "Now Peter, instruct well my body. Teach them to serve as I have served you. Teach them to sell their properties and to assist in the rebuilding of human culture, keeping only what is necessary for worship and service and learning." Then turning to Joseph he continued. "And to my faithful friend, Joseph. Build anew the city of humans, together with my church. Repair the roads and houses. Let the healing sciences grow and expand. Establish among the peoples the kind of industry and lending, buying and selling that will allow each person to live in safety in their own home and eat the fruit of their labors. Honor the land. Allow the vision of Isaiah to lead you. Your goal is to bring to the city of humankind the city of God, so that John's vision is finally and fully realized."

Then looking back into the camera he finished. "I will be with you physically for a season only. But the saints of old and all those who have turned from their wicked ways will be with you in this new Jerusalem.

My holy angels will see that all national armaments are destroyed. They will not be needed any longer. The budgets devoted to war may now be turned to meeting the needs of all people." And looking up, he continued. "May the love of the Father and of the Holy Spirit surround each of you. May my love be in you."

With that Jesus turned. The cameras followed. Two on lookers, I could not tell if they were reporters, yelled out questions. "And what of Satan?" Jesus turned and smiled. "Lucifer and all who followed him without repentance is in a safe place, bound. He will not bother you anymore." Another question followed. "Is he bound forever? If not what follows his release?" Again turning back, Jesus responded. "He is bound for a season. What happens beyond that season is up to, well, him and my Father."

As he was walking away one more questioner yelled out. "But what of you? Where will you stay?" Jesus seemed startled. He stopped and laughed. "I don't know. I hadn't thought of that. Perhaps I will stay with you."

Reflections on "Restoration of Jerusalem's Promise"

In this imaginative story Terry seems to want to have it both ways. Power is needed to restrain evil decisively. Yet Jesus rule seems permissive at every level.

Q: Your thoughts?

Q: Given what Terry has written about the end of the age, is this a satisfactory re-birth?

Q: Does it remain an incarnational work of God?

Q: Is the Church, in this scenario a living sign of Christ impacting culture or simply an irrelevant bystander?

Q: What about Hitler's redemption? ...How do you feel about Satan's possible redemption, hinted at?

Consider your own feelings and thoughts in response to the story and turn it all to prayer.

Week-11: THURSDAY—MATTHEW 22: 23-46

MY THOUGHTS 51—SALVATION HISTORY—IS IT HUMAN, DIVINE OR BOTH? DOES IT MATTER?

An Emerging Focus on Jesus Lived

The unfolding Story of salvation begins in the heart of the Trinity of God; in the fellowship of love between/in the Father—Son—Spirit. As creator and redeemer, Jesus Christ is the central person in the Divine/human story.

His life, death, resurrection, ascension and continuing intercession before the Father (John 17) remain our only hope of salvation. The Holy Spirit pours out and into the Church the historic and continuing life of Jesus. His life is now lived in and through us (his body).

From its inception, the Church has wrestled (Matt 28:17) with the implications of Jesus prayer in the garden of Gethsemane. *"May they also be in us so that the world may believe that you have sent me... May they be brought to complete unity to let the world know that you sent me and have loved them even as you have loved me."* (John 17: 21b, 23b). The promise of unity was all too often fulfilled by the power of the sword—and I'm not talking about the Word. Authority replaced loving and expressive service in Jesus as the source of salvation. The body of Christ increasingly took upon itself the salvational promise of which it breathes. A 'rite of passage' given through the institutional presence of its life replaced the radical and new relationship that every daughter of Eve and son of Adam now enjoy as the Church lives Christ in the human community. Christ was increasingly held captive to the authority of the Church, its ministers and traditions.

In the reformation (Protestant and Catholic) there was a hope of returning the Church to its expressive, subservient and dependent relation to the person and life of Christ. The early reformers called for a return to primary documents and the simplicity of loving and living Christ as remembered by the early Fathers of the Church.

But this hope was quickly hijacked as some in the Protesting Church confused the proclamation of the truth of the Word with the actual living Story inside the proclamation. The authority of the Word and subsequent arguments over it led to a reductionism and Jesus was increasingly held captive to the culturally conditioned versions of His Story. Indeed, His Story was lost in all the experiential details of the message (inerrancy, new birth, doctrines of assurance, Spirit baptism, holiness practices, eschatology). The centrality and mission of the Church as a living of Jesus actual presence in the human community was too often forgotten. By the twentieth century 'proclamation' had largely replaced institutional authority in the evangelical church, sucking out the air that properly belonged to Jesus, alone (uniquely).

Some in the liberal Protestant tradition even suggested that the truth content of the original documents (experience) of the Church were irrelevant, only the proclamation itself. In a convoluted way the fundamentalists were guilty of the same error. For they claimed that the written truth of original documents (which no one possessed) would be sufficient, when correctly believed, to save those who were destined for salvation. Each tradition attempted to place ultimate authority in the message rather than the messenger (Jesus) and hence, the One on whom the message centers.

The foundations of the church shook in December of 1965 when the Catholic reformation reached its apex. Salvation in Christ alone was reaffirmed in the Lumen Gentium, the

Dogmatic Constitution on the Church of the Second Vatican Council. *"...There is salvation only and exclusively in Christ,"* as Pope John Paul II affirms in his book, 'Crossing the Threshold of Hope' (pg#136). Christ alone, as the center of our life and of the Church, is our salvation. The Church is the sacramental expression of His life, by the Holy Spirit. In my adult life I have watched as both the Protestant and Catholic communions have found common ground in the Christ—event.

The Post-modern desire for a Story (a dramatic and sensual connection) has become the historical ground for an Emerging Congregation of Christ, not separate or distinction from the existing visual/institutional presence of Christ on earth, but within each/all.

This 'Emergent' theological tradition (at least as I have watched and lived it) desires to once again connect with the primal story of Christ, as lived. The Emergent tradition searches for Christo-centric meaning in all of our relations, rites and serving. It takes seriously the primary sources in the Written and lived Word of God (Israel's faith, the Gospels and Epistles of the Church and traditions of the Church).

As a conservative Evangelical I remain convinced of the unique authority of the Written Word—not as a courts stenographer, but as the living stories, documents and gathered rites of the People of God who first experienced, remembered, interpreted—often reinterpreted and eventually conveyed in writing this God Story among us. In my limited experience, the Emergent tradition (left and right) understands clearly that the proclamation of the Story cannot be meaningfully lived apart from the whole experience of the Church in history. The Emerging church of the twenty first century has an opportunity to rediscover salvation in Christ alone, as He has been, is and will be lived.

In the Roman Catholic, Evangelical and Emergent traditions our catholicity is being renewed. Such a faith focuses on the 'Acts of God among us' and thus restores the Church to its original mission, to live Christ, as a living sign in the human community.

All we really need is Christ, lived in the Church. We need Jesus who was, is and who is to come. Such a faith requires a trust in the Written and Living Word of God, formed in us by the Holy Spirit. Such a faith is expansive and allows the Church, in all its expressions, to focus on its mission, lived.

Written by Terry following Easter Service Reflections, 2009

Reflections on "Salvation History—Is it Human, Divine or Both—Does it Really Matter?"

All we really need is Christ, lived in the Church. We need Jesus who was, is and who is to come. Such a faith requires a trust in the Written and Living Word of God, formed in us by the Holy Spirit".   Terry (above)

Q: How long should God wait for the Church to become the Church?

Q: Why do you think the Trinity of God keeps waiting for Christ to fully emerge from within us?

Experiment: This week as you reflect on scripture alone or in the body of Jesus—as written or sung or expressed in liturgy; ask 1 question of yourself…

Q: Am I living into this scriptural moment?

Q: Are we living into this scriptural moment?

Then turn it all to prayer.

Week-11: FRIDAY—LUKE 21: 1-4

STORY 42—THE GIFT THAT KEEPS ON GIVING—JERUSALEM'S PROMISE

A Biblical & Imaginative Story—All She Had...

As she made her way up the hill from the lower city, David's Jerusalem in ancient times, she began to feel all the insecurities of her life. She was the only one of her father's children, a girl. 'He had wanted a boy'—the memory of overhearing her papa speaking to her mama seared its way into her mind like a branded lamb. Her mother, long dead always seemed to be delighted with her, 'a gift she had called me'. Her emotions settled a little at the thought. But from her father, it always seemed she could never do enough. 'I am not pretty'. At least she had been told that and often by her peers. Her thoughts continued to betray her; 'If only I had been pretty, at least, my suitor might have offered a hefty price to my papa as a dowry'. But the dowry never came. A soft smile emerged at the thought of her husband, 'may God give him mercy.' He was poor, the last of his family. 'But Papa had liked him' and her gate began to widen in these happy thoughts. 'In fact,' her mind wondered, 'he was the best thing that ever happened to me, ...that is, until he died' a few months later. And so troubled thoughts regained entrance. A decade or more ago, Deborah's papa, 'may Yahweh give him peace', had also passed. With him gone she had no livelihood. Women of her generation were good only for motherhood or prostitution. She had no brothers, sisters or cousins. Her mother, she remembered being told by papa, 'may Yahweh keep her memory alive, had died. I was so young'.

Deborah knew how to work. That is all she had known, from childhood. She was a good cook and her home, what there was of it, never lacked in décor. But she had lost that home as well, to pay off her father's debts.

She was allowed to live in the home and pay a rent that consumed nearly all of the monies she could gather from occasional sewing or cleaning. Mostly she relied on the kindness of neighbors who gave what they could.

Now she was down to the last three coins, Greek Leptas, worth very little and even less when the Temple authorities exchanged it so she could give Yahweh what was his. Anxiety began to impress itself as she approached the Temple. 'Ten percent', she knew, for so 'mama, blessed be her memory, had said'. And, even at an early age—that stuck. She gathered courage to proceed as she remembered another thing her mother had told her of her namesake, 'Deborah the prophetess, leader over all Israel in the times of the judges'. She remembered her mother speaking of Deborah as though her little girl were somehow connected to her, the name being the bridge. 'It's amazing', she wondered at how much she had learned at her mama's knee as a little girl.

Deborah had now passed the Dung gate and entered the court of the gentiles. She made her way without looking at any men, especially Pharisees. She did not want to cause them to stumble, though she never understood how—given her lack of sensual endowment.

Not far from the Holy place and near the wall beyond which no gentile was permitted she turned to her right and made her way toward the Master Gate so that she could exchange her coins. As she approached she dreaded the moment when she presented to the priest her little penance. Her mind played it all out, for she had experienced it often enough. He would say nothing, but his look of disgust would communicate all.

'Why had she even bothered? Her little three coins would not buy a loaf of bread for a priest, let alone pay for the maintenance or improvements constantly being made'. She knew that her three coins were hardly worth the time it took to convert them into Temple coinage. 'But,' her courage strengthened at the thought; 'I am an Israelite, a daughter of Abraham's promise and so I cannot be denied'.

How she wished she could hold onto Yahweh's money until it was large enough that she could hold high her head. Her mind quenched the thought in its infancy. 'But that would be stealing!' It was God's and in whatever amount He saw fit, she would give. Oh, how she longed to have enough to offer a sacrifice acceptable for her sins. She knew they must be great, for—her feelings now betrayed her—'I am a woman, alone, with no husband. Why else would Yahweh inflict upon me so little of life's joys?'

As she left the Master Gate she could not help looking up, for a commotion was stirring in the court of the gentiles. A large number of Israel's children were surrounding someone. Then she saw him. She had only heard of him, but never dreamed she might see him in person. 'It must be Jeshua, the prophet' she thought to herself. Without thinking of where she was or who she was, she kept her eyes up and fixed in his direction. He was moving toward the Holy place, probably to pray or teach. 'Oh no, that is horrible!' she had thought to herself, for the vessels of offering, the trumpets as they were called, were in this sacred place. These trumpets were narrow at the top, wider at the bottom. There were thirteen in all, each assigned to a different temple purpose. The offerings of the rich would make loud noises against the metal sides of the trumpets as they fell through the narrow spout, landing in the bottom, coin upon coin. How she wanted to run. This prophet would be teaching very near the trumpets. But then something revealing, yet strange happened. Jeshua was suddenly about a hundred yards from her when the crowd thinned a little. She could see him, completely. He turned and looked at her. 'Deborah,' her heart cried. 'Look away! Do not cause him to sin.' But she did not look away, nor did he. For just a few moments, maybe only seconds their eyes met. He smiled.

After the crowd had entered into the Holy Place, she quietly entered. Moving past the altar beyond which no gentile could go and through the outer Portico. Always she felt a sense of awe. 'Yes' her mind stilled for just a moment, 'it was the beauty and power of this room'—But it was more. In this nation that had no room for her as a woman, 'God had made room'. The daughters of Israel could enter into His house for worship.

Usually she would quietly, quickly steal away into the corner of the inner sanctuary and wait for a moment when no one else was giving and after praying her little prayer, which she doubted was ever heard, she then would hurriedly give her little offering. But today she waited. For an hour she listened to Jeshua's words. He spoke of God in ways she had never heard before, at least not from a man. Her heart was drawn to him and to His God. He dared to call Him Father.

Suddenly Jeshua, paused. A hush fell over the sanctuary. Even the loud clanging of offering pouring into the vessels of offering had stopped. In that moment Deborah's stomach groaned. Her face turned red. She was sure the whole crowd had heard and would now turn to stare at her. So she turned, quickly, and made her way over to the trumpets and threw in her two coins, for in the exchange the value of her coinage had been reduced. When she dropped her coins in, they made no clanging sound. 'How could they?' her heart skipped, 'They were nothing'.

Turning she glanced around to see if anyone noticed. Fortunately, no one did. No one that is, except Jeshua. He was looking right at her. Again he smiled. She returned his smile and then looked away, a little embarrassed and quietly made her way out of that Holy place and back into the court of the gentiles. Again her stomach growled. But she knew there was nothing she could do about that. She had not eaten in a day and night, nor would she until Yahweh, 'Blessed be His Name', honored her with work or a gift.

Note: Based upon Luke 21: 1-4. The idea for this story and subsequent reading is taken from the devotional writings of another I cannot now remember. It may have been Michael Card's "John: The Gospel of Wisdom."

Reflections on "The Gift that Keeps on Giving—Jerusalem's Promise"

She gave her all. It was not very much. Probably, it was a hassle to count. It would not pay a priest's salary or buy a carpet for the Temple of God. It was insufficient for her to purchase an acceptable sacrifice to atone for her sins, let alone anyone else's.

Yet her gift captured Jesus's attention and his Father's as well. With those two small coins she had moved the heart of the Trinity of God. The inclusion of this story in The Book would seem to infer that she also moved the heart of the Spirit and made an impression on the early church as they relived and remembered the moment.

Would that our gifts today would do the same.

Q: What was it that so attracted Jesus and the church to her gift?

Q: Are gifts given out of our poverty intrinsically more powerful?

Q: Can you think of other Biblical stories with a similar motif?

The sub-title of this story is "The Gift that Keeps on Giving."

Q: Does this story say something about the ability of God to pull lots of small pieces together to form a powerful and larger vision or story or gift?

Q: Have you ever seen or been a part of such a magical God moment—when God shows up in the gifting of something or someone unusual? …Where? …When?

Then turn it all to prayer.

Week-11: SATURDAY—Luke 22: 14-38

STORY 43—THE SIGN OF THE CITY OF GOD—COMPASSIONATE PRESENCE

A Personal Story—Pizza & a memorial Service & Adventure...

From this last Sunday, 09/05/2016

He was homeless and has stayed overnight at our church on, say, a hundred times over several years—sometimes within the building with permission and at others just outside the building at the entrance to my office and without permission. Fred (not his real name) is a hard worker, intelligent and generally free of drugs. He's a perfectionist and avoids all social settings like the plague. He's a fellow believer.

Fred came by my house around 8 pm to advise me that Micah, the 50-year old street preacher by calling and who is currently captured in his own addiction had died. His body lay on the street not ten feet from his street friends; they so inebriated that they did not bother to check on him and call 911. Fred had, once about midnight and later around 6 am, when he discovered him dead. Fred was devastated and asked about a memorial service. We invited him to eat some soup with us (it was dinner time) and he just talked, which for him was unusual. I asked Fred to talk with others on the street and tell them to come by the church on Sunday and we'd do a brief service of remembrance. Only Tre-Shaun showed, a young—maybe 17-year old, creative African American. So I grabbed him and a couple of our guys after the service and we made our way to get some pizza, have a conversation about Micah, read scripture and pray.

What started out rather simple turned into an adventure with Tre-Shaun our new friend. What connected Tre-Shaun to Micah was their mutual love of music; both were guitarists.

As we headed into an upscale pizza place Tre-Shaun shifted the conversation, advising that he really didn't have time because he needed to travel by bus across the city to get his guitar for a gig he had at a pub Sunday evening. Wanting to honor Micah, my friend and Tre-Shaun I offered to take him to his friend's house, about 15 minutes' travel, so he could get his guitar back. Evidently, his friend had taken it from him the evening before at another pub and was too drunk for Tre-Shaun to confront without a bit of a hassle.

"K," Tre-Shaun smiled relaxing, "That'll work". When we got in the car I asked him if he had ten minutes to remember Micah. He did and so the four of us; myself—who knows the struggle of addiction, Gary—who understands human struggle, Nickolaus—who had a 10-year journey on the streets and now manages our church facility and Tre-Shaun proceeded to do the memorial in my car, two up front and two in back. It was a powerful moment as we all shared, Tre-Shaun read scripture and I prayed. Our conversation over our mutual friend, Micah, continued as we drove a rather circuitous route to the home of Tre-Shaun's friend.

I couldn't tell if Tre-Shaun was simply scattered, as he directed me, or like many young persons who do not drive, knew only the routes the bus takes to locations in the city.

Anyway, we got there and he secured his guitar—easily, given his friend was in a significant hangover from the night before. As we left the house of his friend in an upscale neighborhood I drove to a near Panera Bread and got out intending to buy lunch. Tre-Shaun had told us that he was good with the meal invite, that is until we all got out.

The same anxiety or inability to focus reappeared and Tre-Shaun took his leave of us, walking toward the bus to make his way back to West Seattle, now some 18 miles. I had offered to drive him back. He simply smiled and asked me if I wanted to come watch his gig at the pub. I didn't, because I was already exhausted from the journey, but assured him to come by the church and I'd be happy to come order a coke and enjoy his music.

In the restaurant Nickolaus, who is the most loving and effective person in meaningfully engaging our neighbors who live without benefit of rented or owned homes summarized the day. "That was strange. Too bad he wasted our time." I shot back, "That was no waste. It was strange, but our little service and the conversation with Tre-Shaun, helping him to get his gig together was all good." Nickolaus agreed totally. And besides Tre-Shaun gave us all giant hugs as he left—the innocent smile still on his face.

MY THOUGHTS 52—THE SIGN OF THE CITY OF GOD—COMPASSIONATE PRESENCE

Community and Compassion

The promise of the church is not our works of service in the city, but our presence. Anyone can serve and so be the hands of Jesus. But only those who serve as fellow travelers, persons of equal need before the Father—whose children are all about doing their own gig—can truly offer Jesus heart. Whether in Christ or not, it is the person who gives from a spirit of equality and acceptance that touches the Biblical idea of feeding, clothing and visiting Jesus.

Every time we serve out of our own ego needs to prove our worth or as one better, helping with a hand up, we have forsaken Jesus love and short-cut the one essential gift of the Church—Compassionate Presence.

In his short writing entitled "The Only Necessary Thing" Henri Nouwen puts it eloquently:

> *"To follow Christ means to relate to each other with the mind of Christ; that is, to relate to each other as Christ did to us—in servanthood and humility. Discipleship is walking together on the same path. While still living wholly in this world, we have discovered each other as fellow travelers on the same path and have formed a new community.... Compassion always reveals itself in community, in a new way of being together. Fellowship with Christ is fellowship with our brothers and sisters... For where people come together in Christ's name, he is present as the compassionate Lord (see Matt. 18:20). Jesus Christ himself is and remains the most radical manifestation of God's compassion."*
>
> From "Compassion and Community", in the meditative thought "The Only Necessary Thing", by Henri J.M. Nouwen, page #129

Reflections on "The Sign of the City of God—Compassionate Presence"

"Discipleship is walking together on the same path..."
From "Compassion and Community", in the meditative thought "The Only Necessary Thing", by Henri J.M. Nouwen, page #129

The most important discovery along the road of Jesus is that we are all in the same boat. All of us. Compassion is not helping another from above, but entering a listening conversation, especially with persons who need our help. Compassion begins when we discover how badly we need them and their message their faith.

Q: Have you yet discovered the joy and love in serving others as equals?

Reflect and then turn it all to prayer.

Week-11: SUNDAY—EZEKIEL 37: 1-28, HEBREWS 11: 8-
10 & 12: 22-29, COLOSSIANS 1: 24-29, ROMANS 11: 25-
32, REVELATION 21:1-8 & 22: 1-7

STORY 44—THE POWER OF WEAKNESS—JERUSALEM'S GIFT

*"The best metaphor for our world of today is
astronauts speeding through the cosmos, but with
their life supporting capsule pierced by a meteorite
fragment. But the Church resembles Mary and
Joseph traveling from Egypt to Nazareth on a donkey,
holding in their arms the weakness and poverty of the
Child Jesus; God incarnate."*

From "The God Who comes", by Carlo Carretto, from "A Guide to
Prayer for Ministers & Other Servants, page #18

An Imaginative Story—From the Temple Mount to the Heart of God...

It was five in the morning. Jeshua was where he usually was
this time of day, on the Temple Mount, praying for the City of
His Love, Jerusalem. How long he prayed each morning
differed according to the human needs of his glorified body,
once again subject to the laws of earth's gravitational fields
and atmosphere. The lights of the mount were fully lit,
though unneeded given the angel's presence.

There was no one around, save the angels of light, for protection or affirmation or worship, no one on earth yet knew. Construction on the New Temple would be fully engaged in another three hours. This was the time Jeshua chose to be with His Father. He missed the immediacy of the heavenly Jerusalem, where Jeshua would play and talk, weep and pray for his Body on earth. This heavenly Sacrifice of Love, as the Spirit called it, unlike it's earthly counterpart, was not bloody or experienced anew in the time-space continuum. Nor was it born by Jeshua, alone, with the Father's face turned and the Holy Spirit helplessly experiencing the empathetic vibrations, but unable to participate in the actual bio-chemical grief. In the heavenly, eternal and ever deepening sacrifice in the heavens, the love of the Father—Son—Spirit joined in participatory grief—joy—love as the One who is Three received from Jeshua's heart the prayers of his Body for those in time. Jeshua's Word continued to offer to the Father a life-giving drama that reflected human persons and events unfolding. This was the eternal celebration whose counterpart on earth was the Eucharistic celebration.

How Jeshua missed this eternal reality. Yet, he knew that John's prophecy of the city of man becoming the City of God was as yet a future promise. For time had not fully explored the extent to which Israel and Christ's body would together, live out the cross event. Only by love, through love and in love could John's vision be realized.

So Jeshua prayed from inside time's constraints and by the Spirit's interpretative Presence his heart's longing for the city of humankind, especially this city, Jerusalem. When the Temple was completed, Jeshua, together with Joseph and Peter would re-establish a sacrificial liturgy, this time the Eucharistic celebration that mirrored the heavenly One. When this was done, Jeshua knew he would return to His Father, for his presence in time actually constrained the ability of humankind to receive Israel and His body.

Israel had yet to embrace and communicate the 'light of Christ' in the human community. One hundred forty four thousand of Israel's citizens were now being called, equipped and charged with that task. Also, the Church had yet to truly become the 'light of Christ'. The Apostle Paul's vision of the Church completing *"what is still lacking in regard to Christ's afflictions,"* (Colossians 1:24) had not become a living reality in all places where Jesus' body gathered. Jeshua knew there was nothing lacking in his sacrifice in time, made on a hill not so far from this mount. The only lack was in her extension in time by flesh to the whole world. All of Jeshua's prayers and the Spirit's Presence on earth was aimed at this one purpose.

All this weighed heavily upon the Son as the first light of dawn began to cast her golden waves upon the Temple Mount. Jeshua opened his eyes to take in that beautiful scene, remembering his mornings in the garden, nearly two thousand years before. As he lifted his head, tears gently flowing down his cheeks, he noticed one of his oldest human friends.

Over the centuries he had often been given permission to walk the streets of Jerusalem, sometimes even when there were no streets. He would come, listen, pray and return to speak with Jeshua.

"Melchizedek! My friend. Welcome. Please come and sit with me." A silence of some minutes ensued. It was the comfortable kind of silence enjoyed between two friends with common interests. Finally, Jeshua spoke. "It was not far from here, when first we met."

Melchizedek smiled, but it was forced. He had remembered. In fact, in his own prayers, early this morning he had been thinking of that moment and all the events in this city that had transpired. "Yes, I remember, and well. I had left my home in Sodom, some months earlier. I could not stomach any longer Sodom's depravity, especially the sacrifice of their children to the gods and their arrogant pride. You met me, on this very mount, not a hundred yards from here. I thought you an angel at first, at least until we broke bread." Jeshua smiled, even laughed. He stood and came near to his friend and placing one hand on his shoulder, asked. "But you are troubled my friend, once again. Please share with me."

Leaning forward, looking down and starting ever so slowly and with deep respect, Melchizedek began. At first he stumbled over his words, fearful that they might be misunderstood as a challenge, but finally they poured out. "Jeshua, I have walked faithfully ever since that first night. I have watched as this city, Salem, was taken over by the Jebusites. I did not doubt your words. When David conquered and made it his home, my heart was delighted. Jeru-Salem, he called it! I began to understand something of Your Father's ways, his willingness to allow time to work her magic. Even your sacrifice! That bloody, painful, shocking torture that we humans invented, ever perfecting our violent tendencies was beyond me. I turned away. I could not bear to see. Like your disciples I ran, back to the welcome arms of Your Father and mine. But it did not end there! Then the second great destruction came! And the long years when Jerusalem lay in the center of conflicts between the pagans and Your Church. How? I wondered, could You and The Spirit and our Father allow it? How could Your Church so miss the point? You know I did not question. I got it. Only by love and through love and in love! I heard the songs of light. I felt a little of the Sacrifice of Love, what little the colors of light and music could convey to us are not Divine! But, now! Now, We've conquered, not by love but by power! And for what? So that 1.5 billion of your children, of my flesh and blood could die!?"

Standing, Melchizedek moved away from Jeshua, feeling the bitterness of his heart's cry. "I don't understand that kind of math!" He looked at Jeshua again, tears pouring down his face, echoed by the gentle tear drops trickling from Jeshua's eyes. He knew his words stung. He knew that Jeshua, his friend and Jeshua's Spirit and Father were hurting as well, though he could not have imagined the depth of their feeling.

He did not know, as no human could, the nature of the holocaust of love they held together in the continuing and eternal Sacrifice of Love.

Melchizedek stopped, gathered his emotions, softened his voice and returned to sit near and with his friend. "I do not understand why all this is necessary. Is there really a purpose to my life, my prayers, my story as lived and written about, in Your Book? Or was that all background noise for the main event?"

Another silence waited between them. The first crews working on the restored and Holy Temple had arrived. Eliakim, once Hezekiah's trusted architect and builder, responsible for the underground tunnel that saved Jerusalem of old, had arrived and was busy giving instructions, according to the designs he had received from King Solomon. King Solomon had been appointed by Joseph the Prime Minister over all the nations for the rebuilding projects on the Temple Mount. The sun was high in the morning sky, about 9 A.M. in the morning, about the same time Melchizedek had witnessed the first Pentecost. His heart had soared that day in hope. But it was short lived. He did not understand how the Father could build salvation into the human community by means of the Church any more than he had in Israel.

Still, just waiting in Jeshua's presence this morning had been a kind of therapy for him. It had been a long time since they had spoken face to face. The last time was just after the holocaust.

Finally, Jeshua spoke into Melchizedek's heart and mind. "My friend. Have you forgotten? Nothing is ever wasted by my Father. Everything and everyone created, if given back to Him, shall fulfill the promise of his/her creation. No one, not the angels of light or even those turned into darkness, nor any of the daughters of Eve or sons of Adam shall be lost to my father, if they are willing to come home."

Melchizedek looked around him and saw how some of those sons, some of Israel's birth and some of Jeshua's rebirth were now working alongside each other. Melchizedek remembered how both Peter and Joseph were now working with each other to fulfill the mission of bringing to the city of humans the city of God.

Jeshua continued. "My friend, my Body will yet get it. They will rise to become the 'cross' poured out into time. All human suffering is not yet done. Just as my Father turned Israel's rejection into salvation for the world, so Israel's acceptance will now become the foundation upon which We will build the New Jerusalem. In every corner of the earth my Body will serve as priests. They will bring emotional, physical and spiritual healing, in Peter's watch, just as Joseph will reveal how to 'honor the Father' in the public square, without inhibiting those who will yet refuse.

The promise of Ezekiel's bones coming to life, of Israel's fullness in time has now come. But it is not the final time. More rejection and sorrow will be needed before the end of all things. You will yet weep. Only do not despair. I do not even know how the heavenly Jerusalem that John saw comes to be on the earth. Only the Father knows. But this much I do know. It is what I shared with my servant, Ann of Norwich so long ago. 'The cause of pain is sin. But all shall be well, and all shall be well, and all manner of thing shall be well.'"

And Melchizedek smiled, gently, as he remembered the heavenly Temple and what little he had gathered in reflecting upon the color and music of the Sacrifice of Love. Before him, even now he could see in the Temple workers some of that color. He could almost hear the music. The angel nearest began a new song.

Reflections on "The Power of Weakness—Jerusalem's Gift"

Q: Your thoughts?

Join the Trinity of God and pray for the peace of Jerusalem.

Next:
Epilogue

EPILOGUE

So, what is unique about Jerusalem?

What is it about this city, at times just a village, that captures the attention of every great civilization?

Surely one thing is simply the very vulnerable geography on which the city of David existed. Israel and by extension, its capital—Jerusalem was at the cross-roads of every conquering empire; north and south. Sumar, Egypt, Assyria, Syria, Babylon, Persia, Greece, Rome—all passed by its walls on their way from or to Alexandria, Damascus, Nineveh, Babylon, Susa, Athens and Rome; and each person or army or pilgrim was captured by the golden cast of the sun on her sandstone walls.

In each century the struggle to capture and control this sacred real estate carried in it the spiritual longings and hopes of the would be conquers; Egypt, Babylon, Assyria, Greece Rome, Christians, Muslims—all sought to make this golden jewel their own.

But the real story of this city of religions lies in her first citizen, Melchizidek and in David and Solomon; It is a city chosen by God as home and for God to indwell, Israel must live in peace.

So, are we there yet?

No, but in the darkness of this next Sabbath weekend before most of its citizens awake to the rising of the sun an ancient ritual will unfold as it has for centuries between a Rabbi, a Christian Priest and a Muslim Inman—from generation to generation, passed on from father to son to grandson. A key, granting access to the same sacred and shared worshiping space on the holy mountain of Jerusalem will pass from each community of faith to the spiritual leader of the next. It is an untold and hidden sign of God's absolute commitment to Jerusalem and through Jerusalem and all its stories, to you and me.

Terry 09/08/2016

GRATEFUL ACKNOWLEDGEMENTS

Chapter 1

- "Jesus of Nazareth", by Pope Benedict XVI, page #41, 46, 47
- Seattle Times faithpage@seattletimes.com, dated 09/22/07,
- an Article by Rabbi Mark S. Glickman
- "Confessional Holiness", an E-published book by Terry Mattson, pages #91, 92-94
- The Complete works of Oswald Chambers, pg 679, 681

Chapter 2

- "Jesus of Nazareth", by Pope Benedict XVI, page #78, 79, 103-111, 272-274
- "The Complete Works of Oswald Chambers, pages #959-960
- "Three From Galilee", by Marjorie Holmes, pages #103-111

Chapter 3

- Jesus of Nazareth", by Pope Benedict XVI, page #142-144
- "Confessional Holiness", Chapter "Holy—A Little or a Lot?", an e-published book by Terry Mattson
- "Complete Works of Oswald Chambers", pages #655-656
- "Diary of An Old Soul, by George Mcdonald, page #52
- "The Joy of the Saints", edited by Robert Llewelyn, (a reprint of the writings of Julian of Norwich), pages #167-168, 205
- "A Guide to Prayer for Ministers & Other Servants", (a reprint of the writings of Henri J. M. Nouwen), page #262

Chapter 4

- Adapted from "The LORD is My Song" by Lynn N. Austin, pages #236- 240
- "Wesleyan Essentials In a Multicultural Society", page #68, 69, 72, 73 by Ted A. Campbell and Michael T. Burns
- "Confessional Holiness", Chapter 3 "Toward A New Developmental Model?", an e-published book by Terry Mattson
- "Renovation of the Heart" by Dallas Willard, page #30, 38
- "Pastoral Counseling Across Cultures" by David Augsburger, Figure4-3 & 4-2, Comparison of Anxiety, Shame, and Guilt, page #122, 125
- "The Complete Works of Oswald Chambers", page #676, 677

Chapter 5

- "Jesus of Nazareth", by Pope Benedict XVI, page #19, 20
- "The Complete Works of Oswald Chambers", by Oswald Chambers, page #676-679
- Adapted from "Parable of Joy" by Michael Card, pages #96-98 Stories & writing by Terry Mattson

Chapter 6

- "Jesus of Nazareth", by Pope Benedict XVI, page #169-171, 19, 216-217
- "Can You Feel the Mountains Tremble?", by Dr. Suuqiina, page #82

Chapter 7

- "Jesus of Nazareth", by Pope Benedict XVI, page #92
- "Can You Feel the Mountains Tremble?", by Dr. Suuqiina, page #83
- "A Theology as Big As the City" by Ray Bakke, pages 60-61, 38-39, 44-45

> "I Francis" by Carlo Carretto, an account of the life of St. Francis, written in the first person

Chapter 8

> "Can You Feel the Mountains Tremble?", by Dr. Suuqiina, page #84
> "Jesus of Nazareth", by Pope Benedict XVI, pages #160-164
> "His Life is Mine", by Archimandrite Sophrony, page #91
> "The complete Works of Oswald Chambers", page #681

Chapter 9

> From "The Joy of the Saints", page #205
> "Jesus of Nazareth", by Pope Benedict XVI, pages #140, 141

Chapter 10

> "Jesus of Nazareth", by Pope Benedict XVI, page #327, 328, 341, 343

Chapter 11

> "Jesus of Nazareth", by Pope Benedict XVI, page #326, 327
> "The Only Necessary Thing", by Henri J.M. Nouwen, page #129
> "The God Who comes", by Carlo Carretto, from "A Guide to Prayer for Ministers & Other Servants, page #18

I'm sure much of the other material is captured from numerous readings of which, at present, I have no memory plus other writings of mine (always being the result of previous published and unpublished thoughts) and the writings of others who have influenced me. If you recognize

something that appears drawn from other texts, please
advise so I may appropriately credit. Terry :)

OTHER BOOKS BY THIS AUTHOR & THEIR THEMES

This is Terry's seventh paper back published book. He has eight e-published books. His themes and book titles are as follows.

Holiness
(Living into Holy—Love)

They are:

Confessional Holiness

...The Missing Piece of the Puzzle...

(A Theological and personal journey into following Jesus)

Millennial Holiness

... A post-modern invitation to Walk with Jesus...

(To live Jesus in community following him into the renewed earth that He is bringing)

Same Sex Marriage

...the last Prejudice?
...or the last righteous stand?
...or Both?

Terry has written several devotional books around the Liturgical Calendar of the Church. Five are currently e-published and four are now in print and all are available at Amazon.com as well; Two as yet are unwritten.

Devotional Journey's Around the Church's Calendar
(Making Holy—Love Real)

Advent

The Advent of God through Mary

...A Devotional Journey in the Christmas Season as seen through Mary's Eyes

Lent

Who Am I?
...Discovering Jesus through Lent
(A Journey with Jesus from a retreat center on Mount Herman to Mount Calvary)

Sundays of Easter

50 Days of Promise
...A journey from Easter to Pentecost

Ordinary Time

7 Faces of Jesus
...A devotional journey through the American Church

Jerusalem's Gates
...A devotional journey through the Gates of Jerusalem and into the Story of God

The next two books, yet to be written are:

Epiphany (Ordinary Time)

Down & Dirty

...A Narrative & Devotional Journey with Jesus in the Season of Epiphany

Ordinary Time

Generations: A Devotional Narrative about two Sisters & two Brothers
...A look into 'The Greatest Generation' and 'The Millennial Generation'

ABOUT THE AUTHOR
REV. TERRY MATTSON

Terry is an ordained elder in the Church of the Nazarene, having just completed an 18-year pastoral assignment at West Seattle Church of the Nazarene (WSCN). WSCN is a small multi-cultural and cross-generational and economic community historically focused on ministry among Native and Samoan tribal communities, the homeless and the nurturing of Gen-xers and now Millennials.

Prior to Seattle, Terry served in business administration and as youth and worship lay and paid staff in Nazarene churches in Omaha NE, Twin Falls ID and Vancouver WA.

Following high school and college, Terry has continued his interest in theological studies and reflection in classes with Pacific Rim School of Theology, Western Evangelical Seminary and in several still unpublished writings. Terry serves as an associate instructor/facilitator for Kaleidoscope, a Multicultural Learning Center of the Washington Pacific District Church of the Nazarene.

In all Terry's focus has been the cross over point between culture and holiness and in worship as formational in social and personal salvation…especially the 'human' inside The Story of God.

Find out more at: Terrys blog "Musings of a Pastor From a Place In-Between".

http://www.terrymattson-musingsofapastorfromapacein-between.directory/

48752777R00270

Made in the USA
San Bernardino, CA
03 May 2017